Secret
Science

SECRET SCIENCE

Federal Control of
American Science
and Technology

HERBERT N. FOERSTEL

PRAEGER

Westport, Connecticut
London

Library of Congress Cataloging-in-Publication Data

Foerstel, Herbert N.
    Secret science : federal control of American science and
technology / Herbert N. Foerstel.
        p.   cm.
    Includes bibliographical references and index.
    ISBN 0–275–94447–6 (alk. paper)
    1. Military research—United States. 2. Science and state—United
States. 3. Technology and state—United States.
    U393.F64   1993
    355′.07′073—dc20   92–23453

British Library Cataloguing in Publication Data is available.

Library of Congress Catalog Card Number: 92–23453
ISBN: 0–275–94447–6

First published in 1993

Praeger Publishers, 88 Post Road West, Westport, CT 06881
An imprint of Greenwood Publishing Group, Inc.

Printed in the United States of America

∞™

The paper used in this book complies with the Permanent
Paper Standard issued by the National Information Standards
Organization (Z39.48–1984).

10 9 8 7 6 5 4 3 2 1

Contents

Secret Science

CHAPTER 1

Science and the National Security State

SCIENTIFIC DEPENDENCE AND STATE CONTROL

In 1627, a year after Francis Bacon's death, his *New Atlantis* was published, describing an ideal scientific society containing an imaginary research institute called Solomon's House. Bacon told how he and his fellow scientists would decide "which of the inventions and experiences which we have discovered shall be published, and which not: and all take an oath of secrecy, for the concealing of those which we think fit to keep secret: though some of those we do reveal sometimes to the state, and some not."[1]

Historian J.W. Grove contrasts Solomon's House with America's modern scientific community: "Today the shoe is on the other foot. Governments increasingly seek to tell scientists which of their 'inventions and experiences' shall be made public; and they do so not merely for reasons of national security in the older and stricter sense of the term, but also for reasons of commercial advantage and economic dominance over other nations, and especially those nations that are considered potentially hostile."[2]

In Bacon's time scientists often felt the need to keep their work secret from the state, even to the extent of publishing clandestinely or in cipher, largely due to fear of persecution by the state or religious authorities. The striking change since the seventeenth century has been the emergence of the state's authority and inclination to withhold technical information from scientists and the public at large, rather than the other way around. Scientists have taken their place as an influential force in society, even as the state has emerged as the chief sponsor and promoter of scientific research. As a result, scientists have compromised two of the most cherished aspects of the scientific ethos: the freedom to pursue knowledge unhampered by interference from authorities, and the freedom to communicate their ideas without hindrance to the international community of scientists to which they belong.[3]

In his book *Surveillance, Power and Modernity*, sociologist Christopher Dandeker has described the impact of the demands of war on the growth of state surveillance beyond the military sphere into the wider society. The connections between war and what Dandeker calls the "security state" were forged during the two world wars and the subsequent nuclear age, resulting in a breakdown in the division between war and peace and a closer bond between military organization and society. The generalized exercise of bureaucratic surveillance in modern societies is associated with a transformation of the organization of knowledge, which, according to Dandeker, causes a separation of the scientist, technician, and scholar from the means of production of knowledge, and their insertion as elements in bureaucratic organizations like universities and research institutes: "Such organizations are established typically as subordinate adjuncts of the state or of industrial enterprises. The proliferation of knowledge of the natural and social worlds coincides with an extension of hierarchical control over its production and distribution. The independent scholar becomes as outmoded as the self-equipped soldier, the independent tax farmer and the autonomous craftsman in the modern world of technical specialization and bureaucracy."[4] Dandeker concludes that in all modern societies the natural and social sciences become elements of hierarchical systems of military-style command and control.

The peacetime application of such structures became evident in June 1946, when General Dwight D. Eisenhower announced a new War Department research and development policy emphasizing civilian assistance in military planning and the production of weapons, using civilian industrial and technological resources as organic parts of the military structure. In September 1946, *Business Week* provided an unusually candid appraisal of America's postwar science: "Partly by design, partly by default, federal support of pure science is today almost completely under military control. Its general direction is being set by military needs; its finances are coming from military funds. The odds are getting better all the time that pure scientific research will become, permanently, a branch of the military establishment." The need for a civilian agency to restrain, if not replace, the military monopoly over science was clear, but *Business Week* warned, "[E]ven though many scientists deplore the warping of the direction of research inevitable in a military program, some of the university people—with their fields well-established, their file of telephone numbers organized, and the money flowing freely may hesitate to upset a going operation."[5]

In an October 29, 1946, lecture, award-winning physicist Philip Morrison warned that if scientists continued to depend on military funding, science itself would be bought by war, on the installment plan. The war had taught American scientists that significant research could no longer be performed by small groups of men working in modest laboratories. Morrison warned: "About a year has passed since the war ended; and in that year science has not learned how to demobilize. It is my thesis that this is not only a shameful but a dangerous and foolish state of affairs. . . . The armed forces are always sooner or later concerned with secrecy, and with the restrictions such concerns imply on the travels, publications, and even the characters and background of their research workers. Such restrictions will greatly harm our science. It will become narrow, national, and secret."[6]

Scientists worked energetically with Congress to define legislation that would mandate the separation of scientific research from the military. Their efforts were significant in crafting the Atomic Energy Act of 1946. Though the Draconian secrecy provisions of the Act ignored the scientists' pleas for open research and international controls on atomic energy, the Act did succeed in assigning responsibility for American atomic research to a new civilian agency, the Atomic Energy Commission (AEC). Still, many scientists believed that the only hope for weaning science from the military was a well-funded civilian science foundation, and they lobbied effectively for its creation. The National Science Foundation Act of 1950 authorized and directed the NSF to initiate and support basic scientific research in the environmental, physical, life, and social sciences as well as in mathematics and engineering. The creation of the NSF was indeed a critical step in the demobilization of science after World War II, and though it occasionally functions as a middle man for the military, the NSF remains the primary restraint on the military domination of American science.

America's postwar science policy attempted to reconcile the military role of scientists with the inability of the military to keep them on the payroll. It was decided that scientists had to be demobilized, but they could be maintained on strategically valuable projects by having the government subsidize their research. The American government was faced with the question of how much wartime scientific information and technology to declassify and make available to civilian scientists. The military was particularly reluctant to make public any scientific instruments they considered strategically important, unless considerably downgraded from military models. Scientists who were allowed to work with classified machinery were required to derive military applications from their research, and the view that the associated technological data constituted "sensitive" information became an accepted part of the unequal relationship between science and the military. By accepting this arrangement, scientists helped to create a dependency relationship that persists to this day. In *A Fragile Power: Scientists and the State*, Chandra Mukerji concludes: "Scientists generally contribute to the inequality of their relationship to the military—first, by developing machinery under these conditions, and secondly, by accepting as fundamentally legitimate military interest in secreting technological information."[7]

The United States emerged from World War II as the preeminent global superpower, holding all the military and technological advantages. It controlled two-thirds of the world's capital as well as its science and industry. More important, it held a nuclear monopoly. The nearest thing to a rival power remaining in the world was its wartime ally, the Soviet Union, which had suffered over 20 million dead, including 7.5 million soldiers. The major Soviet cities had been devastated along with the nation's economy: 31,000 factories, 40 million head of livestock, one-fourth of the nation's material wealth had been destroyed by the Nazis. The Soviets had no modern navy and no long-range air force, but their victorious ground armies remained a powerful force in Eastern Europe. Because the ideology of communism still seemed to offer hope to the world's colonized peoples, it remained a threat to the Western colonial powers and their reluctant patron, the United States of America.

How could the Soviet Union compete with the United States in the international contest for military and technological power, given its desperately inferior postwar position? The United States assumed espionage to be the most likely Soviet plan to achieve parity, and took unparalleled and often heavy-handed domestic action to prevent the Soviet Union from closing the military/technological gap through theft of sensitive information. In the 1950s J. Edgar Hoover warned, "Day and night the Russian spy machine is digging for facts about scientific research and development of atomic energy, electronics and aeronautics. . . . The battle to control Russian espionage is a primary phase of our struggle for freedom. Every loyal American can help by being alert; any information in your possession regarding subversion activities should be reported immediately to the FBI."[8]

The FBI questioned the loyalty of American scientists more than any other group—and even Albert Einstein became one of Hoover's targets. On October 23, 1950, Hoover sent a secret and confidential letter to the Pentagon expressing his concern about the alleged use of Einstein's office in Berlin, *prior to 1933*, by Communists. The letter also requested that the European Command conduct an investigation of Einstein's secretary because of her activities "on behalf of the Soviet Union." Hoover asked the Pentagon to provide "legal evidence and the identity of informants who can testify to the information furnished if the need arose in connection with any action taken against Dr. Einstein or his secretary by the United States Government. It is pointed out in this connection that the immigration and naturalization service is presently considering an investigation of Dr. Einstein for possible revocation of his citizenship." The Bureau began investigating all of Einstein's former associates and any "communist intellectuals who may have moved in Einstein's circle of acquaintances."[9]

During the McCarthy era, Melba Phillips of the American Association of Scientific Workers deplored the federal information control that resulted from the growing public financing of scientific research: "Freedom of thought and of communication has always been considered essential to science. Yet it is taken for granted that the scientist, as a valuable but untrustworthy piece of property, must have his speech constrained and his freedom of movement restricted. Every scientist employed by the government, whether on secret military work or not, is screened genealogically and politically. Educators in public institutions are rapidly coming under the same kind of surveillance."[10]

Throughout the Cold War the American government placed the highest priority on preventing the loss of scientific and national security information to its potential adversaries, particularly the Soviet Union. Ironically, the most heavily guarded secret in human history, the atomic bomb, was the most quickly and easily lost. With the explosion of the first Soviet atomic bomb in 1949, four years after U.S. use of such a weapon on Hiroshima, and the first test of a Soviet hydrogen (fusion) weapon in 1953, just nine months after the initial U.S. test,[11] an approaching balance of power (or terror) was signaled; indeed, a nominal military parity was assumed until the recent Soviet demise.

As many in the United States feared that the nation might lose its unquestioned superiority in advanced science and technology, our na-

tional security focus began to shift from atomic weapons to atomic information, from military technology to high technology. National doubt
and anxiety increased with the launching of *Sputnik* in 1957, when it
seemed that the Soviets had assumed world leadership in space technology. The United States soon adopted the position that any high-
technology information, no matter how remote or tenuous its connection
to national security, must be kept from Soviet or other adversarial eyes.
American officials argued that the national security rested not so much
on maintaining a military lead over adversaries as in maintaining a technological lead over competitors.

Today there is strong indication that the desire to regain international
industrial competitiveness is leading American science to an even greater
dependence on the Pentagon. Late in 1988, the Pentagon commissioned
a Defense Science Board (DSB) study on America's diminishing technological edge. The DSB panel's final report recommended that, in order
to reverse "an increasing loss of technological leadership to both our
allies and adversaries," the Department of Defense (DoD) should increase its guidance of civilian research and development and become
more directly involved in shaping the nation's economic policies. The
President was urged to issue an Executive Order establishing an Industrial Policy Committee including Pentagon representatives. Panel member Richard DeLauer, former Under Secretary of Defense in the Reagan
Administration, defended the recommendation that the Secretary of
Defense be made a member of the nation's Economic Policy Council.
The Defense Secretary, he said, "has to be an important member of the
economic decision-making process. The Defense Department's point of
view should be a strong influence on decisions."[12]

The DSB proposals were resuscitated in 1992 when a panel of the
National Academy of Sciences recommended a broad program to increase the government's support of basic scientific research to improve
U.S. competitiveness. In particular, the Defense Advanced Research
Projects Agency would be expanded to include dual-use technologies,
and the DSB notion of an Industrial Policy Committee was reworked in
the form of a quasi-public Civilian Technology Corporation.

DoD is allocating an increasing proportion of its technology budget
to its "in-house" laboratory system rather than to universities. By 1991,
these in-house labs were using more than two-thirds of the $21 billion
spent annually on the federal laboratory system. The Pentagon also was
exercising not only financial but also *administrative* influence over private
industry. In October 1991, Eleanor Spector, the Pentagon's Director of
Procurement, told a House investigations subcommittee that the Pen-

tagon was prepared to offer extraordinary financial assistance to its biggest contractor, McDonnell Douglas Corp., if cost overruns threatened the company's solvency. More important, the involvement of Pentagon officials in the *management* of McDonnell Douglas was disclosed in a letter from Donald J. Yockey, Deputy Secretary of Defense, to the company's chairman, outlining the administrative steps the Pentagon expected the company to take, including selling divisions and real estate, reducing salaries, and cutting travel, advertising, and lobbying expenses. In addition, Yockey demanded that the company's top executives exercise tighter control over its operating divisions. McDonnell Douglas did its best to comply with DoD's demands, selling its information systems division and laying off 15,000 employees, but the Pentagon rejected the company's broader fix-up plan as "inadequate."[13]

Today's "soft-money researchers," dependent on government funding and maintained by the government as an elite reserve labor force, provide the authoritative voice on scientific ideas, ratifying the advice given to politicians on all technical matters. Chandra Mukerji says that "like the unemployed on welfare, scientists on research grants are kept off the streets and in good health because of the interests and investments by elites." These scientists have also been compared to the eighteenth-century writers who were the kept pets of the aristocracy, telling their patrons what they wanted to hear. But today's scientific dependence presents a more somber image whose consequences are more ominous. The issue at stake is not a change in the direction of poetry but the control of nuclear arsenals.[14]

THE LEGAL BASIS FOR SCIENTIFIC FREEDOM

In 1954, at the height of McCarthyism, Mark de Wolfe Howe, professor of law at Harvard University, described the "internal security" investigative committees of the day, which exploited that phase of our legal tradition which seems to deny any freedom that lies beyond an individual's liberty. Howe claimed that the Constitution and the law make no explicit commitment to academic or scientific freedom as such: "Our law still looks upon intellectual freedom as a right of individuals and not as an obligation of groups. When government denies the scholar or the scientist the enjoyment of this right, he stands essentially alone against the state. In any such conflict, particularly when the people's fears support the state, the outcome is readily predictable.... The community of scholars will feel that tragedy more intensely than will the body of citizens, but there being no constitutional commitment to the enterprise of scholarship, an appeal to law made in those terms will be unavailing."[15]

The current view of the First Amendment status of scientific expression is somewhat more sanguine than Howe's pessimistic and somewhat passive McCarthy era assessment. Thomas I. Emerson, professor of law at Yale University, points out that not only is scientific inquiry a fundamental element of our system of free expression, it is in fact the basis for that system. "The theory of freedom of expression, indeed, developed in conjunction with, and as an integral part of, the growth of the scientific method. Locke, following Hobbes, based his philosophical and political theories on the premises of science."[16]

A system of free scientific expression is essential to the operation of the scientific method, which has as its central principle the notion that scientific knowledge is determined by a freely accepted consensus of professional opinion. But are the conduct and communication of scientific research constitutionally protected? In recent years the Supreme Court has suggested a hierarchical structure of First Amendment protection, with different levels assigned to different kinds of expression. For example, the Court has held that commercial speech deserves only a "limited measure of protection, commensurate with its subordinate position in the scale of First Amendment values."[17] Still, the Court has held that commercial information is sufficiently akin to other varieties of expression to warrant some degree of constitutional protection. It has stressed that commercial speech promotes three fundamental First Amendment interests: an individual interest in self-expression; a social interest in the free flow of ideas; and a political interest in enlightened public decision making.

Using these guidelines, James Ferguson in the *Harvard Civil Rights-Civil Liberties Law Review* analyzed the constitutional status of scientific speech and found it to have a more compelling claim to protection than commercial speech. First, he noted that the scientist's personal satisfaction in creative intellectual work motivates his interest in a system of free scientific expression. Second, the scientist's professional standing is largely dependent on the prompt publication of his research and the critical evaluation of his peers. Finally, free scientific expression clearly promotes enlightened self-government. Indeed, in an industrial world, the major policy issues of our time are rooted in a technical base, making scientific expression essential to enlightened public decision making.

From all of the above, Ferguson concluded: "[S]cientific expression is so crucial to the individual concerns of scientists, so vital to the material and cultural concerns of the public-at-large, and so important to the policy concerns of a democratic state that it warrants more than the 'limited measure of protection' that the Court has extended to commercial speech. . . . On this basis, it seems clear that the first amendment value of scientific speech is at least equal to that of any other category of expression."[18] It follows that restraints on scientific and technological expression should rely on settled principles of First Amendment law to determine if the state's interest in regulating the information justifies restraint on fully protected speech.

The application of standard First Amendment principles will generally provide a satisfactory basis for deciding the constitutional issues that arise from governmental attempts to regulate scientific and technological information. Law professor Ruth Greenstein has affirmed that scientific exchange is a form of free speech, and she particularly questions the authority of the government to control "disembodied scientific information," as opposed to the products of technology. Greenstein says the government has argued in the past that technical information is not covered by the First Amendment, but this argument has never been accepted by the courts: "Controls aimed at disembodied scientific information do not have regulation of speech as a mere incident of regulation of something else. Here the government's objective is the restriction of the information itself. Regulatory schemes aimed specifically at restricting communication require as their justification a 'compelling' governmental interest, a more rigorous requirement than that applicable to incidental regulation. It becomes questionable whether the government could persuade a court that the interest in suppression of such information is compelling."[19]

Greenstein's distinction between information and technology is found frequently in the law, usually on the basis of pure versus applied science and more recently on the basis of thought versus action. But when does science become action? Philip Handler claims that for scientists, experimental research involving empirical observation and testing of hypotheses is an inseparable aspect of free scientific inquiry. While the protections of the First Amendment can extend to actions, the extent to which research, as action, is thus protected is as yet untested in the courts. Handler concludes: "We must, therefore, be ever vigilant against the argument that the Government must decide what is safe for the American people to learn and, hence, to know, or that the Government should be the arbiter of knowledge. In this sense it is not so much the courts as the Congress, by its authorizations and conferral of regulatory authority, that is keeper of the first amendment."[20]

Some have claimed that government restraint on access to information is not constitutionally protected in the same way that *expression* is protected. But historian J. W. Grove rejects the argument that freedom of inquiry is not a basic right like freedom of speech: "On the contrary, it is exactly like freedom of speech, with the same kinds of moral and practical dilemmas that face those who seek to exercise it."[21] In a number of cases, the Supreme Court has suggested the existence of a right to receive ideas and information. Justice Thurgood Marshall has written: "The freedom to speak and the freedom to hear are inseparable; they are two sides of the same coin. But the coin itself is the process of thought and discussion. . . . The first amendment means that Government has no authority to thwart the process of free discussion, to 'abridge' the freedom necessary to make the process work."[22]

In a similar opinion, Justice William Brennan claimed that "the right to receive ideas follows ineluctably from the *sender's* First Amendment right to send them. . . . More importantly, the right to receive ideas is a necessary predicate to the recipient's meaningful exercise of his own rights of speech, press and political freedom."[23] These statements may seem like strong pronouncements of law, but they are dicta rather than actual holdings of the Court. At this time they do not represent the view of a majority of the Court, and thus fall short of establishing a constitutional right to receive information.

In any case, since scientific information is wholly derived from or verified by experimental research, it follows that restraints on scientific inquiry are also restraints on scientific speech. However, there is a growing public sentiment that science may need to be restrained from research that threatens life and the environment. Who will impose such restraints? Science historian Leonard Cole has analyzed perversions of science in nineteenth-century Italy, Stalinist Russia, and Nazi Germany, concluding that when the state has imposed dangerous or corrupt policies or mandated truths, scientists have offered as little resistance as other groups, sometimes less. He concludes, "Neither science nor scientists will save us from externally imposed scientific truth or from irreversible hazards. Only the nexus of structures and values that comprises the political system can."[24] Yet it is important to note that even those who advocate restraints on certain areas of modern science make no argument for keeping it secret from the American public or the international scientific community. For society's protection they insist that American scientists conduct their work in the full view of their fellow citizens.

NATIONAL SECURITY

Historian J. W. Grove warned: "There are no limits in principle to the power of the state to declare the open communication of *any* scientific knowledge contrary to the interests of national security. . . . Yet the unrestricted use of this power would do irremediable harm to the progress of science, and it is scientific progress on which, paradoxically, the welfare and security of nations now increasingly depend."[25]

Paranoid government behavior in the name of national security was never more evident than in the Watergate scandal, revealed in the testimony of former Nixon aide Egil Krogh, chief of the notorious White House "plumbers": "I see now . . . the effect that the term 'national security' had on my judgement. The very words served to block critical analysis. It seemed at least presumptuous if not unpatriotic to inquire into just what the significance of national security was."[26]

Just what is meant by "national security," a term invoked at every turn in the government's effort to restrict access to information? The Office of Technology Assessment (OTA) of the U.S. Congress sees it this way: "National Security may be defined as the military, defense, and foreign relations objectives of this Nation. This definition has implicitly been broadened over time to include protection of economic and trade objectives."[27] The OTA says national security and foreign trade interests have converged to the point where they are frequently confused. In addition to direct military threat, the term "national security" now includes the long-term risks of change in the military, economic, and political balance of power between nations, and relative scientific and technological capabilities are considered critical to this balance. Most areas of advanced industrial technology have potential military applications, and therefore America's scientific leadership seems to translate directly into military advantage.

During the Pentagon Papers controversy, Deputy Under Secretary of State William Macomber, Jr., presented the government's case for suppression: "Perhaps if we could talk only to the American people, we could tell a lot of secrets, but there is no way you can talk only to the American people. Other people listen in."[28] The logical corollary to this claim is, of course, that if the information were already known to these snooping foreigners, there would be no possible justification for withholding it from Americans. On the contrary, we have seen that government secrecy is frequently aimed exclusively at the American public, withholding or distorting information well known to U.S. adversaries.

Today, in peacetime, citizens are denied scientific information that even the enemy already knows. For example, in November 1988 at Cape Canaveral, the all-military crew of the space shuttle *Atlantis* wore black Lone Ranger-type masks when meeting with reporters and joked about the secrecy of their mission. In contrast with the previous launches of *Discovery* and *Challenger*, there were no news conferences, no media kits, and the crew was issued flash cards containing our government-approved responses to reporters' questions: "Yes. I don't know. I can't tell you. I can tell you, but I'd have to kill you."[29] Such extreme secrecy in the name of national security was rendered absurd by the capability of Soviet sensors to determine the nature of the shuttle's payload once it was in space. In fact, even before launch time, the Soviet news agency TASS reported a description of the "secret" payload, suggesting that American secrecy may have been directed at Americans. Military officials insisted that the national interest was served by "denying the Soviets' certitude," perhaps costing them a bit more time, money, and resources to verify the correctness of their information about the shuttle. But the government has also attempted to orchestrate, and even distort, the information released about *Atlantis*.

The pattern of information control surrounding *Atlantis* is all too commonly applied to American science in general, often to an absurd degree. In 1989 the Pentagon classified as secret a set of rocks—Russian rocks gathered by Americans, with Moscow's approval—from below the surface of Soviet territory. The rocks were described as follows: "They have been weighed, photographed and logged in. When they are moved, they get logged out. . . . Those who want them must be government-certified to handle secret rocks." Soviet officials said they were ordinary rocks, but a team of American researchers received a DoD grant of $750,000 to study how the rocks absorb shock waves. The purpose was to assist in determining if the Soviets were violating a 1974 treaty limiting the size of underground nuclear tests. But why keep the rocks secret from the American scientific community? The Lawrence Livermore National Laboratory and the Congressional OTA disputed the charge of Soviet cheating on underground tests, and Christopher Scholz, a geophysicist at Columbia University, said the rocks were being withheld out of concern that the research data would disprove the cheating allegation. Whatever the Pentagon's real reason for invoking its rock secrecy, Scholz said, "It is obviously not being used to hide information from the Russians."[30]

A former Army engineer working for the Defense Nuclear Agency described a researcher from the Rand Corporation who was told to acquire all the information he could from open Soviet publications about nuclear weapons in space. When he presented his report in the United States, the information had to be discussed in a closed, classified meeting. Similarly, at a 1989 conference in Albuquerque, New Mexico, a Soviet delegation from Moscow's Kurchatov Institute presented dramatic details on their nuclear reactors that would have been classified in the United States.

In the past, the United States has had the curious tendency to place access restrictions on scientific information that the *Soviets* provided in their lectures and open literature. From whom was this information being withheld? One of many such oddities occurred in 1988 when a Freedom of Information Act request revealed that many of the "limited access" (U.S. citizens only) reports at the Department of Energy's Office for Scientific and Technical Information were, in fact, translations of articles that appeared originally in the Soviet technical literature! Yet it took a lengthy court battle, initiated by the National Security Archive, to allow *Americans*, other than the government and its contractors, to read this Russian technical literature. Explain that one in terms of adversarial eyes!

A committee of scientists concluded that the U.S. government has opposed the free communication of unclassified university research, not because it feared gains to the Soviet military but because such information might have helped the Soviet Union improve its industrial capacity. The committee stated: "Were we to accept the long-term considerations which the government seems to advance as appropriate reasons for limiting the exercise of academic freedom, claims on behalf of national security no matter how broad or indefinite could be used to justify any manner of restraints on academic freedom at any time."[31]

Most of the mechanisms that make it more difficult and expensive for foreign competitors to acquire technology also make it more difficult and expensive to conduct U.S. technology and research enterprises. Physicist Robert Park says, "[T]he government is playing a dangerous game. The same actions that delay technology transfer to our military adversaries or economic competitors inevitably impede the transfer of information within our own borders. Whether the government likes it or not, the price of maintaining a free and informed society is that sometimes the neighbors listen in."[32]

Whereas in the 1970s the United States produced about 50 percent of the world's technical information, today, at best, it is producing about 20 to 25 percent of such knowledge. Robert Park describes a 1987 conference on high-temperature superconductivity at which President Ronald Reagan addressed 2,000 businesspeople, engineers, and scientists. The meeting was limited to U.S. citizens, by order of the President's science adviser, despite the fact that the superconductivity materials which inspired the conference were discovered in Zurich and confirmed in Tokyo and Beijing. Park described the added irony that the principal U.S. superconductivity research leading up to the conference was done by a group of Chinese-surnamed scientists from the University of Houston, most of whom would not have been permitted to attend.

From the growing morass of government secrecy and xenophobia, Park concludes: "What these cases tell us is that information cannot be only a little secret. Once we accept any restraint on communication we are drawn inexorably, by a series of logical steps, to a total prohibition against public disclosure. . . . We are eventually led to treat 'sensitive' information like any other classified material—that is, to keep it secure and release it only to persons with proper clearance and a need to know. Proper clearance is coming to mean U.S. citizenship." But almost half of all Ph.D. engineers entering the U.S. work force today are not U.S. citizens, leading Dr. Park to infer that "The work force we propose to keep ignorant by citizenship restrictions is to a large extent our own."[33]

Park warns that the United States is in no position to erect a wall around its scientific research. When asked how we can simultaneously prevent foreign interests from exploiting commercially or strategically useful information while preserving its accessibility to Americans, Park responded, "The answer is, we can't. . . . In our open, democratic society, the practical result of citizen-based restrictions on information is to deny access to U.S. citizens and aliens alike. . . . It is a dangerous myth that America's problems in competitiveness result from some one-sided flow of technical secrets."[34]

In 1987 the National Academy of Sciences released its report, *Balancing the National Interest: U.S. National Security Controls and Global Competition*, which warned that the government's fixation on secrecy was costing American industry an estimated $9.3 billion a year in lost sales. Analyst Robert Kuttner says that restricting the ability of domestic manufacturers to export new technologies no longer assures that advanced technologies will stay out of unfriendly hands: it only diverts the business to Japanese or European manufacturers. Kuttner warns that the contradictions between America's national security goals and its economic goals are only going to get worse: "The national-security establishment has understandably concluded that America's military security depends in part on our technological leadership. But, to keep our most advanced technology from falling into the wrong hands, the intelligence agencies are shackling the ability of U.S. companies to exploit the very technologies they need to retain that leadership. This leads to making much of America's high-technology a ward of the military establishment...." Kuttner concludes that we are destroying free scientific inquiry in order to save it, with predictable costs to the U.S. economy and to scientific freedom.[35]

In 1982, former CIA Director Bobby Inman predicted that by the latter half of the decade, the United States would be defining strategically important technology in economic, not military, terms. More recently Inman stated: "Science and national security have a symbiotic relationship.... In the long history of that relationship, the suggestion is hollow that science might (or should somehow) be kept apart from national security concerns, or that national security concerns should not have an impact on 'scientific freedom.' "[36] Clearly, the current view of national security depends at least as much on the strength of the nation's industrial base as on its stock of military weapons, and the community of scientists within academia has been conscripted to build both pillars of national power. We have entered an era in which national advantage, not national security, is considered sufficient justification for government control of science.

NOTES

1. Francis Bacon, *Advancement of Learning and New Atlantis* (Oxford: Clarendon Press, 1974), 246.

2. J. W. Grove, *In Defense of Science: Science, Technology, and Politics in Modern Society* (Cheektowaga, NY: University of Toronto Press, 1989), 59.

3. Ibid., 49, 189.

4. Christopher Dandeker, *Surveillance, Power and Modernity* (New York: St. Martin's Press, 1990), 12.

5. "Science Dons a Uniform," *Business Week*. 14 September 1946, 19.

6. Philip Morrison, "The Laboratory Demobilizes," *The Bulletin of Atomic Scientists*, 1 November 1946, 5–6.

7. Chandra Mukerji, *A Fragile Power: Scientists and the State* (Princeton, NJ: Princeton University Press, 1989), 115.

8. Donald Cruse Fisher, "J. Edgar Hoover's Concept of Academic Freedom and Its Impact on Scientists During the McCarthy Era, 1950–54" (Ph.D. diss., University of Mississippi, 1985), 205.

9. Secret and confidential letter to the Assistant Chief of Staff, G–2, Department of the Army, The Pentagon, from J. Edgar Hoover (23 October 1950), Einstein File, File No. 61–7009, Sec. 1, FOIPA Reading Room, FBI.

10. Melba Phillips, "Dangers Confronting American Science," *Science*, 24 October 1952, 439–441.

11. American officials claimed that without the technical information passed to the Russians by atomic spy Klaus Fuchs, the Soviets would have been unable to build an H-bomb. On the contrary, Fuchs's last contact with the Soviets, in 1946, occurred five years before Edward Teller's crucial breakthrough, at a time when American scientists still doubted the theoretical basis for a thermonuclear explosion. More significant, the Soviet H-bomb operated on a much more sophisticated process than the American bomb, a process the U.S. subsequently copied for its bombs.

12. "Defense Science Board Urges President to Coordinate Military with Economic Plans," *Physics Today*, December 1988, 87–88.

13. "Pentagon Says It Would Aid McDonnell Douglas," *Washington Post*, 4 October 1991, F1–2.

14. Mukerji, *A Fragile Power*, 7.

15. Mark de Wolfe Howe, "The Legal Basis for Intellectual Freedom," *The Scientific Monthly*, March 1954, 135–37.

16. Keith Wulff, ed., *Regulation of Scientific Inquiry: Societal Concerns with Research* (Boulder, CO: Westview Press, 1979), 130.

17. James R. Ferguson, "Scientific Inquiry and the First Amendment," *Cornell Law Review*, 64 (1979), 648.

18. James R. Ferguson, "Scientific and Technological Expression: A Problem in First Amendment Theory," *Harvard Civil Rights-Civil Liberties Law Review*, Fall 1981, 543.

19. Ruth Greenstein, "National Security Controls on Scientific Information," *Jurimetrics Journal*, Fall 1982, 79.

20. Wulff, *Regulation of Scientific Inquiry*, 101–102.

21. Grove, *In Defense of Science*, 67.

22. *Kleindienst v. Mandel*, 408 U.S. 753, 775–76 (1972).

23. *Board of Education, Island Trees Union Free School District No. 26* v. *Pico*, 457 U.S. 853 (1982).

24. Leonard A. Cole, *Politics and the Restraint of Science* (Totowa, NJ: Rowman and Allanheld, 1983), 171.

25. Grove, *In Defense of Science*, 67.

26. John Shattuck, "National Security a Decade After Watergate," *Democracy* 3 (Winter 1983): 57.

27. Office of Technology Assessment, *Science, Technology and the First Amendment: Special Report* (Washington, DC: GPO, 1988), 40.

28. David Wise, *The Politics of Lying: Government Deception, Secrecy and Power* (New York: Random House, 1973), 31.

29. "Secrecy Prevails at Shuttle Site," *Washington Post*, 30 November 1988, A3.

30. "Pentagon Labels Soviet Rocks 'Secret,' " *Washington Post*, 13 August 1989, A4.

31. "Federal Restraints on Research," *IEEE Spectrum*, May 1982, 63.

32. Robert L. Park, "Restricting Information: A Dangerous Game," *Issues in Science and Technology*, Fall 1988, 62.

33. Ibid., 66.

34. Ibid., 55–56, 65.

35. Robert Kuttner, "Spooks and Science: An American Dilemma," *Washington Post*, 20 August 1989, B7.

36. "Federal Restraints on Research," 60.

CHAPTER 2

National Security Controls
on Science

CLASSIFIED INFORMATION

Military and state secrets have been protected by the American government since George Washington's presidency, but without clear statutory authority. Instead, the authority of the Presidency itself has been the principal basis for the entire network of security classification, with the possible exception of the Atomic Energy Act. The specific criteria used in imposing secrecy on government documents through classification were introduced by President Franklin Roosevelt in 1940, with authority claimed under a defense installations law. After Pearl Harbor, the First War Powers Act gave the President the power to control all communications with foreign powers, eventually including the publication of any information that might compromise American military or foreign policy interests or aid U.S. adversaries. The use of classification categories, ranging from Confidential to Top Secret and beyond, was established through a series of Executive Orders, and the fundamentals of that system remain in effect today.

At the conclusion of World War II, Dr. Vannevar Bush, science adviser to the President, warned that the nation must proceed with caution in carrying over wartime methods to the very different conditions of peace. He recommended removal of the rigid controls in order to recover freedom of inquiry and the healthy competitive spirit necessary for the expansion of the frontiers of scientific knowledge.

Instead, the prompt declaration of the Cold War introduced a period of intense ideological conflict that was used to justify a continuation, and even expansion, of the wartime information controls. President Harry Truman assumed broad constitutional and statutory authority to classify information, and he extended the classification system far beyond traditional defense matters while authorizing virtually every federal agency to classify information. Since Truman, almost every President has issued his own Executive Order on information classification, always transcending military matters and invoking national security in such areas as foreign policy, economics, and law enforcement.

By 1970 the unchecked increase in the classification of technical information was approaching unmanageable proportions, and a Defense Science Board task force recommended the declassification of as much as 90 percent of existing classified information. The task force also affirmed that basic scientific research should never be classified, with classification most profitably applied in areas close to design and production. Its recommendations were followed by similar advice and counsel from concerned agencies and organizations. All went unheeded.

President Jimmy Carter at least attempted to follow the spirit of the many recommendations for increased openness. New classification guidelines were designed by the Carter Administration requiring government officials "to balance the public's interest in access to government information with the need to protect certain national security information from disclosure." Such information was not to be classified unless "its unauthorized disclosure reasonably could be expected to cause at least identifiable damage to the national security." The policy posited that "[i]f there is a reasonable doubt which designation is appropriate, or whether the information should be classified at all, the less restrictive designation should be used, or the information should not be classified."[1] Even so, a 1979 study by the General Accounting Office (GAO) revealed massive overclassification within the Department of Defense (DoD). The GAO reported that despite the official Carter policies, DoD classifiers were assigning the higher levels of classification whenever in doubt. They were also classifying information unrelated to national security, and even classifying mere references to classified documents.[2]

Information paranoia reached its pinnacle in 1982 when President Ronald Reagan issued Executive Order 12356, which dramatically reversed the previous official inclination toward openness, and either eliminated or drastically altered the fundamental features of the previous system. Under the new Executive Order, classifiers were no longer required to weigh the public's need to know against the need to classify information. Instead, they needed only to have a "reasonable expectation of damage" to national security. Classifiers were now told, "[I]f there is a reasonable doubt about the need to classify information, it shall be safeguarded as if it were classified . . . and if there is a reasonable doubt about the appropriate level of classification it shall be safeguarded at the higher level of classification."

Unlike President Carter's Executive Order, which prevented the re-classification of information already declassified and released to the public, Reagan's Executive Order 12356 specified that "information may be classified or reclassified after an agency has received a request for it under the Freedom of Information Act or the Privacy Act." The review of information for classification is thus conditioned upon outside requests for it, with the odd result that much information will be classified only if the American public shows an interest in it.

E.O. 12356 authorized the reclassification of publicly released information if that information relates to national security and "may reasonably be recovered." The government argued that such information should be retrieved in case of classification error or, more important, when shifts in international events have made previously harmless information sensitive. The Reagan administration did indeed pursue this new policy of information reclassification and retrieval, stalking authors such as James Bamford and Ralph McGehee. Bamford's problems began when Lt. Gen. William E. Odom, Director of the National Security Agency (NSA), criticized his 1982 book on the history of the NSA, saying Bamford should be prosecuted under a 1950 law barring disclosure of U.S. communication intelligence activities.

In researching his book, *The Puzzle Palace*, Bamford had used a Freedom of Information Act (FOIA) request to acquire documents dealing with illegal activities by the NSA. Two years later, despite the fact that these documents were unclassified, the Reagan Administration demanded that Bamford return them, threatening to use the Espionage Act against him if necessary. Using the footnotes in Bamford's book, government agents then went to the George C. Marshall Research Library in Virginia, where they removed from the shelves many of Bamford's sources, stamping them SECRET in the process. All this despite the fact that Bamford's sources were all unclassified and 150,000 copies of his publicly available book quoted the same information. The NSA then sent Bamford a letter stating, "You are currently in possession of information that requires protection against unauthorized disclosure. . . . Under the circumstances I have no choice but to demand that you return the . . . documents." NSA Director Lincoln D. Faurer subsequently explained, "Just because information has been published doesn't mean it shouldn't be classified."[3]

Another disturbing aspect of Reagan's Executive Order 12356 was the elimination of previous provisions for automatic declassification of dated material. Many officials now question whether the growing mountain of classified information can *ever* be declassified. At a workshop led by Scott Armstrong, former Executive Director of the National Security Archive, a work group did a bit of arithmetic to estimate the magnitude of the problem. Taking 1986, when about 20 million documents were classified, we assumed 5 copies of each document, averaging about 10 pages per document, for an approximate total of 1 billion pages. DoD says it takes at least 20 minutes per page to declassify documents, meaning it would take about *38,000* man-years (24 hours a day) just to declassify one year's accumulation, not to mention the massive backlog.

Beginning with President Truman's Executive Order 10290 in 1951, all classification orders had limited classified information to "official information" in which the government holds some form of proprietary interest. But President Reagan's Executive Order 12356 extended government classification control to any information that "is owned by, produced by, produced for, or is under the control of the United States Government." As a result of the drastic new inclination toward secrecy introduced in Executive Order 12356, 1982 set an all-time record for newly classified documents, and in fiscal year 1984 alone, 19,607,736 "classification decisions" were made. The number of documents classified annually was averaging 15 million during the Reagan years, and the amount of classified information continued to grow rapidly.[4] The unmanageable mountain of classified information soon became a matter of concern even to leaders of government and industry, with Attorney General Edwin Meese admitting that the federal government was classifying far too much information.

E.O. 12356 gives unprecedented authority to government officials to intrude upon academic research by imposing classification restrictions *after* projects have been undertaken. Harvard's John Shattuck notes that this "appears to allow classification to be imposed at any stage of a research project and to be maintained for as long as government officials deem prudent."[5] In 1982, at the request of the DoD, the National Academy of Sciences appointed a panel chaired by Dale R. Corson to determine how and where controls should be imposed on scientific research. The panel first made it clear that relatively little of the harmful leakage of technical information to hostile countries came from universities or open scientific literature, and recommended that no restriction of any kind should be placed on access to or communication of university research unless *all* of the following apply:

1. The technology is in a rapidly developing area, with a short time between research and application

2. The technology has direct military applications or is dual use

3. Technology transfer would provide the Soviet Union with significant short-term military benefit

4. The United States or its allies are the only source of the information.

In summary, the Corson panel's report recommended "security by accomplishment" rather than "security by secrecy."

Still, many in academia were disappointed by the Corson panel's easy acceptance of DoD's claim that technology transfer was a threat to national security. Rosemary Chalk of the American Association for the Advancement of Science wrote, "Such an approach translated the national policy debate between openness and military controls into a problem of minimizing the impact of military objectives on other national interests." Chalk concluded that "there has been no public assessment of the costs to national strength when the values of openness and public communication traditionally associated with American scientific work are compromised."[6] Eventually, despite the major influence exerted by the DoD on the Corson panel, DoD rejected the panel's recommendations as too difficult to translate into operational consideration.

The arbitrary and unrestrained use of classification has led many to conclude that the edifice of formal information control is collapsing under its own weight. Over 1 trillion classified documents are in existence, and the amount is growing out of control. This vast overclassification of information continues to damage the credibility of appropriately classified documents, ultimately compromising national security. Former Solicitor General Irwin N. Griswold, who in 1973 argued the Nixon Administration's national security case against publication of the Pentagon Papers, recently admitted, "I have never seen any trace of a threat to the national security from the publication. Indeed, I have never even seen it suggested that there was such an actual threat. ... It quickly becomes apparent to any person who has considerable experience with classified material that there is massive overclassification and that the principal concern of the classifiers is not with national security, but rather with governmental embarrassment of one sort or another."[7]

When the Supreme Court decided that President Nixon did not have the right to prevent the *New York Times* from printing the Pentagon Papers, Justice Potter Stewart reminded Americans: "When everything is classified, then nothing is classified, and the system becomes one to be disregarded by the cynical or the careless, and to be manipulated by those intent on self-protection or self-promotion. I should suppose, in short, that the hallmark of a truly effective internal security system would be the maximum possible disclosure, recognizing that secrecy can best be preserved only when credibility is truly maintained."[8]

SENSITIVE COMPARTMENTED INFORMATION: ABOVE TOP SECRET

In 1968, Secretary of Defense Robert McNamara, testifying before Congress on the Gulf of Tonkin incident, claimed, "Clearance is above Top Secret for the particular information involved in this situation." To which a bewildered Senator responded, "I thought Top Secret was Top Secret?"[9] Special access programs (SAPs) and the Sensitive Compartmented Information (SCI) that forms its most highly guarded subset are the ultimate in security confusion. They represent an ultrasecret classification defined by a set of codes and markings imposed by individual federal agencies on existing classification categories. The Pentagon alone has 10,000 of these classification compartments, and as a result the government is crippled by a blizzard of classified information within which truly important information is lost, and espionage and leaks become much easier. These new levels of secrecy *above* Top Secret have confused even political leaders.

During World War II, American scientists working on the atomic bomb project were deliberately compartmented, isolated from their colleagues, a situation often preventing the acquisition of data badly needed by project workers. As it turned out, the British, who were not burdened with a system of compartmented information, were able to provide American scientists with valuable nuclear information denied to them by their own government. In 1948, Dr. Edward Condon, then Director of the National Bureau of Standards, stated that "we would have had a much harder time with the atomic bomb project had our British friends not short-circuited compartmentalization for us.... The moral here is self-evident: excessive compartmentalization threatens our goal."[10]

In 1950 Walter Gellhorn warned the scientific community of this growing aspect of government secrecy: "Secrets, it is thought, are most likely

NATIONAL SECURITY CONTROLS

to remain so if they are known to only a few people.... To minimize what any one person may be able to tell, the secrecy administrators have evolved the homespun security principle that he ought to be told only as much as may be necessary to get on with his immediate job. And so it is that scientific labors come to be done in separate compartments, which tend to limit the interchange of knowledge."[11]

Gellhorn warned that by placing scientific information in isolated compartments the government would be fragmenting knowledge, narrowing fields of inquiry, and encouraging the duplication of unsuccessful research. Such an approach prevents the exchange of scientific ideas and the stimulation that comes from a comparison of experience. In addition, it takes no account of the needs of scientists working outside the area of secrecy. Indeed, among the multitude of secrecy procedures introduced during World War II, none was more dubious than compartmentalization. Employed by the military on national security grounds, the imposition of this philosophy on scientific research was uniformly counterproductive. One government official admitted that "more harm in arresting research and development was done by this compartmentalization of information than could ever have been done by the additional scrap of information that the enemy might have picked up by a more general dissemination of knowledge."[12]

Despite the lessons of World War II, the Atomic Energy Commission (AEC), from its inception, continued the discredited compartmentalization philosophy. The AEC required that no person receive more classified information than was needed for the particular tasks entrusted to him or her, though it acknowledged that such restrictions "may work against progress since often one person or group will be in possession of information of great value to others."[13]

The intelligence agencies have also demonstrated almost blind faith in compartmentalization. During the Kennedy Administration the Central Intelligence Agency (CIA) compartmented its projects to such extremes that few CIA officials knew what anyone else was doing. Internal review of projects was almost impossible. Intelligence analysts in the CIA's Directorate of Intelligence were isolated from their supposed colleagues in the Directorate of Operations. CIA officers in charge of espionage in a given country could remain ignorant of planned covert action there, and hence incapable of judging or influencing such plans. The Bay of Pigs fiasco was a good example of this.

On May 13, 1976, George Bush, then Director of Central Intelligence (DCI), issued DCID No. 1/14, a directive titled "Minimum Personnel Security Standards and Procedures Governing Eligibility for Access to

Sensitive Compartmented Information." In diffuse prose, Bush defined
this ultra-secret category to include "all information and materials bearing special community controls indicating restricted handling within
present and future community intelligence collection programs and their
end products for which community systems of compartmentation have
been or will be formally established." The directive's detailed secrecy
provisions applied to "all United States Government civilian and military
personnel, consultants, contractors, employees of contractors and other
individuals who require access to Sensitive Compartmented Information."[14] Regardless of where one might find SCI, the authority to control
this highest level of secret information resided with the DCI.

On April 2, 1982, President Ronald Reagan's Executive Order 12356
unleashed a host of information controls and enshrined SCI as the jewel
of a broader category of ultra-secrecy: SAPs. Section 4.2 of E.O. 12356
states: "Agency heads ... may create special ... programs to control access, distribution and protection of particularly sensitive information
classified pursuant to this Order or predecessor orders. Such programs
may be created or continued only at the written direction of these agency
heads."[15]

New categories of supersecrecy continue to emerge. In the five years
following E.O. 12356, funding for "gray," "black," and special access
programs increased eightfold. SAPs imposed controls beyond those required for access to confidential, secret, or top secret information. "Gray"
programs covered activities that required protection above the level of
top secret but not quite at the SAP level. "Black" programs were a subset
of SAPs whose very existence and purpose were classified. One disturbing aspect of the rapid growth of these compartmentalized programs
was the absence of adequate management, investigative, and auditing
capacity. There has never been an accurate identification and count of
all such programs, and legislative oversight has been severely hampered
by security restrictions.

THE BLACK BUDGET

Today, most scientific research in the United States is federally funded.
Most federally funded research is conducted for the military, and much
of that research is on SAPs, sometimes called "black" programs. In his
book *Blank Check*, Tim Wiener writes: "The black budget is the President's secret treasury. It funds every program the President, the Secretary of Defense and the Director of Central Intelligence want to keep
hidden from public view. It pays for the weapons for the Cold War, and

the Third World War—and World War IV. The money is kept off the books, erased from the public ledger."[16]

The documentation for these secret accounts is kept sealed in covert compartments of the Pentagon's ledgers. The Constitution requires of the government that "a regular Statement and Account of the Receipts and Expenditures of all public Money shall be published from time to time." But the public budget that the Pentagon submits to Congress is a cover story, containing hundreds of programs camouflaged under code names, with costs deleted and goals disguised.

The origins of this secret treasury can be traced to Franklin D. Roosevelt's earliest decision to proceed with research on the atomic bomb. Prior to World War II, the President decided he could finance the atomic research from a hidden reservoir of funds, and over the next four years $2.19 billion was transferred secretly from the Treasury to the Manhattan Engineer District, the code name for the atomic bomb account. General Leslie R. Groves, the commander of the atomic bomb project, described the need for some "rather unorthodox" methods and "unusual procedures" to spend such vast amounts of secret money. Those methods and procedures remain today as the blueprint for the black budget. General Groves said "the overriding need for security" required "a determined effort to withhold all information on the atomic bomb project from everyone,"[17] especially the Congress. Eventually, three members of Congress—House Speaker Sam Rayburn, Majority Leader John McCormack, and Minority Leader Joseph Martin, Jr.—were given a briefing on the secret program. They agreed to keep the project money buried in the Army's budget, and they vowed to keep their colleagues from asking questions.

When Harry S. Truman became President, he and his staff knew so little about the atomic bomb that they were unable to create coherent policy. Truman had no idea of how many warheads the nation had, how many were needed, or what plans the military was preparing. "Secrecy—and also awe—constrained even those with an obvious need to know," recalls McGeorge Bundy. "The subject, for everyone, was surrounded by taboos. The result was enormous ignorance, even at the top."[18]

The U.S. secret atomic weapons policy was formally expressed in a 1950 National Security Council directive, NSC–68. It became the central document of the Cold War, providing for a permanent war economy that made every national interest secondary to the military. Paul Nitze, the principal author of NSC–68, deliberately withheld all cost estimates from the President. That veil remained in place through the coming decade. Though Dwight Eisenhower made an effort to challenge the

secret military control of U.S. nuclear arsenals, he was unable to establish
Presidential control over nuclear weapons and, more important, he was
prevented from sharing his concerns with the nation. The issue was too
secret. But on January 16, 1961, in his farewell address to the nation,
he felt compelled to deliver as clear a warning as he could.

> [W]e have been compelled to create a permanent armaments industry of
> vast proportions. . . . In the councils of government, we must guard against
> the acquisition of unwarranted influence, whether sought or unsought, by
> the military-industrial complex. The potential for the disastrous rise of
> misplaced power exists and will persist. We must never let the weight of
> this combination endanger our liberties or democratic processes. We
> should take nothing for granted.[19]

Eisenhower's carefully worded warning has had no effect on the
growth of the black budget. When President Reagan announced that
the cost of national security would be $180 billion, he failed to mention
the additional 100 billion black dollars for the Stealth bomber, the advanced cruise missile, the spy satellites, and the host of other secret
weapons. The National Reconnaissance Organization, which creates and
operates U.S. spy satellites, remains so secret that even its name may not
be mentioned on the floor of the Congress or in any unclassified document. Yet, under the cover of the Air Force Office of Space Systems
in the Pentagon, it receives the largest black funding of any government
agency. Its letterhead remains classified. Officially, it does not exist.

At the request of Congress, Bruce Blair, a former missile launch-
control officer, member of the Strategic Air Command, and current
analyst at the Brookings Institution, produced a pioneering study of
black programs. But upon its completion, the report was seized by the
Pentagon and hidden away under the highest security classification. Only
the President, the Secretary and Deputy Secretary of Defense, and the
Chairman of the Joint Chiefs of Staff were cleared to see it. Congress
commissioned Blair's study, but Congress can't see it. Blair himself cannot see it, and he is prohibited from discussing its details. Today he says,
"Part of the story of black programs is this loss of faith in the democratic
system, the adversarial system, to produce consensus on weapons programs. . . . The black programs are a travesty of our political system. What
it means is that nuclear-weapons decisions, decisions that have always
eluded democratic control, are now being delegated to a small inside
group."[20]

Tim Wiener has described the obsessive secrecy of the Reagan Administration, which dramatically expanded the black budget, enshrouding the most expensive weapon systems. From 1981 to 1985 the secret spending for black weapons increased eightfold, with no outside scrutiny, even by the Pentagon's own auditors. By the end of the Reagan Administration the black budget had grown to $36 billion. This was larger than the federal budget for transportation or agriculture, twice the cost for the Education Department, eight times more than the Environmental Protection Agency, and more than the entire military budget of any nation in the world except the Soviet Union. The black budget imposes an annual tax of about $150 on every man, woman, and child in the United States, though no citizen has the right to know how this tax is spent.

Only a few senior members of Congress have access to the details of the black budget, and should they dare to discuss that information on the floor of Congress, a virtual act of treason, they would be subject to censure or expulsion. The Reagan Administration wanted reporters or public officials who published information about black programs to be convicted of high treason. Strictly speaking, those convicted could be executed by firing squad.

Congressman John Dingell (D-MI) complained: "The Pentagon keeps these programs of almost unbelievable size secret from Congress, from the General Accounting Office, from its own auditing agencies. And every time they have kept secrets from us, the facts, when they come out, have been surrounded by a bodyguard of lies." On January 16, 1986, Dingell asked Secretary of Defense Caspar Weinberger for a list of all black programs costing over $10 million. He got nothing. Soon thereafter, Weinberger received a letter from Les Aspin (D-WI), Chairman of the House Armed Services Committee, and Bill Dickinson (R-AL), the ranking Republican on that Committee, speaking for the full Committee. The letter began: "We are concerned over the growing volume of defense programs that now fall under the . . . 'black' umbrella. . . . [I]t is essential that the maximum portion of our defense effort be conducted in the open. The need to mobilize support for our defense programs alone demands that." The letter asked that the "basic numbers" associated with special access programs like the Stealth be made public, and concluded: "In fact, it appears to us that about 70 percent of the funds contained in [the black budget] could be declassified." Weinberger responded by releasing a superficial and doctored "fact sheet" on the Stealth bomber.[21]

When asked why it was necessary during the Reagan Administration to keep secret not just our weapons but also their cost, Weinberger claimed that revealing such funding would give additional information to the enemy. Tom Amlie, a Pentagon financial analyst, described the possible justifications for the Pentagon's black programs. "One, you're doing something that should genuinely be secret. There's only a couple of those, and Stealth ain't one of them. Two, you're doing something so damn stupid you don't want anybody to know about it. And three, you want to rip the money bag open and get out a shovel, because there is no accountability whatsoever."[22]

The Stealth bomber went through its research and development in total security, so highly classified that Congress could not debate it. The security procedures surrounding the B2 were the most intense in the nation. Videotaped lie detector tests were imposed on 2,500 workers a year, and there were massive backlogs in security checks. In 1988, when the Stealth emerged from its blackness, its secret cost was revealed. When Congress was finally allowed to debate the Stealth, it approved $4.3 billion for 1991 but imposed the requirement that the bomber be subject to the same kinds of tests that any new weapon would have to pass. Rep. Mike Synar (D-OK) noted, "Maybe we have learned a lesson. That lesson is that special access programs may be the worst thing we can do, not only in behalf of the taxpayer, but in behalf of our national security."[23]

No part of the black budget is growing faster than the Pentagon's secret research and development fund. It multiplied sixteenfold in the 1980s, growing from $626 million in FY1981 to $10.27 billion in FY1990. Thirty percent of the Navy's $6.1 billion research budget for tactical warfare is black, and 95 percent of the Air Force's budget for intelligence and communications research is black. In 1988, Les Aspin, Chairman of the House Armed Services Committee, attempted to discuss the advanced cruise missile (ACM) with his committee colleagues. "A report has been done," he told them, "but because of the high classification, the report remains locked in the committee safe. The ACM is not classically a black program. I am not barred from acknowledging its existence. I may speak its name. But it is protected in nearly all interesting details by high classification. There is one interesting thing I can tell you. It is a procurement disaster. The ACM is the worst of the programs the committee has looked at.... Why? Because of classification the reasons will have to remain sketchy, almost nonexistent."[24]

In the 1991 budget almost 25 cents of every dollar proposed for Pentagon research was black, and estimates are that more than *$100 billion* will be spent on secret weapons in the next few years, unless the Pentagon is forced to open its ledgers to public scrutiny. No one in the Pentagon knows how many black programs exist, but more than 100 multimillion-

and multibillion-dollar weapons systems are being built in secret. The armed forces refuse to tell their civilian overseers about their black programs, but the GAO estimates that there are several thousand special access compartments containing hundreds of unauthorized black programs. The Pentagon insists that defense contractors are not abusing the secret cover of the black budget, but the history of corruption and criminality among the major black contractors suggests otherwise.

On February 14, 1991, Rep. John R. Kasich (R-OH), a member of the House Armed Services Committee, released a statement calling for reform of "special access" or "black" programs. "Do not go looking for them in the budget," advised Kasich, "because for all practical purposes, information about them has been blacked out." Kasich, who characterizes himself as a "cheap hawk," agrees that some technological advances need to be shielded from potential adversaries, but he claims that the cloak of secrecy has been overused to the point where it prevents adequate oversight. "Special access designations not only conceal poor management, they also stifle public congressional discussion on the merits of these programs in the first place. . . . The debate on whether the B–2 was indeed necessary became clouded in the minds of many by a second debate over how we could terminate a program on which so much had already been spent. The longer we are kept in the dark, the more difficult it is to make good decisions."[25] Unofficial estimates indicate that President Bush's 1992 budget contained as much as $35 billion of special access funding, with 16 percent of all research and development money hidden in these black programs and one out of every six Pentagon dollars in special access line items.

There is some hope for improvement. Les Aspin, Chairman of the House Armed Services Committee, has stated that reform of the SAPs would be a top priority of his Committee during 1991. Sen. Howard Metzenbaum (D-OH) has campaigned to unveil the intelligence budget, arguing that "in a democratic society, it's totally inappropriate to classify what's being spent." In an attempt to make the black budget comport with the constitutional requirement for public disclosure, Metzenbaum sponsored a measure that calls for official publication of three separate multibillion-dollar intelligence figures: how much the President requests each year; how much the Congress authorizes to be spent; and how much was actually spent in the previous fiscal year. The Senate Intelligence Committee approved the Metzenbaum proposal by a 10 to 5 vote, stating, "Disclosure of the amount actually spent each year will enable the American people, in due course, to gain an appreciation of how much of the national treasury has gone to this function of government, as opposed to competing national priorities."[26]

Kasich has introduced legislation to remove the special access cloak from any program costing more than $50 million, and there is a growing recognition that the government must comply with the openness and accountability the Constitution demands. There should be no more secret spending hidden behind blank spaces and code words in the public budget. The practice of black budgetary should be discarded as a relic of the Cold War.

NATIONAL SECURITY DECISION DIRECTIVES

Termed "secret laws" by Rep. Jack Brooks (D-TX), Chairman of the House Judiciary Committee, National Security Decision Directives (NSDDs) have been issued through the NSC by each President since Truman, but they do not appear in any register, even in unclassified form. They have no prescribed format or procedures, and are not revealed to Congress or the public, except under arbitrary or accidental circumstances. The NSC claims that even a list of NSDDs would be classified. President Ronald Reagan alone signed about 300 NSDDs; Congress and the public remain ignorant of most of them. President George Bush has maintained total secrecy over *all* of his NSDDs.

Not even Congressional intelligence committees have been allowed to review most NSDDs, nor do they know how many have been issued or what subjects they cover. The Congressional Research Service has described NSDDs as "secret policy instruments, maintained in a security classification status," and it warns: "National Security Decision Directives clearly pose a problem for a free and open society and bring the U.S. and all of us very close to one of the most dangerous condition [*sic*] of authoritarian or totalitarian government, rule by secret law."[27] A 1987 Congressional analysis of NSDDs claimed that the implementation of policy decisions through undisclosed directives poses a significant threat to Congress's legislative and oversight responsibilities under the Constitution. "Operational activities undertaken beyond the purview of the Congress foster a grave risk of the creation of an unaccountable shadow government—a development that would be inconsistent with the principles underlying our republic."[28]

What some regard as the growing Imperial Presidency has developed a system of secrecy that functions as a source of executive power beyond any reasonable need to protect national security. Some Reagan Administration NSDDs imposed restraints on the fundamental ethic of science: information access, free association, and open communication. For example, President Reagan's NSDD–189, "National Policy on the Transfer of Scientific, Technical, and Engineering Information," issued on September 21, 1985, authorized the use of the classification system to control information generated during federally funded fundamental research in science, technology, and engineering at colleges, universities, and laboratories. Such information was to be classified prior to the award of grants, contracts, or agreements, and periodic review of all such agreements was to be conducted for "potential classification."[29]

NSDD–189 represented a decision to apply secrecy controls to information that is neither classified nor government-owned, including such scientific communication as visits to the United States by foreign scholars. The presidents of 17 American scientific and engineering societies wrote to Defense Secretary Caspar Weinberger in September 1985, complaining that a new system of classification had been imposed on research. The letter declared that their scientific organizations would not sponsor restricted sessions at their meetings, and said that if the Pentagon wanted to restrict particular scientific subjects, it should set up classified meetings.

Among the many awkward incidents resulting from NSDD–189 was the forced cancellation of a 1985 session of the Society for Photo-Optical Instrumentation Engineers, due to the government's claim that its unclassified papers could not be presented in open session. Eventually, 28 of the 43 papers were presented in closed session, but only after they were revised under DoD review.

On November 1, 1985, President Reagan secretly issued NSDD–197, "Reporting Hostile Contacts and Security Awareness." The directive, which was declassified in 1986, required all government agencies to prepare and implement guidelines for security awareness and the reporting of foreign contacts, and to provide a copy of their procedures to the NSC. NSDD–197 states that these procedures should "be tailored to meet the particular functions of the agency or department" and directed at "employees who, through either their job functions or access to classified or sensitive information or technology, invite targeting or exploitation by foreign intelligence services." The wording suggests that these tight controls on the behavior of federal workers would be focused on agencies where the vast majority of employees must have security clearances. Predictably, workers in science and technology have been severely affected by this NSDD.

On March 11, 1983, President Reagan issued NSDD–84 ("Presidential

Directive on Safeguarding National Security Information"), requiring, among other things, that all government employees with access to SCI submit to lifelong censorship of their publications and even their public speech. In addition to sweeping prepublication review requirements, NSDD–84 mandated the heavy use of polygraph tests to prevent government leaks and imposed restrictions on media contacts by government employees with access to any classified information. It provided for an SCI Nondisclosure Agreement, which referred to SCI as highly restricted information that is "classifiable" and available only to a separate and narrower category of employees among those with security clearances.

Those signing the form acknowledged that "by being granted access to SCI, special confidence and trust shall be placed in me by the United States Government," and that direct or indirect unauthorized disclosure, retention, or negligent handling of SCI could cause "irreparable injury to the United States or could be used to advantage by a foreign nation." The form required government employees to submit for security review "all materials, including works of fiction," that might relate to SCI, with such restraints to apply during the course of the employees' access to SCI "and at all times thereafter." All royalties or remunerations that "have resulted, will result, or may result from any disclosure, publication, or revelation not consistent with the terms of this Agreement" are assigned to the U.S. government. Breach of the Agreement may result in termination of security clearances, removal from "any position of special confidence and trust," termination of employment, and criminal prosecution.[30]

Thomas Ehrlich, Provost of the University of Pennsylvania, says NSDD–84 was "virtually alone among important issues in recent times" in receiving a "completely uniform and completely negative . . . reaction of those in academia." He predicted that NSDD–84 would cast a "deep freeze over any inducement for academics to serve in government by denying them the primary benefit of using government experience and information in scholarly publications and classroom lectures."[31]

The American Library Association's Executive Director, Robert Wedgeworth, wrote President Reagan requesting that NSDD–84 be rescinded. C. Peter Magrath, President of the University of Minnesota, told Congress: "Scholars who contribute a period of their careers to government service or who carry out federal research should not be forced to take lifelong vows of silence. The laboratory is not the monastery; the scientist is not a Trappist monk. To misunderstand these differences is to discourage the best and brightest from lending their talents to national objectives, and, in that case, our security will truly be jeopardized."[32]

Congress responded with consternation to the heavy-handed provisions of NSDD–84, and a group of Republican Congressmen issued a report stating that (1) there was no serious problem of former government employees divulging SCI; (2) no compelling overriding governmental need for prior restraint had been established; (3) the few instances of unauthorized disclosure did not justify the imposition of a lifelong censorship system.

On February 24, 1984, Congress held hearings on a bill that would prohibit prepublication review and polygraph exams for government employees other than those at the CIA and NSA. In the face of these hearings, the Assistant Attorney General claimed that the President had suspended and withdrawn these provisions and promised to give Congress 90 days' notice if they were to be reinstated. However, National Security Adviser Robert McFarlane subsequently advised Congress that the DoD was proceeding with prepublication restraints independently of NSDD–84 and that other executive branch departments were using an earlier CIA version (Standard Form 4193) of the SCI Nondisclosure Agreement. Signers were tied to a lifetime pledge that they will seek approval from government censors for any book, speech, or publication that deals with classified subjects, even if fictionalized. Government workers who refuse to sign SF4193, or the other pledges imposed on them, can lose their security clearances and, inevitably, their jobs. SF4193 applies to about 150,000 current employees, and the number of former employees affected is substantial.

In 1985 President Reagan issued NSDD–196, which, like NSDD–84, was aimed at employees with access to SCI. It imposed nondisclosure agreements and periodic lie detector tests upon government employees and contractors, and its restrictions extended all the way to cabinet officials. Secretary of State George Shultz drew public attention to NSDD–196 when he proclaimed, "The minute in this government that I am told that I am not trusted is the day that I leave." Departing U.N. Ambassador Jeane Kirkpatrick refused to sign the prepublication review agreement, claiming "it binds you not to write, not even from unclassified material that may have come to you in the course of your work in the State Department. It is an extraordinary document. You could never write after signing it."[33]

The agent of NSDD–196's heavy-handed controls on expression was Standard Form 189, which pledged almost 4 million government employees not to disclose "classifiable" information. Critics like Sen. Charles Grassley (R-IA) said the term "classifiable" could mean anything. It would produce a chilling effect on government employees, who would not communicate anything for fear that at a later date it might turn out to have been classified. Grassley added, "We in Congress must ask ourselves this question: is SF–189 a legitimate attempt to prevent disclosures of classified information, or is the Administration over-reaching its authority, seeking to gag public servants, in order to prevent embarrassing disclosures of waste and abuse?" Grassley's answer: "My personal involvement and dealings with executive branch officials on this matter indicate to me an attempt on their part to go way beyond the legitimate protection of classified information. Their intent, in my view, is to place a blanket of silence over all information generated by the government."[34]

The National Federation of Federal Employees and the American Federation of Government Employees challenged the constitutionality of SF189 in a lawsuit that focused on the term "classifiable." One plaintiff stated, "My interpretation was that if at any time I were to write or speak something that displeased the government, they would have the opportunity to declare the information classified and charge me with violating the agreement."[35]

In August 1988, U.S. District Court Judge Oliver Gasch ordered the government to notify 2 million affected federal workers of what its form SF189 meant when it prohibited employees from revealing "classifiable" information. Gasch gave government departments and agencies 30 days so to notify its employees, but he commented that the government had been so uncooperative that he was almost tempted to declare the whole thing unconstitutional. The government responded by issuing Standard Form 312, replacing the term "classifiable information" with the equally vague term "classified information marked and unmarked." Ominously, the government's Information Security Oversight Office insisted that "Notwithstanding the changes in some of its language, the SF312 does not in any way differ from its predecessor nondisclosure agreements with respect to the substance of the information that each is intended to protect."[36]

In addition to its loose definition of classified information, SF312 restricts documents that might meet the standards for classification but are in the process of classification determination. In dealing with such information, an employee has no easy way to determine the appropriate level of restriction, yet SF312 holds the employee liable for unauthorized disclosure. Even worse, there is evidence to suggest that an employee who asks a supervisor if a particular document is really classified may become the subject of an investigation to determine fitness for a security clearance. Because federal employees are required to sign SF312 as a precondition to receiving a security clearance, the effect is to chill communications between employees, including those who have a genuine need to know.

Steven Katz of People for the American Way has compared this kind of institutionalized secrecy with the policies of the McCarthy era. "Today, loyalty oaths are replaced by secrecy contracts; information disclosure is defined in terms of 'leaks,' and the espionage law is wielded by government officials beyond the intent of the law. Government employees are sworn to secrecy."[37]

Traditionally, the President has claimed that executive agencies have the authority to impose nondisclosure agreements, even in conflict with existing law. Congressional uneasiness with this executive assertion emerges each year in debate on the annual appropriations agreement. Among the issues in dispute has been the vague definition of the information being protected by these nondisclosure agreements. Whenever the appropriations bill has attempted to restrain the use of nondisclosure agreements within executive agencies, the President has challenged the constitutionality of the bill, claiming it impinged on his powers.

In 1990, for the first time, a President failed to challenge the wording of an appropriations bill that affirmed the primacy of existing law over nondisclosure agreements. Among the binding statutes mentioned in the appropriations bill were some requiring that restricted information be "marked" or "so identified." As a result of the new bill, before agencies may receive further funding to implement or enforce nondisclosure forms, the forms must be amended to specify that when their secrecy provisions conflict with statutory rights to free expression, those rights will prevail. These new requirements were described in the October 22, 1990, *Federal Register*: "No funds appropriated in this or any other Act for fiscal year 1991 may be used to implement or enforce the agreements in Standard Forms 312 and 4355 of the Government or any other nondisclosure policy, form or agreement if such policy, form or agreement does not contain the following provisions: 'These restrictions are consistent with and do not supersede, conflict with or otherwise alter the employee obligations, rights or liabilities' " under existing law.[38] On November 5, 1990, President Bush's signature put these restraints on nondisclosure agreements into effect. Their practical effect remains untested.

THE LOYALTY-SECURITY SYSTEM

The U.S. government administers an information security system and a personnel security system. The former controls information through classification, while the latter controls people through security clearances, thereby restricting their access to information, equipment, and jobs. Ostensibly, a level of security clearance is associated with each position, and is pegged to the kind of information the incumbent would have a need to know. As always, a significant percentage of the positions requiring security clearances are in scientific work, particularly in atomic energy, weapons systems, aerospace, and satellites. Unfortunately, the security badges worn around the necks of millions of scientists and technicians have become badges of honor, bestowed arbitrarily and withheld punitively on the basis of questionable judgments on the employees' loyalty and patriotism.

For over a century and a half, through civil and global war, depression and panic, the United States of America survived quite nicely without a repressive loyalty-security program. The laws against espionage and treasonous acts were adequate to deter or punish those who would threaten national security. In fact, in 1884 this presumption of loyalty was enshrined in America's first Civil Service Law, whose very first rule stipulated:

> No question in any form or application, or in any examination shall be so framed as to elicit information concerning the political or religious opinions or affiliations of any applicant, nor shall any inquiry be made concerning such opinions or affiliations, and all disclosure thereof shall be discountenanced.

From 1884 until 1939 all federal employees were hired without a loyalty screening, but the early winds of World War II introduced a new form of security investigation for many government employees. Today's extensive security system had its origins in President Truman's government loyalty programs, initiated in 1947. The system was expanded and formalized in Executive Order 10450, signed by President Eisenhower in 1953. Under E.O. 10450, federal departments or agencies must ensure that their employees are "reliable, trustworthy, of good conduct and character, and of complete and unswerving loyalty to the United States." To this end, each agency must ensure that the employment of any individual is "clearly consistent with the interests of national security."[39]

All data suggest that Americans are no less "loyal" today than they were during the first century and a half of the nation's history. The political spy has been replaced by the market-oriented mercenary, with greed replacing ideology as the motivation for espionage. This renders the politically charged security investigation an anachronism. For example, since the inception of America's loyalty-security system, millions of government employees have been investigated and required to swear that they were not members of the Communist Party. Not one employee has been prosecuted for falsifying that denial. According to Professor Ralph S. Brown, Jr., of the Yale University Law School, "We find no responsible claims that the loyalty security programs have caught a single known spy."[40]

Yet at least a dozen persons who were cleared by the security screening were later indicted for espionage. What is worse, the security system has hounded some of the best and brightest scientists from government, denying their skills to the nation and thereby compromising national security. Perhaps the most notorious example of this adverse effect on the nation and its science was seen in the Oppenheimer case, described in detail in Chapter 3. J. Robert Oppenheimer, "father of the atomic bomb," a brilliant scientist whose advice and skills had been essential to the U.S. government during World War II and the Cold War, was subjected to a demeaning security clearance trial that eventually denied him access to the atom bomb research that he had created. Oppenheimer had been cleared in earlier security investigations, but an additional trial was considered necessary, not because Oppenheimer had changed but because the political winds had altered.

The Personnel Security Board of the Atomic Energy Commission (AEC) and the Commission itself found Oppenheimer disloyal, primarily on the basis of his youthful political associations. By removing his security clearance it rendered him unemployable within modern American science. The separate but reinforcing verdicts of the AEC's Security Board and full Commission each had a single dissenting opinion, expressed by the lone scientist within each group. These scientists questioned not only the majority verdict against Oppenheimer but also the security system that hounded him. Henry D. Smyth, the scientist on the AEC, stated, "In my opinion, the conclusion drawn by the majority from the evidence is so extreme as to endanger the security system."[41]

The Federation of American Scientists (FAS) said that the AEC findings were unfair and demonstrated "the dangers and the bitter fruits of a security system which is motivated more by the risks of politics than the risks of disclosure of information." Because the FAS saw no threat in a man who had proven himself in the most secret councils of government, it recommended that attention be directed to the security system under which the case had arisen:

> The threat lies in the use of security machinery to dispense with technical consultants whose views may no longer be acceptable to the administration in office. The danger lies in the discouragement of independent minded men, including many scientists, from lending their talents to government. ... But beyond that we urge strongly that the entire machinery of security must itself come under review.... Security machinery has only one justification, to protect a small area of vital national information ... ; it cannot do more without sapping our national strength and eventually destroying our traditions and practices as a free people.[42]

Writing for *Science* magazine, Dael Wolfle said the Oppenheimer security trial brought out "some of the difficulties of the security regulations, some of the troublesome aspects of the attempt to judge who is a security risk, some of the tremendous cost to the nation that must lose the services of a uniquely qualified advisor in order to comply with regulations of unknown validity and perhaps temporary applicability." Wolfle said the AEC's verdict left the status of Dr. Oppenheimer in doubt, but left even more doubts about the security regulations under which he was judged.[43]

The isolation and ignominy that befell Oppenheimer were a sad consequence of the security system, but a number of Oppenheimer's colleagues and protégés suffered even more tragically. Not even his brother Frank was spared. During World War II, Frank Oppenheimer had worked on the Manhattan Project at the Berkeley Radiation Lab and at Los Alamos. He had been a trusted colleague of scientific luminaries like Hans Bethe and Edward Teller. But in July 1947 a Washington newspaper ran a front page story stating that Frank Oppenheimer had been a "card-carrying member of the Communist Party who worked on the Manhattan Project and who was aware of many secrets of the bomb from the start."[44] In 1949 Frank Oppenheimer was called before the House Un-American Activities Committee (HUAC). He admitted that he had once been a member of the Communist Party, but had quit long before he had engaged in atomic research. He provided the HUAC with a 1945 letter from the Manhattan Project's director, General Leslie Groves, praising his work as "an essential factor in our success" and expressing "grateful thanks" for his "indispensable part in the project."

Nevertheless, the publicity surrounding the charges was devastating to Frank Oppenheimer's career. Less than an hour after he had appeared before the HUAC, he learned that he was no longer employed at the

University of Minnesota.[45] This doctor of physics, suddenly unable to find a teaching position at any American university, fled the world of science to become a sheep rancher in Colorado. Even there, FBI agents maintained constant surveillance of his activities, asking neighbors if he was performing any physics experiments at the sheep ranch. In 1959, after ten years of exile, Frank Oppenheimer was invited to join the physics department at the University of Colorado, where he was permitted to teach college-level physics.

A similar fate befell Giovanni Rossi Lominitz, a brilliant young physicist who in 1942 had worked with Oppenheimer at Berkeley on a new method of isotope separation that played a major role in the atomic bomb project. Because of Lominitz's leftist political associations, security investigators determined that he represented a grave danger to the Radiation Lab, and they developed a scheme to have him drafted into the Army. When Lominitz received notice that his draft deferment had been revoked, he spoke to his friend Oppenheimer, who, knowing the desperate shortage of trained scientists at the Lab, immediately sent a telegram to the secret headquarters of the atomic bomb project:

BELIEVE UNDERSTAND REASONS BUT FEEL THAT VERY SERIOUS MISTAKE IS BEING MADE. LOMINITZ NOW ONLY MAN AT BERKELEY WHO CAN TAKE THIS RESPONSIBILITY.... THEREFORE URGE YOU SUPPORT DEFERMENT OF LOMINITZ OR INSURE BY OTHER MEANS HIS CONTINUED AVAILABILITY TO PROJECT.... I REGARD [THIS] AS URGENT REQUEST.[46]

Oppenheimer had no way of knowing that the security people he was appealing to had secretly arranged Lominitz's induction. Nine days later Lominitz received his notice to report for induction. As Oppenheimer had warned, a badly needed physicist from Los Alamos had to be transferred to Berkeley to replace the brilliant and talented Lominitz, who became a clerk in the Army's 44th Division.

When Lominitz was released from the Army in May 1946, he returned to Berkeley's Radiation Lab, and subsequently taught at Berkeley, Cornell, and Fisk University. But in 1949 he was summoned before HUAC; he asserted his loyalty but invoked the Fifth Amendment rather than testify about his friends and political associations. The day after his HUAC appearance, Lominitz lost his position at Fisk University and suddenly found it difficult to obtain work in his field. He returned to his native Oklahoma City, where he worked, successively, tarring roofs, loading burlap bags, placing bearings in boxes, trimming trees, bottling hair oil, mixing paint and putty, and painting and loading iron girders. During this period he was incessantly surveiled by the FBI, resulting in frequent loss of employment. Years later, Lominitz was able to return to teaching at a small college in Washington, but the possibility of work at a major university was denied him and his important research was lost to the nation. All under the imprimatur of the security system.

Physicist David Bohm, a close friend of Lominitz and Oppenheimer, was another scientific casualty of the Cold War security system. Oppenheimer attempted to bring Bohm to Los Alamos to assist the atom bomb project, but security officers blocked his assignment there. Like Lominitz, Bohm was summoned before HUAC; he was indicted for contempt of Congress, and acquitted. Like Lominitz, Bohm immediately lost his university position, but he chose to seek scientific work outside the United States. On the basis of a highly complimentary reference from Albert Einstein, Bohm assumed a position at the University of São Paulo, Brazil, but within a few weeks he was summoned to the U.S. consulate in São Paulo, where his passport was confiscated. He was told that it would be kept at the consulate and stamped "VALID ONLY FOR RETURN TO THE UNITED STATES."

Fearing further restrictions on his movements, Bohm acquired Brazilian citizenship and a Brazilian passport, which allowed him to teach in Israel and England, where he became a full professor at the University of London. In 1961, Bohm was offered an attractive position at Brandeis University in Massachusetts, but American security and immigration officials insisted that he must first make the equivalent of a public recantation of his political views. Bohm refused, and, though regarded by the international scientific community as one of its most creative minds, remained an exile.

Bernard Peters was another friend and former student of Oppenheimer who was dragged before the 1949 HUAC. Peters had been one of Oppenheimer's protégés at Berkeley's school of physics, where he was selected to draft the notes from Oppenheimer's lectures on quantum mechanics and assist him in preparing them for publication. In 1942, Oppenheimer asked Peters to join him at the Los Alamos laboratory, but Peters declined. Two years later, the chief security officer at Los Alamos, Peer de Silva, inquired further about the incident in a conversation with Oppenheimer, during which Oppenheimer allegedly described Peters as "quite a Red." That derogatory information came back to haunt both Peters and Oppenheimer. In September 1948, while attending a European scientific conference, Peters had his passport and other credentials taken from him by an officer who said that he was acting on orders from Washington. Peters was forced to cancel his speech and return to America, where he learned that his work for the Office of Naval Research had been terminated. An inquiry revealed that the source of Peters's problems was the "derogatory information" provided by Oppenheimer in his informal conversation with de Silva.

In June 1949 both Peters and Oppenheimer were called before the HUAC. A week after the HUAC hearings, the *Rochester Times-Union*, Peters's home-town newspaper, headlined: "Dr. Oppenheimer Once Termed Peters 'Quite Red.' " In response to protests from colleagues, Oppenheimer wrote a letter to another Rochester newspaper, which published it under the heading "Dr. Oppenheimer Explains." In it Oppenheimer described Peters as not only brilliant, but also a man of strong moral principles and high ethical standards, who had never committed a dishonorable or disloyal act. Oppenheimer said that his 1944 comments about Peters had been taken out of context, and he expressed his profound regret "that anything said in the context should have been so misconstrued, and so abused, that it could damage Dr. Peters and threaten his distinguished future career as a scientist." Oppenheimer concluded:

> Beyond this specific issue, there is ground for another, more general, and even greater concern. Political opinion, no matter how radical or how freely expressed, does not disqualify a scientist for a high career in science; it does not disqualify him as a teacher of science; it does not impugn his integrity nor his honor. We have seen in other countries criteria of political orthodoxy applied to ruin scientists, and to put an end to their work. This has brought with it the attrition of science. Even more, it has been part of the destruction of freedom of inquiry, and of political freedom itself. This is no path to follow for people determined to stay free.[47]

Surprisingly, Peters's employer, the University of Rochester, refused to fire him, and when the State Department withheld Peters's passport, the University's president, Alan Valentine, complained: "A man's reputation and career have been greatly threatened and perhaps even ruined without his being given the opportunity to hear the grounds for such action, to identify and face his accusers and to offer his defense. It was my impression that our government protected its citizens against such practice. In this case the citizen appears to need protection from his own government."[48]

In 1951 the State Department agreed to return Peters's passport, allowing him to accept a professorship at the Tata Institute of Fundamental Research in Bombay, India. In 1959, Peters joined the

Ionosphere Laboratory at Copenhagen's Technical University, and he soon came to supervise all European cosmic-ray experimentation. Still, like David Bohm, Peters remained a scientific exile, his talents lost to America.

The loyalty-security system that banished Oppenheimer and other scientists remains largely intact today, but the scientific community and the nation at large have been spared a recurrence of the bizarre witch-hunts of the McCarthy era. There persists a serious legal and political dispute over what kinds of employment the security system is authorized to address. It has been claimed that President Eisenhower's authorizing E.O. 10450 could even "require general loyalty to the United States for all federal employment regardless of the nature of the functions the person is expected to perform."[49] The Reagan Administration said that the security apparatus could apply to any positions requiring

    a. Access to classified information

    b. Proximity to classified information, with or without actual access

    c. Sensitive functions unrelated to access.

Many indirect legal vulnerabilities accrue to those scientific and technical employees who require security clearances. One example of this vulnerability appeared in 1987 when the National Aeronautics and Space Administration (NASA) sought to impose suspicionless, random drug testing on its employees. The employees to be drug-tested under NASA's plan were scientists and technicians in "national security" positions, and their security clearance was the sole basis for testing them.

When NASA employees challenged the imposition of drug testing, the question of whether an employee with a security clearance cedes Fourth and Fifth Amendment protections became a paramount issue. On April 4, 1989, several unions working within NASA filed a Motion for a Preliminary Injunction and Declaratory Relief, to prevent NASA from conducting suspicionless random drug tests on employees with security clearances. It soon became clear that most of the security clearances at NASA were gratuitous. An examination of the actual work assignments showed that few incumbents had access to classified information. Though the clearances had little to do with the work performed, the employees harbored fears, real and imagined, of career roadblocks, job opportunities lost, and a perceived reduction in the prestige of their work if they did not retain a security clearance. Eventually, NASA's national security drug testing was put on hold.

The law regarding security clearance procedures and the free speech rights of employees is unsettled. The government typically maintains that a security clearance is a privilege, not a right, and therefore no due process is appropriate when a clearance is revoked or denied. Case law indicates that the courts will usually defer to the judgment of executive agencies. Frequently, the employee who requests a review of a security clearance revocation will receive no response for months or even years, effectively encouraging the employee to resign. The internal review process is usually shrouded in secrecy, but in most agencies a review panel is eventually established. The employee is not advised of the right to appear before the panel, or of the right to present evidence relating to the case. The case law for government contract employees is the same as for federal employees, the courts holding that neither has a right to a security clearance, nor to due process upon the denial or revocation of same.

In recent years, the government has circulated Executive Orders that address the issue of due process within the security clearance structure, but the thrust of these E.O.s has been to recommend that the individual agencies maintain full discretion to summarily deny or revoke security clearances. The most recently floated E.O. was drafted by an interagency group created through President Reagan's 1983 NSDD–84, "Safeguarding National Security Information." The NSDD–84 study group recommended that a new E.O. be drafted to address access or proximity to classified information for all persons. One provision of the draft E.O. imposes penalties on any employee with a security clearance who fails to report inquiries involving classified information by persons without a security clearance, even if they are congressional investigators or the press. More disturbing, Section 7.2 of the draft E.O. explicitly denies due process rights to job candidates who are denied an initial security clearance or an upgrade in clearance level. Not only would review and appeal rights be denied, but the candidate would be given no indication of the reason for denial.

The Justice Department's position is that, technically, individuals do not apply for clearances. Employers apply for clearances for individuals, who need not be told of adverse action. When Congressional hearings on the proposed E.O. were held in 1989, the Subcommittee Chairman, Gerry Sikorski (D-MN), said it would "inevitably lead to uninformed, inaccurate and unwise security clearance decisions grounded on undisclosed gossip, distortion, mistake, innuendo or worse and motivated ... by malice, competition, envy, greed, prejudice, treason, or the like."[50]

The Justice Department's counsel, Mary Lawton, had the following exchange with Chairman Sikorski.

Mr. Sikorski: You pointed out that it [denial of security clearance] may, in fact, mean that you do not have a job.

Ms. Lawton: There are agencies where it does mean that. . . .

Mr. Sikorski: . . . No procedural due process rights?

Ms. Lawton: That is right.

Mr. Sikorski: That is right. Why?

Ms. Lawton: Because as a matter of law the employee has no right.[51]

Perhaps. But on April 15, 1992, U.S. District Judge Harold H. Greene brought some relief to civilian employees of the Pentagon by barring the use of an intrusive DoD questionnaire as the basis for security background investigations. The questionnaire, part of Form DD–398–2, inquires about previous arrests, financial status, and past drug use. A Pentagon spokesperson said the questionnaire was filled out by more than 500,000 people each year, including all contract personnel with access to classified or "sensitive" information. Judge Greene said that with the end of the Cold War it was difficult to justify such invasion of privacy. "To put it another way," he said, "while the department may be entitled to *some* information with respect to *some* employees, it may not under our system of laws require all employees with security clearance . . . to provide replies to blanket inquiries."[52]

NOTES

1. E.O. 12065, 43 *Federal Register* 28949 (28 June 1978).

2. General Accounting Office, *Continuing Problems in DOD's Classification of National Security Information* (Washington, DC: GPO, 1979).

3. Statement of James Bradford in *Hearings Before the Subcommittee on Courts, Civil Liberties, and the Administration of Justice, Committee on the Judiciary, House of Representatives, 3 November 1983* (Washington, DC: GPO, 1984), 40–41.

4. "Administration Keeping More Facts Secret," *Washington Post*, 8 May 1985, A21.

5. "Reagan Issues Order on Science Secrecy: Will It Be Obeyed?" *Physics Today*, November 1985, 56.

6. Rosemary Chalk, "Commentary on the NAS Report," *Science, Technology and Human Values*, Winter 1983, 22–24.

7. "Issues Larger Than Lives," *Washington Post*, 17 February 1989, A2.

8. *New York Times Company v. United States*, 403 U.S. 713 at 729 (1971).

9. Senate Committee on Foreign Relations, U.S. Congress, *The Gulf of Tonkin, the 1964 Incidents*, 90th Cong., 2nd Sess. 20 February 1968 (Washington, DC: GPO, 1968), 38–39.

10. E. U. Condon, "Science and Security," *Science*, 107 (1948), 659.

11. Walter Gellhorn, *Security, Loyalty, and Science* (Ithaca, NY: Cornell University Press, 1950), 39.

12. Ibid., 47.

13. Ibid., 39–40.

14. *Federal Government Security Clearance Program*, Hearings before the Permanent Subcommittee on Investigations of the Committee on Governmental Affairs, U.S. Senate, 99th Cong., April 16, 17, 18 and 25, 1985 (Washington, DC: GPO, 1985), 454.

15. "Presidential Documents," 47 *Federal Register* 14881 (6 April 1982).

16. Tim Wiener, *Blank Check: The Pentagon's Black Budget* (New York: Warner Books, 1990), 5.

17. Leslie R. Groves, *Now It Can Be Told* (New York: Harper & Row, 1962), 359–366.

18. McGeorge Bundy, *Danger and Survival: Choices About the Bomb in the First Fifty Years* (New York: Random House, 1988), 201.

19. Ibid., 38.

20. Ibid., 71.

21. *Blank Check*, 94–95.

22. Wiener, *Blank Check*, 12–13.

23. Ibid., p. 106.

24. Les Aspin, *Acquiring Strategic Weapons: Are Working Nukes Just Flukes?* (June 1988), privately printed report.

25. "It's Time to Lift the Special Access Veil of Secrecy," 14 February 1991 press release by U.S. Rep. John R. Kasich.

26. "Shedding Light on the Black Budget," *Washington Post*, 20 July 1991, A13.

27. *Computer Security Act of 1987: Report*, U.S. House of Representatives, 100th Cong., 1st Sess., Rpt. 100–153, Pt. 2 (Washington, DC: GPO, 1987), 31–32.

28. Ibid., 33.

29. National Security Decision Directive 189, "National Policy on the Transfer of Scientific, Technical and Engineering Information," 21 September 1987.

30. Steven D. Katz, *Government Secrecy: Decisions Without Democracy* (Washington, DC: People for the American Way, 1987), App. D.

31. Testimony of Thomas Ehrlich before a joint hearing of the House Subcommittee on Science, Research and Technology and Investigation and Oversight, *Scientific Communication and National Security*, 24 May 1984, 1–5.

32. *1984: Civil Liberties and the National Securities State*, Hearings before the House Subcommittee on Courts, Civil Liberties and the Administration of Justice, 3 November 1983, 58.

33. Katz, *Government Secrecy*, 28.

34. *Classified Information Nondisclosure Agreements*, Hearings before the Subcommittee on Human Resources of the Committee on Post Office and Civil Service, House of Representatives, 100th Cong., 1st Sess., 15 October 1987 (Washington, DC: GPO, 1987), 8.

35. "Secrecy Pledges Challenged Openly," *Washington Post*, 2 September 1987, A21.

36. *Federal Register*, vol. 53, 38278–38280 (29 September 1988).

37. Katz, *Government Secrecy*, 34.

38. *Congressional Record*, 22 October 1990, p.H11460.

39. *Federal Government Security Clearance Programs*, 1256.

40. Ralph S. Brown, Jr., *Loyalty and Security: Employment Tests in the United States* (New Haven: Yale University Press, 1958), 36.

41. "Science and the Citizen: Verdict," *Scientific American*, August 1954, 36.

42. "Science News," *Science*, 11 June 1954, 827.

43. Dael Wolfle, "The Trial of a Security System," *Science*, 18 June 1954, 886.

44. James Walter, *Washington Times-Herald*, 12 July 1947, 1.

45. Philip M. Stern, *The Oppenheimer Case: Security on Trial* (New York: Harper & Row, 1969), 131.

46. *In the Matter of J. Robert Oppenheimer: Transcript of Hearing Before Personnel Security Board* (Washington, DC: GPO, 1954), 123.

47. Ibid., 213.

48. Memorandum from University of Rochester President Alan Valentine, dated 28 September 1948 (reprinted in Stern, *The Oppenheimer Case*, p. 439).

49. *Federal Government Security Clearance Programs*, 1276.

50. *Proposed Changes to Security Clearance Programs*, Hearing before the Subcommittee on Civil Service of the Committee on Post Office and Civil Service, House of Representatives, 101st Cong., 1st Sess. (Washington, DC: GPO, 1989), 2.

51. Ibid., 18–19.

52. "Judge Curbs Pentagon Questionnaires," *Washington Post*, 16 April 1992, A16.

CHAPTER 3

Atomic Secrets

INFORMING THE PUBLIC

When the hypothesis of nuclear fission was confirmed in January 1939, there was an immediate interest in the military use of nuclear energy and official concern over the spread of such information. In the spring of 1939, a group of physicists attempted to stop international publication of nuclear research by voluntary agreement. Leading American and British physicists agreed to such restrictions, but Frédéric Joliot, France's foremost nuclear physicist, refused. Consequently, publication continued for another year, though some papers were withheld voluntarily by their authors. At the April 1940 meeting of the National Research Council, a censorship committee was proposed to control publication in all American scientific journals. Though the intent was primarily to control papers on uranium fission, the Reference Committee set up later that spring was authorized to control publication in *all* fields of possible military interest. The first subcommittee formed dealt with uranium fission, and it required the editors of various journals to submit all papers for review. The subcommittee would later inform the editors of the appropriateness of publication. This procedure was very successful in preventing publication, though the absorption of most physicists into military research soon reduced the number of papers submitted almost to the vanishing point.

Indeed, in May 1942, *Time* magazine noted that no papers on chemistry or physics were presented at a meeting of the American Philosophical Society. "Such facts as these," said *Time*, "add up to the biggest scientific news of 1942: that there is less and less scientific news. Today's momentous scientific achievements will not be disclosed until the war's end."[1]

The veil of atomic secrecy was even more evident in the mass media than in scientific symposia, due to a "voluntary" system of censorship overseen by the government's Office of Censorship. This system was voluntary only in the sense that it was implemented by the nation's editors and reporters themselves rather than by squads of federal censors located at each newspaper or magazine. But the guidelines for the control of information were created, monitored, and administered centrally by the Office of Censorship. Byron Price, the director of that Office, formed a Press Division from editors and reporters around the country, and on January 14, 1942, he enunciated the "voluntary" code of censorship for all newspapers, magazines, and periodicals. One part of the code stipulated that no press accounts of new or secret military weapons and experiments should be allowed.

The heavy government secrecy surrounding the development of an atomic bomb kept even the Office of Censorship ignorant of the project until March 30, 1943. An Army officer in the atomic bomb project, code-named the Manhattan Engineer District, complained to the Office about press coverage of construction work on nuclear project sites near Oak Ridge, Tennessee, and Pasco, Washington. The stories had mentioned nothing about atomic energy, but the Army wanted a total news blackout concerning the two sites. On April 1, the head of the Office of Censorship's Press Division wrote to the Army explaining that a blackout was impossible, because the press accounts came from public court records.

Soon the Office of Censorship, the Office of War Information, and Military Intelligence prepared a confidential note to all editors, stating that nothing should be printed or broadcast about wartime experiments on the production or utilization of atom smashing, atomic energy, atomic fission, atom splitting, or any of their equivalents. Similarly prohibited were stories on the military uses of radium or radioactive materials, heavy water, high-voltage discharge equipment, or cyclotrons, and information about the following elements or any of their compounds: polonium, uranium, ytterbium, hafnium, protactinium, radium, rhenium, thorium, and deuterium. The June 28 directive was mailed to 2,000 daily newspapers and 11,000 weeklies as well as all radio stations.

In response to the June 28 directive, the American media attempted to place a cap on "atomic" stories, but the Office of Censorship was soon unhappy with media compliance. On July 27, 1943, the *Schenectady Ga-*

zette was reprimanded for printing a letter to the editor in which a former state assemblyman referred to U–235 as "the most potent stuff on earth." The *Gazette* gave its assurance that no such letter would be printed in the future. On July 31, when *Business Week* referred to Oak Ridge as the Army's "most secret project," the Office of Censorship objected, claiming that the article should have referred only to a war project in Tennessee.[2] Simultaneously, the Office of Censorship halted the distribution of Ohio State University's promotional booklet about its atomic research. Military Intelligence cautioned Ohio State scientists to keep their work secret.

In October 1943, the Office of Censorship's Broadcast Division examined a Westinghouse radio script about peacetime atom smashing, but allowed the show to be broadcast with minor changes because it did not violate the June 28 directive against "wartime" applications. However, when Jack Lockhart, the new head of the Office's Press Division, reviewed the decision, he decided that the broadcast should not have been aired. On October 20 he wrote to Byron Price, warning that the Westinghouse laboratory was a potential target for sabotage. Lockhart claimed that the broadcast could have told the enemy that the United States was making progress in atom smashing, even though there was no mention of military applications. He concluded, "In view of the importance of this matter as I understand it, I feel it better to lean to the side of extreme caution."[3] The Office of Censorship agreed with Lockhart's approach, and suggested the possibility of altering the June 28 directive to cover *all* experiments, not just wartime research. It was eventually decided that the Office should simply be more cautious in handling such matters in the future.

On October 31, 1943, the International News Service (INS) ran a story about an atomic scientist who was hopeful of an important breakthrough bearing on the war effort. The Office of Censorship immediately contacted INS, which sent a bulletin to editors saying the story must be killed. On December 13, 1943, Lockhart wrote that he was not objecting to the general subject of atom smashing but was concerned that the subject not be related to U.S. thinking and activity. He explained, "We are trying to lead the enemy to believe that we never think about such a thing—even though he says he is busy at work on it. Maybe that's silly, but maybe not."[4]

The government's code of atomic censorship allowed information to be published if it came from "an appropriate authority," which the Office of Censorship defined to be a qualified government source. Brig. Gen. Tom Frazier was considered such a source when he spoke of the secret war production of a weapon that could possibly end the war. The Associated Press (AP) ran the story at 12:24 P.M., but the Office of Censorship had the story killed by 2 P.M. This caused considerable difficulty for the afternoon papers that had already completed half of their press runs but, at substantial cost, most of them deleted the story.

On March 15, 1944, the *Cleveland Press* became the first publication to write about the atomic bomb project at Los Alamos, New Mexico. Under the headline "Forbidden City," the paper referred to an American mystery town under the direction of scientist Albert Einstein. The Office of Censorship made certain that no other newspaper received the story, and it convinced *Time* magazine to abandon a similar story it had been working on.

Not even fiction was free from the scrutiny of the Office of Censorship. On April 11, 1944, the Army asked the Office to determine whether an already published detective novel, *The Last Secret*, had violated the code. The novel contained no actual atomic information, but the Army felt that a brief reference to atomic energy in the first chapter was unacceptable. Accordingly, Lockhart wrote to rebuke the publisher, Dial Press, stating that "when fiction incorporates factual information dealing with restricted subjects, it can give information on to the enemy as readily as any other form of published material."[5] Lockhart asked Dial to be more careful in the future.

Universities across the nation conscientiously complied with the atomic censorship guidelines, but there were occasional misunderstandings. In May 1944, the University of Illinois put out a press release on atom smashing that referred to campus experiments that could not be discussed because of the secrecy surrounding them. The Office of Censorship complained to the University that the press release might encourage a spy to inquire further about the experiments. Illinois apologized and expressed embarrassment over the incident. The Office of Censorship had an awkward confrontation with Dr. S. C. Lind, Dean of the University of Minnesota's Institute of Technology. In the spring of 1944 Lind had given three talks on atomic power and planned to publish an article on the subject. The Office of Censorship asked him to halt the talks and scrap the article. Lind responded: "I regret that one in authority in this country should so underestimate the enemy. You are probably aware that atomic fission was discovered in Germany.... If Germany does not know far more about it than I or any other scientist in this country except those who are actually engaged on the project, I would be very pleased to think that their Intelligence Service had completely broken down."[6]

Lockhart replied that he did not want to hand the enemy anything on a platter, and he subsequently convinced the *Bulletin* of the Minnesota Federation of Engineering Societies not to publish Lind's article until the war had ended.

The first mention of the atomic bomb project's code name "Manhattan" in the press occurred on June 26, 1944, when *Steel* magazine referred to the work at Pasco, Washington. Five days later the *New Leader* noted that the Manhattan Engineer District was one of the most amazingly kept secrets of the war. In both cases, the Office of Censorship exacted promises that no further mention of the Manhattan Project would occur.

On August 24, the *Minneapolis Tribune* printed an editorial-page column bylined by a former employee of the Office of Censorship, William Mylander. The article noted that the government's War Production Board had placed tight controls on the sale of uranium. The article concluded, "To physicists it's a scalp tingler. The uranium atom has shown more promise than any other of yielding to science's quest for a key to release sub-atomic energy.... All known explosives are popgun affairs compared to the dreadful power sub-atomic energy might loose."[7]

The Office of Censorship immediately ordered postal censors not to send that issue of the *Tribune* outside of the United States. The Army offered to send an officer to the paper to "put the fear of God" into the editors. Buy Mylander was unrepentant, claiming that the article did not violate the code because no war experiments were mentioned. The Office of Censorship insisted that a reader could see the word "war" between every word and line, and in a letter to Bill Steven, managing editor of the *Tribune*, the Office asked for assurances that such an article would not again be published. In his response, Steven said he did not believe that the war effort was better served or the enemy kept unenlightened by insisting that newspapers not mention the element uranium or prewar experiments involving it. Shortly thereafter, the head of the nation's atomic bomb project, Gen. Leslie Groves, visited the head of the newspaper chain that owned the *Tribune*. No more articles of this sort appeared in any of the chain's newspapers for the remainder of the war.

Time magazine had for some time been working on an article on the Danish physicist Niels Bohr, who had escaped from the Germans in 1943 and secretly joined the American atomic bomb project. On September 16, 1944, Lockhart wrote to *Time* and, without mentioning Bohr's name, asked that the magazine not interview or run a story on such a famous foreign scientist. Lockhart explained that the scientist's specialized field would make him vulnerable to enemy intelligence. *Time* responded that all of their bureaus had been instructed to avoid the subject.

On October 25, 1944, Brig. Gen. Frederick H. Smith, Jr., speaking at a weekly Pentagon press conference, said that the Germans were probably working on an atomic explosive that he did not expect them to perfect. Because Smith was considered an "appropriate authority," and his comments were not designated "off the record" by Army screening officers, the press assumed his remarks could be published. When the comments appeared on the wires, Lockhart called the Army, which insisted that the Office of Censorship have the story killed for security reasons. Lockhart pointed out that the story had come from an appropriate authority, and it had been on the wires for over four and a half hours. The best that the Office could do was to prevent Smith's remarks from being reported outside the United States. The War Department actually tried to revise his remarks by issuing a confidential note to editors and broadcasters, telling them that any inference that the United States was working on atomic explosives was in error. The War Department note claimed that Brig. Gen. Smith had actually intended to state his ignorance of any such activity. The media were asked to report no further on this matter and to avoid discussing any possible U.S. activity in atomic explosives. The note concluded, "It is requested that no further mention or reference be made to this incident."[8]

The problem of how to handle stories emanating from foreign publications was difficult, particularly when the stories came from the very enemy from whom we were withholding information. On December 27, 1944, the AP carried a short story noting that a German radio station claimed that Field Marshall Karl von Rundstedt's army had just used an atomic bomb in its Belgium offensive. The German broadcast supposedly described the effects of the bomb, including huge areas of scorched land on which any human being was shattered to smithereens. The Army immediately asked the Office of Censorship to ensure that the media carry no enemy statements about atomic bombs. Lockhart said it would be difficult to reverse a long-standing policy that news from foreign media sources was not prohibited by the code. The only purpose Lockhart could see for censoring the German information was to avoid stirring up comment and interest in atomic energy generally. The compromise reached with General Groves was that American media should not use foreign sources as an excuse to write about the American development of the atomic bomb.

On January 13, 1945, the *Atlanta Constitution* carried a column by Ralph McGill that said: "Atomic energy bombs are just around the corner. God help us all if Germany comes up with this one. If she really should be first with controlled energy she can conquer the world in two weeks."[9]

Lockhart quickly complained to the *Constitution*'s managing editor that such articles could tell the Germans how close we were to developing the atomic bomb. He concluded, "No doubt the Germans know that we are devoting some attention to this matter—but by not spotlighting our undertakings we hope we can keep them from learning how extensive our efforts are."[10]

Perhaps the war's most bizarre leak of atomic information occurred on April 14, 1945, when the national comic strip "Superman" showed the Man of Steel in a university physics lab. An arrogant professor addresses Superman and assembled guests: "Gentlemen—the strange object before you is the cyclotron—popularly known as an 'atom smasher.' Are you still prepared to face this test, Mr. Superman?" The Man of Steel answers, "Why not?" Superman's friends are horrified, and one shouts, "No, Superman, wait! Even you can't do it! You'll be bombarded with electrons at a speed of 100 million miles per hour and charged with three million volts! It's madness!!"[11] Lockhart wrote to the McClure Newspaper Syndicate, which distributed the comic strip, saying that while the government was not normally in the business of censoring fiction or comic strips, nonetheless any discussion of atomic energy should be discouraged for the duration of the war. McClure promptly rewrote the "Superman" plot to eliminate atom smashing for the remainder of the war.

When the Germans surrendered in May 1945, ending the war in Europe, the Office of Censorship mailed confidential letters to editors in Tennessee, Washington, and adjoining states warning them to maintain the secrecy of the Tennessee and Washington projects until Japan was defeated. A May 15 revision of the Code of Wartime Practices relaxed general censorship restrictions, but a confidential insert to editors noted that the secret provision against writing about atomic energy was still in force.

Nonetheless, the Office of Censorship was powerless to halt the increased flow of atomic stories from overseas publications. On May 21, the *London Daily Express* ran a front-page story from Oslo, revealing the five-year struggle between British and German scientists to perfect the atom bomb. Though the article contained nothing about U.S. work on the bomb, the Office of Censorship expressed concern. Impatient American journalists were now beginning to complain that they were prevented from covering stories that their foreign peers were publishing daily.

On June 8 the Army complained about a *Newsweek* story that predicted a lifting of the rigid censorship restrictions on scientific experiments in nuclear physics. The first disclosure, claimed the story, would come from a major electric company that was conducting atom smashing experiments. General Groves wrote to Byron Price on June 11, claiming that the *Newsweek* article was the most serious violation of the Code of Censorship yet to occur, representing greater potential harm to American security than any previous breach.

Theodore Koop, the new head of the Office of Censorship's Press Division, quickly wrote to *Newsweek*, lamenting the fact that the existence of a censorship code had been revealed to the public for the first time. *Newsweek* promised that it would clear all future stories about nuclear research before running them. However, the *Newsweek* story led to an AP follow-up on June 9, which said that many of America's top scientists wanted to give immediate approval to disclose hitherto secret scientific activities. The AP was promptly reprimanded by the Office of Censorship for providing valuable hints to people who might "combine bits and pieces of information." This concern with isolated detail was acknowledged by the Office of Censorship when it complained to the *Detroit News* about a passing reference to atomic energy: "This may be what Jack Lockhart in a letter to you earlier this year on the same subject called 'straining at gnats,' but we have come to expect you to bear with us even in such cases."[12]

When an atomic bomb was tested for the first time on July 16, 1945, at a remote desert site near Alamogordo, New Mexico, there were, remarkably, no press leaks. The Office of Censorship had been warned in advance about the test, and the Army had prepared a 50-word press release claiming that the blast was the result of an ammunition dump explosion. The phony press release also said that the Army had considered evacuating nearby civilians because of the danger of gas liberated by the explosion.

Because the Alamogordo atom bomb was visible for many miles, there were numerous eyewitnesses, and the Office of Censorship asked the wire services to submit any of such persons' accounts for approval before sending them out. The AP submitted one such story, quoting several persons who had seen the blast from 150 miles away. The story also claimed that the blast was heard 200 miles northwest, at Gallup, New Mexico. The Army wanted the stories killed, but the Office of Censorship said that suppressing the story would tip off the press and the eyewitnesses that this was something special. Thus, the wire services were allowed to carry the accounts, but nothing could be sent out of the country except the Army's 50-word statement.

On July 18, a column by Arthur "Bugs" Baer, distributed by the King Features Syndicate, called the atomic bomb "as dangerous as a quack with a diploma." Baer's column concluded: "By arrangement with the governments of America, England and Russia, this is all I can tell you about the atomic bomb."[13] Byron Price complained bluntly to King Features that "serious" writers might now claim that if "Bugs" Baer could tell the enemy that we have perfected the atomic bomb, then they could as well. Worse still, Price feared that many writers would now conclude that they could publish without consulting the Censorship Office. The King Features Syndicate agreed to caution all editors and writers about the censorship guidelines of June 28, 1943.

On August 6, 1945, the White House announced that an atomic bomb developed by Allied scientists had been dropped that day on Hiroshima. Thirty minutes later the Office of Censorship sent a message on all wire services to editors and broadcasters rescinding the 1943 secrecy order on scientific experiments. The message nonetheless cautioned them to continue to withhold information, without appropriate authority, concerning U.S. uranium stocks, scientific processes, formulas, and mechanics of operation of the atomic bomb, as well as information on the relative importance of the various plants and their functions or efficiencies. The media were also to suppress information on the quality and quantity of production of the bombs, their physics, characteristics, and future military employment.

The Office of Censorship was quickly deluged with inquiries about stories on the atomic bomb. The AP was given permission to interview Niels Bohr. *Blue Book* magazine was allowed to run a fiction story that it had been holding because it mentioned atomic experiments. The *Boston American* was given approval to run prewar cyclotron and atom-splitting photographs. The *Chicago Tribune* had an editorial on atomic explosives cleared. But the Press Division took the position that no description of how the atom was split or how the bomb worked could be published. For example, the *Chicago Tribune* received a statement from a former Undersecretary of the Navy saying that the explosive charge in the atom bomb was about the size of a softball. At the request of the Office of Censorship, the *Tribune* agreed not to publish the statement. The *Tribune* also submitted an article for approval that told of four different warheads developed for the new bomb. One was said to employ radar to detonate the bomb above ground, in order to maximize its destructive force. Because the source was a scientist who did not wish his name to be used, the Office of Censorship did not consider him an "appropriate authority."

On August 7, the INS submitted an article by a nuclear scientist, Harold Jacobson. The article discussed the bomb's radioactive effect, concluding that it would kill anything within a wide radius, that the land would be sterile for 70 years, and that rescue workers entering the area for some days would be killed by the radiation. The Office of Censorship approved the story, on the assumption that the radioactive properties of uranium were already well known. When the story was run, the Army claimed that much of it was untrue and that it should never have been cleared for publication. Jacobson himself was soon visited by the FBI and Army Military Intelligence, which threatened him with prosecution under the Espionage Act for violation of a government secrecy pledge he had signed. To counteract the effects of the story, physicist Robert Oppenheimer, the father of the atom bomb, was enlisted to issue a statement challenging Jacobson's article.

The *Philadelphia Bulletin* sent a sensational eyewitness account of the Alamogordo bomb test to the Office of Censorship for approval. The story described the dangers of radioactivity to the towns surrounding the bomb site. Price returned the story to the *Bulletin* with two-thirds of it deleted. He advised the *Bulletin* that Army officials feared pressure from unfriendly sources on anyone known to have participated in the Alamogordo test. For this reason, publicity about such people should be minimized.

Even in the final week of the war, the Office of Censorship found the need to suppress stories. On August 9, for example, the INS submitted an interview with a Congressman who said that the "atomic substance" was about the size of a nugget. The Office of Censorship said this description had never been published and should be deleted. The wire service complied.[14]

On August 14, the day of the Japanese surrender, General Groves thanked the Office of Censorship for doing a fine job in protecting the secrecy of the atom bomb project. Indeed, not one instance had occurred where the press deliberately violated the Office of Censorship's regulations concerning atomic energy. On the following day, Byron Price, the Director of Censorship, announced the closing of the Office and the end of the Code of Wartime Practices. On August 17, 1945, Price wrote a final letter to General Groves, in which he pointed out an important lesson learned from the voluntary censorship imposed on information about atomic energy. "Had we been similarly taken into the confidence of military authorities on other projects they were trying to protect, the results would have been better."[15]

HOLLYWOOD TELLS THE TALE OF THE BOMB

Up to the day in August 1945 when the atomic bomb was dropped on Hiroshima, most Americans were unaware of the federal government's monumental program of research on atomic weapons, code-named the Manhattan Engineer District or Manhattan Project, or its associated network of massive production plants and laboratories in a dozen states across the nation. Even after the war, only a handful of civilian and military officials had access to the full scope of this information. What the public was given was a movie, *The Beginning or the End*, an MGM spectacular that told the story of the bomb in terms that were intended to be good for national security and good for the box office. The film's original impetus grew out of the "scientists' movement" in the United States, which lobbied for national legislation to ensure civilian control of atomic energy while advocating international controls as well. In November 1945, the various local groups of these scientists merged to form the Federation of Atomic Scientists, which, in December, changed its name to the Federation of American Scientists (FAS). These concerned scientists were committed to the education of the lay public on the fearful nature of the atomic bomb and its political and foreign policy implications. They believed that the media, and Hollywood in particular, could be an ally in conveying their ideas about atomic energy. The scientists planned to influence the film by withholding permission to portray them by name unless the script was acceptable. Scientists like Robert Oppenheimer, wartime director of the Manhattan Project's crucial Los Alamos site, hoped that the movie would enhance the reputation and influence of scientists. He wrote to Vannevar Bush, the President's science adviser: "You and I both know that it is not primarily men of science who are dangerous, but the policies of Governments which lead to aggression and war."[10]

Perhaps the earliest discussions of the movie's concept occurred in correspondence between a Hollywood movie star, Donna Reed, and Edward Tompkins, a former scientist at the Oak Ridge site of the Manhattan Project. Three Hollywood studios showed interest, and eventually MGM hired Tompkins as technical adviser to the film. He was subsequently asked to assist the studio "in getting permission to use names of prominent scientists," in return for which MGM would make a "substantial donation" to the scientists' organizations.[17]

The studio obtained government approval for the movie at a brief meeting of President Harry S. Truman, producer Samuel Marx, and Tony Owens, Donna Reed's husband. Whatever conditions were attached to this approval have never been revealed. The scientists failed to obtain a contract granting them control over the final script, and they were rushed by the studio and their own idealism into hasty, informal agreements. MGM's screenwriter Robert Considine prepared a story in consultation with representatives from the atomic scientists' movement, and drafts of a screenplay based on Considine's story were prepared by Commander Frank Wead. The screenplay was roundly criticized by the American scientists, who, by early 1946, withdrew their support for a script they felt glorified the military, "put foolish words" in the mouths of scientists, and provided little insight into the awesome responsibility this new weapon required of society.

Late in 1945 Gen. Leslie R. Groves, the military man who had headed the Manhattan Project, signed an agreement with MGM giving him $10,000 and the right to review the script. Nathan Reingold writes, "Even without the agreement with Groves, there is little, indeed, to suggest an inclination on MGM's part to present the antimilitary viewpoint of the atomic scientists' movement so soon after the conclusion of a popular, victorious conflict." While the military personnel depicted in the film received cash for their permissions, all scientists gave their permissions gratis. J. Robert Oppenheimer signed a release in May 1946, claiming that though the screenplay was not "beautiful, wise, or deep... it did not lie in my power to make it so."[18]

The scientists soon realized they would have to compromise. One of them wrote to Tompkins: "Let me say that many [scientists] feel that we can afford to sacrifice a little on scientific accuracy so far as the picture is concerned if the story of the atomic crisis is gotten across well." The entertainment mission of MGM quickly became the overriding influence on the script, as producer Samuel Marx insisted that "it was not important how a scientist would talk but how the public thought he would talk."[19] MGM sent a memo to Albert Einstein emphasizing the need to fictionalize the A-bomb story for dramatic purposes: "It must be realized that dramatic truth is just as compelling a requirement on us as veritable truth is on a scientist."[20] Eventually the conflict between Marx and Tompkins became so intense that Tompkins resigned his position and returned to Oak Ridge.

Foreign scientists like Niels Bohr, Lise Meitner, and Sir James Chadwick refused to participate in the movie or to allow themselves to be depicted in it. Bohr, whose research was central to the development of the atomic bomb, cited the many inaccuracies in the plot. For example, to justify dropping the bomb on Japan, the original MGM script showed Bohr announcing that the Germans were sending atomic experts and materials to Japan by submarine. A fictional German physicist named Schmidt was depicted delivering atomic secrets to Tokyo, where he was joyously welcomed and spirited off to a modern nuclear laboratory—in Hiroshima, of course. All of this "history" was created from MGM's dramatic imagination, and fortunately little of it survived in the final film. But the ultimate compromises between scientists, the military, the government, and the studio produced historical distortions and misrepresentations, which, according to a *Life* review, oversimplified nuclear physics "to the level of an Erector set."[21] *The Beginning or the End* presented selective images of the Manhattan Project and the atomic bombing of Japan that reassured American viewers.

In the film, Groves was played by Brian Donlevy and J. Robert Oppenheimer by Hume Cronyn. The film invoked the names of various historical personages, excluding the prominent European scientists who refused permission, but the plot centered on a fictitious young scientist, Matt Cochran, whose character, according to MGM publicity, was drawn from interviews with personnel at Oak Ridge and Los Alamos. By emphasizing and embellishing the secret American success story and the arms race, *The Beginning or the End* exploited melodrama and distorted history in order to justify the secrecy of the Manhattan Project and the ultimate decision to bomb Hiroshima. President Roosevelt is shown authorizing over $1 billion for the bomb while admitting, "Congress would be justified in impeaching me if I spent that much on a secret project and it failed."[22] Corporate America is shown providing unquestioning, patriotic support for the atom bomb project. In the original screenplay, a DuPont spokesman generously (and fictionally) waives all patent rights associated with the bomb. Such a gesture would have been empty, since the government had made clear its intention to keep such patents out of private hands.

In the film, Truman implies that leaflets warning of the atomic attack would be dropped in advance. More explicitly, on the flight to Hiroshima one crew member remarks, "We've been dropping warning leaflets on them for ten days now. That's ten days more warning than they gave us before Pearl Harbor."[23] In fact, there is considerable doubt that leaflets of any kind were dropped before the Hiroshima attack, and it is known that no explicit warning of the impending attack was communicated by any means. In his review of the film, Harrison Brown decried what he called "The most horrible falsification of history . . . that Hiroshima had been warned of the approaching attack."[24]

General Groves maintained the closest contacts with MGM as the film proceeded, perhaps reassured by his aide's report that security was maintained throughout the film, and there was no danger of arousing popular revulsion toward the bomb. In any case, the aide insisted that the public impact would be minimal because the film would be a flop. Movies were an important source of public information in the pre-TV era, but at the time of the release of *The Beginning or the End* only 33 percent of all Americans polled said they had seen newsreels on the atomic bomb. Michael Yavenditti concludes: "If only a fraction of these people saw *The Beginning or the End*, its impact and distortions could have been significant; countervailing information was still classified, unpublished, or available to the public in fragmentary or highly technical accounts. Contemporary reviews suggest a tendency to accept the film uncritically as historically and morally valid."[25] Yavenditti says the film reassured Americans that "those who guided and worked on it [the atomic bomb] were ingenious and humane, resourceful and responsible. America used the bomb, but only after ritualistic doubts, agonies, and even human sacrifice."[26]

The Beginning or the End was not only an artistic and box office disaster. It was a particular embarrassment to the scientific community, which maintained an almost total public silence on the film from the moment it was released. The scientists had hoped for a film that would educate the public on the need for national and international control of atomic energy. Instead, according to Yavenditti, the movie offered quite different propaganda themes stressing "the superiority of the American Way of Life, the end-justifies-the-means morality of the Manhattan Project, and the 'necessary evil' of dropping the bomb on Japan." Yavenditti concludes, "*The Beginning or the End* illustrates certain perils of dependence, just as did the scientists' participation in war work generally and on the Manhattan Project in particular. . . . [S]ome scientists drew similar lessons from their wartime dependence on Washington and their postwar dependence on Hollywood."[27]

As bits of information about the dangers of atomic energy were revealed, there was a loss of public confidence not only in governmental agencies but also in scientists as sources of objective truth. Nathan Reingold concludes: "In all sorts of contexts, it did not matter that veritable truth was compromised. It is hard to avoid the conclusion that compromises with veritable truth are more likely the further the medium from familiar forms of professional communication. And a Hollywood saga was far from the style of *Physical Review*."[28]

THE ATOMIC ENERGY ACT

Shortly after the bombing of Hiroshima and Nagasaki, a superficial description of the scientific principles used to produce the atom bomb became public, but all technical specification of the process remained classified, including the most fundamental physics of heavy elements. Most American scientists, led by those who had developed the bomb, argued for the removal of wartime restrictions on nuclear information and research. As was the case with the MGM fiasco, the scientists had minimal influence over the ultimate political decisions.

In the Fall of 1945 a scientific panel advised Secretary of State James Byrnes of the possibility of a dangerous nuclear arms race among the scientifically advanced nations, and the panel recommended immediate international cooperation toward control of the atom. But Byrnes claimed that international controls were impractical, and he joined President Truman in introducing the notion that has dominated U.S. nuclear policy to this day. They argued that though the principles of atomic physics were well known, the engineering aspects could and should be kept secret. America's political leaders felt that our atomic "secret" should be hidden from potential enemies, but the scientists who had worked on the Manhattan Project rejected this view as simplistic and uninformed. The American people seemed comfortable with the government's claim that a significant portion of modern physics could be bottled up and kept secret indefinitely from all but a tiny coterie of privileged insiders. After all, the government had successfully denied the American people any knowledge of the atomic bomb until after its use against Japan.

The War Department began working with Congress to draft legislation for postwar control of atomic energy, giving every indication that rigid restrictions on American scientists would continue into the postwar period. But America's most prominent nuclear scientists urged a return to the traditional openness of scientific research. Enrico Fermi warned, "Unless research is free and outside of control, the United States will lose its superiority in scientific pursuit."[29]

Indeed, the first draft of an atomic energy bill, introduced in the Senate on December 20, 1945, reflected the scientific community's concern about federal control of science. The McMahon Bill, as it was called, placed great emphasis on "fostering private research and development on a truly independent basis" in order to encourage "free dissemination of basic scientific information and for maximum liberality in dissemination of related technical information." The bill defined "basic scientific information" to include, "in addition to theoretical knowledge of nuclear and other physics, chemistry, biology and therapy, all results capable of accomplishment, as distinguished from the processes or techniques of accomplishing them." The latter was referred to as "related technical information."[30]

Despite its generally liberal approach to dissemination of scientific information, the original McMahon Bill authorized the new Atomic Energy Commission (AEC) to withhold technical information on national security grounds, but only "within the meaning of the Espionage Act." The bill's most restrictive provisions concerned the control of fissionable materials and the facilities using them. Private ownership of such materials and facilities was to be prohibited, and all associated patents were to be assigned to the AEC. Richard Hewlett, former Chief Historian of the AEC, recalls that the McMahon Bill would have created "an absolute government monopoly over the production and use of fissionable materials."[31]

In hearings and executive sessions the McMahon Bill moved steadily toward an even more conservative approach to information access, conflicting with what the scientific community had advocated. In April 1946, the Special Senate Committee on Atomic Energy changed the name of the bill's Section 9 from "Dissemination of Information" to "Control of Information," and removed the declaration on free dissemination of scientific information as a cardinal principle. The Committee also abandoned the distinction between "basic scientific" and "related technical" information, establishing instead a special category of classified information to be called "Restricted Data." This new category was defined as "all data concerning the manufacture or utilization of atomic weapons, the production of fissionable material, or the use of fissionable material in the production of power, but shall not include any data which the Commission from time to time determines may be published without adversely affecting the common defense and security." This was the seed of the concept of "born classified," the notion that certain kinds of scientific information were classified from the moment they were conceived, whether generated in a government lab or in the mind of a private citizen working in his own home.[32] Such information could be declassified only at the initiative of the Commission.

In its final form, the Atomic Energy Act of 1946 introduced a broad array of controls, but the most revolutionary was the new category of Restricted Data. Until that time, the process of classifying information anywhere within the government required a careful and prescribed procedure to determine the specific national security threat involved. But under the Atomic Energy Act, all Restricted Data is born classified, despite the fact that it includes the kind of elementary scientific information contained in college textbooks. Atomic information can thus see the light of day only if the AEC determines that it "may be published without adversely affecting the common defense and security."

Even in the areas of health and biology, where research is traditionally regarded as open literature, the AEC has maintained strict controls and, oddly, has been even more reluctant to declassify research in the biological sciences than in physics or chemistry. From the beginning, the AEC's classification/declassification policies have been withheld from public scrutiny, but its Fifth Semi-annual Report (1949) revealed the preliminary guidelines. Subjects in which research and publication are allowed without prior AEC clearance are termed "Unclassified Areas." They include the following:

1. Pure and applied mathematics, except as related to classified projects

2. Theoretical physics, except the theory of fission, of reactors, of neutron diffusion, and weapon physics

3. All physical (except nuclear) properties of elements of atomic number less than 90

4. The basic chemistry of all elements (except the technology of the production of fissionable materials) and the physical metallurgy of elements with atomic number less than 83

5. Instrumentation, including fission chambers

6. Medical and biological research and health studies, excluding work with elements of atomic number 90 and above

7. Chemistry and technology of fluorine compounds, except for applications in AEC installations.

All other knowledge in the world of science was regarded as Restricted Data.

CONTROL OF PRIVATE INFORMATION

Because the Atomic Energy Act of 1946 defines Restricted Data to include *all* data in the prescribed subject areas, many have assumed that the Act was intended by its authors to apply not only to government information but also to data generated in the private sector without Government support or involvement. Two Senate staff members, J. Newman and B. Miller, who played a major role in drafting the 1946 Act, stated, "It does not matter whether these [restricted] data are discovered or compiled in a government laboratory or in connection with the private research of an individual scientist." They claimed, "[I]f the Act does not restrict the liberty of scientific thought, it without question, abridges freedom of scientific communication. The controls on information were deliberately designed to regulate the interchange of scientific ideas."[33]

On July 21, 1947, the Attorney General wrote to the Chairman of the AEC stating that there was considerable indication that Congress intended the Atomic Energy Act to apply to nongovernment information, and recommending an amendment to the Act to resolve the question. Private industry was increasingly demanding access to nuclear technology, particularly on reactor development, and by 1953 pressure for major revisions in the Atomic Energy Act of 1946 was undeniable. In the rapidly developing field of nuclear power, the government felt obliged to protect American interests in the international competition for the power reactor market. The result was an entirely new statute, the Atomic Energy Act of 1954. The 1954 Act left the original provisions on information control and Restricted Data virtually unchanged, but it allowed private companies access to *some* Restricted Data, primarily power reactor technology, if they agreed to impose the AEC's regulations on information classification and security.

Though the 1954 Act again failed to directly address federal control of private American research, it did include a provision controlling information developed in other countries, thereby implicitly stating that data wholly outside the U.S. government could be Restricted Data. But despite the absence of any unambiguous statutory authority to restrict privately developed information, the AEC and its successors, the Energy Research and Development Administration and the Department of Energy, continued to apply the concept of "born classified" almost comprehensively. In Senate hearings in 1955 the AEC's General Counsel claimed that research produced in a private lab with no government connection was subject to AEC controls, so long as the data produced *would have been* regarded as Restricted Data in an AEC facility.

In 1960, several American companies began preliminary research on a gas centrifuge process for producing uranium–235, a fundamental ingredient of the atomic bomb. The process was already undergoing research in Western Europe, and to exclude American companies from competing in this field would put them at an international economic disadvantage. Yet the AEC regarded the centrifuge as a potential threat to national security, and in June 1960 it decided that the Atomic Energy Act's access restrictions (10 C.F.R. Part 25), including classification and security controls, should apply to gas centrifuge technology. But as written, Part 25 would apply only to companies seeking access to the *Commission's* Restricted Data. Because the AEC desired access to and control over *privately* generated information on the gas centrifuge, it chose to amend its access permit regulation to apply "to all permits for access to centrifuge information, whether or not the permittee desires access to AEC 'Restricted Data' information." Without using the words or acknowledging their legitimacy, the AEC was here applying the "born classified" concept to private research. As Richard Hewlett recalls, "The Commission was not saying, but clearly implying, that private research on the centrifuge would inevitably result in the generation of Restricted Data, which in turn would subject the private company to the terms of the regulation." By April 20, 1961, when this revision of the Atomic Energy Act took effect, it contained the general provision that access restrictions would apply "irrespective of whether access to the Commission's Restricted Data information is desired."[34]

For several years the Commission relied upon the new regulation to control the dissemination of Restricted Data by private companies, but some companies began to negotiate foreign contracts to develop nuclear devices relevant to weapons manufacture. The AEC had always claimed that the scope of its authority rested entirely on the use of the words "all data" in the definition of Restricted Data. But to make clear to the public the broad reach of the "born classified" concept, the AEC staff proposed a new regulation (10 C.F.R. Part 26) that would cover Restricted Data generated by private companies or foreign countries. In July 1964 new wording for Part 26 was proposed to make this authority explicit: "The statutory definition is not limited to information ... that is generated or owned by the Commission or the Government. It includes also any information within the scope of the definition that is generated by any person even though he may never have been engaged in any Government atomic energy activity."[35]

Because the AEC's own contractors had made substantial progress in developing the gas centrifuge, the Commission no longer felt obliged to allow private companies to access its Restricted Data in this field, even if they agreed to impose the AEC's security controls. There was considerable debate over the legal question of whether individuals were being deprived of free speech and property rights without due process. The Commission's legal experts concluded that to the extent that the regulations impinged on such rights, they were a reasonable exercise of sovereign power in the interest of the common defense and security, as authorized in the Atomic Energy Act. On March 26, 1965, the Commission gave tentative approval to Part 26 with its explicit restrictions on private scientific research, on the condition that the AEC staff would resolve any remaining legal questions with the Department of Justice. For the first time, the AEC would bring its Draconian edifice of scientific thought control under legal scrutiny. Like the emperor's clothes, the legal cover for the concept of "born classified" was found wanting.

On June 4 Wayne Barrett at the Justice Department told the AEC that the Office of Legal Counsel was "not completely satisfied that the

Atomic Energy Act (1) was applicable to Private Restricted Data and (2) authorized the issuance of the proposed regulation [Part 26]." In the absence of direct evidence of Congressional intent, the Office of Legal Counsel doubted that the original legislation intended to provide such sweeping authority. Through a systematic analysis of the Atomic Energy Act, Barrett concluded that in the absence of a contract, the Commission would be without authority to control dissemination of private information. Barrett also cited language in the Act to mean that the Commission "shall not itself disclose" rather than "shall not permit anyone else to disclose" Restricted Data. In addition, Barrett held that the Act's enforcement provisions were designed to deal with treasonable conduct or conspiracies, providing no authority to control private and commercial research.[36]

The AEC's General Counsel did not deny the merit of the Justice Department's legal analysis, but he thought Barrett had ignored the historical context of the Act and the need in 1945 to protect the "secret of the bomb." With minor revisions, the AEC published the proposed new regulation, giving the public an opportunity to submit comments. The Atomic Energy Committee of the New York Bar Association submitted a comprehensive analysis, noting the uniqueness of the "born classified" concept: "In all other areas of national defense secrets affirmative action by the responsible agency is required in order to classify information as secret or restricted; the data in all other such cases is 'born free.' " The Bar Association noted that all reports, testimony, and hearings on the 1946 and 1954 Acts were silent on whether privately generated Restricted Data were "born secret." The Bar Association characterized the Commission's justification for these controls as "indeed fragile support for such a significant limitation on the rights of private individuals." It concluded that the proposed regulation was "unconstitutional substantively as an undue interference with the exercise of free speech as protected by the First Amendment, and the application of the criminal sanctions to enforce the Regulations would be unconstitutional as a deprivation of liberty and property without due process of law, as prohibited by the Fifth Amendment."[37]

In a separate response to the proposed regulation, the Atomic Industrial Forum commented: "Given the extremely important and fundamental rights which the Commission's regulations would limit . . . [we] would recommend that the Commission consider seeking legislation more clearly defining (and refining) its authority."[38]

The AEC made repeated attempts to meet these legal objections to Part 26, but even the Commissioners were unconvinced that they were on solid legal ground. In 1969, when the Commission was once more forced to refer the statutory and constitutional problems to outside authorities for study, the five-year attempt to promulgate Part 26 ended. The AEC dropped its proposal for Part 26, and until its demise in 1975, continued to impose its sweeping controls without explicit legal authority. The AEC's successors, the Energy Research and Development Administration and Department of Energy, have assumed the same arbitrary authority.

THE OPPENHEIMER AFFAIR

Though he AEC spent most of its early years closeting Restricted Data, its most dramatic act of secrecy may have been the notorious Oppenheimer security trial. In 1943, J. Robert Oppenheimer had been chosen to head the prestigious Los Alamos Laboratory and thereby lead America's scientific race to develop an atomic bomb before the Nazis could do so. When Oppenheimer assumed this staggering scientific and political responsibility, he was just 38 years old but already widely acknowledged within the scientific community as a supremely gifted physicist and professor at the University of California, Berkeley. Throughout his work on the dramatically successful and highly secret atomic bomb program, known as the Manhattan Project, Oppenheimer enjoyed the full confidence of the Project's director, Gen. Leslie R. Groves, though Army Security officers never felt comfortable with Oppenheimer's prewar associations with the political left. Because of his essential role in leading America's scientific and military team to a functioning atom bomb, Oppenheimer soon became known as "the father of the atom bomb." After the war he became the government's most trusted adviser on atomic policy and related security, heading numerous governmental advisory committees, including the General Advisory Committee (GAC) of the AEC.

Oppenheimer's tragic descent from governmental favor and his corollary loss of scientific prestige began in 1949, when he and the GAC he chaired recommended that the United States should delay a crash program to develop a thermonuclear bomb until an attempt had been made to reach an agreement with the Soviet Union on forswearing development of the "super weapon." President Truman quickly overruled that recommendation, and the AEC conspicuously failed to reappoint Oppenheimer to the GAC in 1952. When Lewis L. Strauss, a strong advocate of the H-bomb, became Chairman of the Atomic Energy Commission in 1953, he initiated a review of "derogatory information" about

Oppenheimer, whose influence within the government and the science it controlled quickly evaporated. Oppenheimer's only remaining connection with the government was as a rarely called consultant for the AEC, and even that appointment was scheduled to expire in June 1954. But the government seemed intent on publicly humiliating Oppenheimer in a way that would banish him forever.

On November 7, 1953, William Liscum Borden, formerly the Executive Director of Congress's Joint Committee on Atomic Energy, wrote a letter to FBI Director J. Edgar Hoover, claiming:

> (1) Between 1939 and mid–1942, more probably than not, J. Robert Oppenheimer was a sufficiently hardened Communist that he either volunteered espionage information to the Soviets or complied with a request for such information;
>
> (2) More probably than not, he has since been functioning as an espionage agent; and
>
> (3) More probably than not, he has since acted under a Soviet directive in influencing United States military, atomic energy, intelligence and diplomatic policy.

Perhaps because there was little hard evidence supporting Borden's charges, he emphasized that the central problem was *not* determining if Oppenheimer had ever been a Communist but, rather, whether "he in fact did what a Communist in his circumstances, at Berkeley, would logically have done."[39]

The FBI sent the letter to President Eisenhower, who immediately called AEC Chairman Strauss to the White House. In his memoirs, prominent columnist Joseph W. Alsop suggested that the Red-hunting Senator Joseph McCarthy had confronted Strauss with the option of jettisoning Oppenheimer or becoming a McCarthy target himself. Because Strauss had approved Oppenheimer's security clearance several years earlier, he was forced to choose between standing up for his own past judgment or, in Alsop's words, "to offer Oppy, bound on the altar, as a sacrifice to appease McCarthy's wrath."[40]

The President told Strauss to convene a hearing on the charges against Oppenheimer, and he ordered that a "blank wall" be erected between Oppenheimer and the atomic secrets that originated in his work. Eisenhower then made the following curious entry in his diary: "It is reported to me that this same [security] information, or at least the vast bulk of it, has been constantly reviewed and re-examined over a number of years, and that the over-all conclusion has always been that there is no evidence that implies disloyalty on the part of Dr. Oppenheimer. However, this does not mean that he might not be a security risk."[41]

The AEC quickly named a three-man board, headed by Gordon Gray, President of the University of North Carolina and former Secretary of the Army, to conduct hearings on Oppenheimer's fitness to retain a security clearance. The two other members of the board were retired industrialist Thomas A. Morgan, former President and Chairman of the Sperry Corporation, and Ward Evans, a chemistry professor at Northwestern University. Evans was a staunch Republican whose conservatism extended to his science. Never distinguished for his research, he rejected much of modern science, including quantum theory. The AEC appointed a tough, conservative prosecutor, Roger Robb, who had seven years of experience as an Assistant U.S. Attorney. Oppenheimer's choice for chief counsel was Lloyd K. Garrison, a prominent New York attorney relatively inexperienced in adversarial courtroom proceedings. Joseph Alsop described Garrison as follows: "An eminently well-groomed New Yorker, Garrison was the epitome of high-mindedness, and it is always a mistake to pay for high-mindedness when you are hiring a lawyer. In the end, Garrison allowed himself to be so hustled by Robb's well-practiced nastiness that he failed to get it squarely on the record that Strauss had . . . seen fit to approve Oppenheimer's security clearance only a little before the case was brought on."[42]

In February 1954, the Eisenhower Administration announced that 2,429 government employees had been fired as "security risks"; of them, 422 were "subversives." The Communists-in-government issue quickly became the backdrop for Oppenheimer's security trial. Even before the trial, Oppenheimer had been the subject of shocking government intrusions on his personal life. For 11 years his home and office had been bugged, his phone calls monitored, and his mail opened. He was followed everywhere by government agents. Senator Joseph McCarthy said the AEC's action to suspend Oppenheimer was "long overdue—it should have been taken years ago. . . . I think it took considerable courage to suspend the so-called untouchable scientist—Oppenheimer."[43] Most scientists, including Albert Einstein, came to Oppenheimer's defense. Unexpected support for Oppenheimer came from former President Harry Truman, and even from then Vice President Richard Nixon, who said, "On the evidence I have seen, Dr. Oppenheimer in my opinion is a loyal American" who, if "he is not subject to blackmail, should have a right to work for the government."[44] Gen. Leslie Groves, former head of the Manhattan Project, said that nothing in the AEC charges convinced him that he had been mistaken in choosing Oppenheimer to head the supersecret Los Alamos Lab. Yet now, years later, Oppenheimer was to face the arbitrary and fearsome judgment of the loyalty-security system.

Oppenheimer was apparently offered the option of voluntarily terminating his AEC consultant's contract rather than face a hostile hearing, but he declined. "I have thought most earnestly of the alternative suggested," he wrote to AEC Chairman Strauss. "Under the circumstances this course of action would mean that I accept and concur in the view that I am not fit to serve this Government, that I have now served for some 12 years. This I cannot do. . . . If I were thus unworthy, I could hardly have served our country as I have tried, . . . in the name of science and our country."[45] And so Oppenheimer cast his fate with the AEC's Security Board, which convened its hearing on April 12, 1954.

The distinction between the prosecution (Roger Robb) and the judge/ jury (the AEC Board) quickly eroded, and Board Chairman Gray was soon referring to Robb as the AEC's prosecutor. Whereas it would have been unthinkable in a normal trial for a judge and jury to meet alone and discuss the case with the prosecuting attorney, that is exactly what occurred before the Oppenheimer hearing began. The three members of the AEC Board spent a week reading the government's investigative reports on Oppenheimer, while Robb and the rest of the prosecuting team explained and interpreted the information for them. Garrison's request for a similar courtesy for the defense was denied. Indeed, throughout the hearing, Garrison seemed unduly timid and passive in dealing with the combined force of Robb and the Board, usually deferring to their every presumption of authority.

As Robb and Garrison prepared for the hearing, it became clear that they would need security clearances to function effectively. But the path Robb followed into that privileged world was quite different from the one available to Garrison. The special atomic "Q" clearance required a full field investigation by the FBI, normally taking a minimum of 60 to 90 days. Just a week before Robb was to begin work, the AEC requested an "emergency Q" clearance for him, and it was granted in just 8 days. Robb's full field investigation and permanent clearance were accomplished in just 22 days.

Garrison initially requested a clearance for himself and his two associates, but the AEC denied that request. Oppenheimer's attorneys then told Strauss that they would forgo any security clearances, so long as the AEC would agree to declassify certain secret documents, like the minutes of the GAC's 1949 H-bomb meeting. At the very least, Garrison said, he expected the AEC's cooperation in providing unclassified summaries of such documents. When the AEC refused both requests, Garrison

realized that he faced the possibility his entire legal team could be expelled from the hearing room each time the prosecution introduced
secret materials. With 17 days remaining before the commencement of
the hearing, Garrison requested a security clearance for himself. Given
the ease and dispatch with which Robb's clearance had been provided,
there appeared to be no cause for concern. But the AEC not only failed
to process Garrison's clearance request in time for the opening of the
hearing, it claimed that it could not clear Garrison before the *end* of the
hearing, eight weeks later. Nothing in the personal or political back-
grounds of Robb or Garrison could explain the dramatic disparity in
the handling of their clearance requests.

Once the hearing began, Garrison and his associates were denied access to the secret documents available to prosecutor Robb, information
on which the final judgment of Oppenheimer would be based. Just as
Garrison feared, there were occasions when the entire defense team was
forced to exit the hearing room for security reasons, leaving Oppenheimer alone and unrepresented. Throughout the hearing, the AEC
repeatedly refused Garrison's requests for unclassified summaries of
relevant documents. The motive behind this rigid secrecy was rendered
questionable during the hearing, when the government introduced into
the public record documents that had been denied to Garrison.

On one occasion, when Robb introduced portions of unidentified,
previously classified AEC documents and Garrison complained of his
lack of knowledge of the origin or authenticity of these documents, Robb
angrily responded: "If [Garrison] does not want to hear this, and wants
the Board to go ahead and consider it without him hearing it, that is
alright with me.... This report is before the board in its entirety. I can't
see why putting a portion in the record seems to be such a horrible step
to take."[46]

All participants in the trial, witnesses and interrogators alike, seemed
captives of the McCarthyite assumptions of guilt by association. In his
Foreword to the subsequently published transcript of the trial, Philip
Stern warned: "[I]f in these pages the reader feels that witnesses (especially Oppenheimer) succumbed in unseemly fashion to the brow-
beating of the prosecutor, Roger Robb, he should bear in mind the fear
that polluted the political atmosphere of 1954."[47]

Throughout the AEC hearing, Oppenheimer was harassed mercilessly
by the prosecutor. After the first week of the hearing, former AEC
General Counsel Joseph Volpe privately advised Oppenheimer and his
attorneys that if the hostile and one-sided atmosphere continued, they
should simply leave the hearing room and advise the AEC Board to

conclude the case in any way they saw fit. Oppenheimer decided to stick it out. Former AEC Chairman David Lilienthal, appearing as a witness before the Board, was shocked to see Oppenheimer's attorneys expelled from the hearing room during the discussion of a classified document. "When I saw what they were doing to Oppenheimer," he later recalled, "I was ready to throw chairs. How can a lawyer defend his client's interests if he isn't even in the hearing room? There hadn't been a proceeding like this since the Spanish Inquisition."[48]

Another former AEC Chairman, John J. McCloy, testified on the concept of a "security risk," drawing on his World War II experience in the War Department. "I don't know just exactly what you mean by a security risk. . . . I think there is a security risk in reverse. . . . We are only secure if we have the best brains and the best reach of mind. . . . If the impression is prevalent that scientists as a whole have to work under such great restrictions and perhaps great suspicion in the United States, we may lose the next step in this [nuclear] field, which I think would be very dangerous for us." McCloy pointed out that AEC regulations require that security risk judgments give "due recognition to the favorable as well as unfavorable information concerning the individual and . . . balance the cost to the program of not having his services against any possible risks involved."[49]

Vannevar Bush, leader of the American mobilization during World War II, appeared before the Board and immediately accused it of making a serious mistake by including Oppenheimer's opposition to the H-bomb among the "security risk" charges. "[H]ere is a man who is being pilloried because he had strong opinions, and had the temerity to express them. . . . No board should ever [decide] whether a man should serve his country or not because he expressed strong views. If you want to try that case, you can try me. I have expressed strong opinions many times. They have been unpopular opinions at times. When a man is pilloried for that, this country is in a severe state."[50]

Many believe that the most damning testimony in the hearing came when Edward Teller, the "father of the H-bomb," testified for the government against Robert Oppenheimer, the "father of the atomic bomb." A colleague of Teller's claims that Teller was reluctant to testify against Oppenheimer, his former intellectual companion, but he believed his debt to AEC Chairman Strauss, an early H-bomb supporter, outweighed his obligation to Oppenheimer, who allegedly had tried to block the H-bomb program.

A few hours before Teller's testimony, Roger Robb had shown him a dossier containing information unfavorable to Oppenheimer. Teller re-

calls that Robb characterized Oppenheimer as a devil. With this prep-
aration, Teller began his testimony. He said that he had always assumed,
and continued to assume, that Oppenheimer was a loyal American. Robb
then asked if Teller considered Oppenheimer a "security risk." Teller
answered, "I feel that I would like to see the vital interests of this country
in hands that I understand better, and therefore trust more." When
Robb asked for examples of behavior that he found difficult to understand or trust, Teller mentioned an Oppenheimer proposal to share
plutonium with other countries and his opposition to early A-bomb detection devices. Teller admitted that the second of these alleged behav-
iors was "definitely in the hearsay category, and I might just be quite
wrong on it."[51]

Chairman Gray asked Teller, "Do you feel it would endanger the
common defense and security to grant clearance to Dr. Oppenheimer?"

Teller initially responded that Oppenheimer would never knowingly
and willingly do anything to endanger the United States. Therefore,
with respect to Oppenheimer's *intent*, he saw no reason to deny clearance.
But Teller quickly added, "If it is a question of wisdom and judgement,
as demonstrated by actions since 1945, then I would say one would be
wiser not to grant clearance." Teller made clear that he was concerned
about Oppenheimer's "wisdom and judgement" on matters of *policy*, not
security. For example, when asked about the danger of Oppenheimer
having access to Restricted Data, Teller answered that there would be
no danger so long as Oppenheimer would "refrain from all advice in
these matters."[52]

Luis Walter Alvarez, a professor of physics at Berkeley and staunch
supporter of Edward Teller, testified at great length about his own efforts to promote the H-bomb and Oppenheimer's lack of support. Board
member Ward Evans asked Alvarez, "It doesn't mean he was disloyal?"
Alvarez answered that it did not, but it did mean that Oppenheimer had
shown "exceedingly poor judgement."[53]

The final witness against Oppenheimer was William Liscum Borden,
the man whose letter to the FBI had set this trial in motion. Borden did
little more than read his letter aloud. Surprisingly, Chairman Gray commented that there was no evidence before the Board to support Borden's
charges that Oppenheimer had complied with any request for espionage
information, or that he had been functioning under a Soviet directive.
Oppenheimer's attorneys decided there was no point in cross-examining
a witness whose charges had been largely rejected by the Board, and
Borden's brief appearance was concluded.

Robert Oppenheimer was then called to the stand by his own counsel.

He once more attempted to place his lifetime of service to science and his country against the AEC's political charges. In the course of cross-examining Oppenheimer, Robb asked: "Doctor, I am a little curious, and I wish you would tell us why you felt it was your function as a scientist to express views on military strategy and tactics?" Oppenheimer responded, "I felt, perhaps quite strongly, that having played an active part in promoting a revolution in warfare, I needed to be as responsible as I could with regard to what came of this revolution."[54]

The final voice in the hearing was Garrison's three-hour summation, which, by all accounts, was eloquent. He said that the compelling fact "is that for more than a decade Dr. Oppenheimer has created and has shared secrets of the atomic energy program and has held them inviolable."[55] Garrison asked that the case be disposed of on the basis of the fact that Dr. Oppenheimer had been trusted and had not failed that trust. But Garrison knew that the judgment on Oppenheimer would hinge on matters such as his H-bomb policy. "[T]he only question you have here," Garrison said, is "whether his own advice [on the H-bomb], unlike every other member of the GAC, was motivated by a sinister purpose to injure the United States of America and to help our enemy— the mere utterance of that proposition is shocking to me." Garrison concluded: "There is more than Dr. Oppenheimer on trial in this room. . . . The government of the United States is here on trial also. Our whole security process is on trial here, and is in your keeping, as is his life. . . . America must not devour its own children. . . . If we are to be strong, powerful, electric and vital, we must not devour the best and the most gifted of our citizens in some mechanical application of security procedures and mechanisms."[56]

On May 27, 1954, the Board submitted to AEC General Manager Kenneth D. Nichols its 15,000-word report: "Subject: Findings and Recommendations of the Personnel Security Board in the Case of J. Robert Oppenheimer." The wording in its introduction was vintage Cold War, emphasizing the "central" nature of "security" during the "present peril," which therefore made some "undue restraints upon freedom of mind and action" necessary. It said the "protection of all our people" must be "paramount to all other considerations." It concluded that what "may seem to be a denial" of freedom might in fact be the "fulfillment" of that freedom, "For, if, in our zeal to protect our institutions against our measures to secure them, we lay them open to destruction, we will have lost them all, and will have gained only the empty satisfaction of a meaningless exercise."[57]

Having placed their judgment of Oppenheimer in context, the Board explained its findings on the AEC charges. Despite its conclusion that Oppenheimer was loyal and discreet, with "an unusual ability to keep to himself vital secrets,"[58] the Board found 20 out of 24 charges to be "true" or "substantially true." Though the three-man Board was divided in its judgment of Oppenheimer, the majority, led by Chairman Gray, concluded:

1) We find that Dr. Oppenheimer's continuing conduct and associations have reflected a serious disregard for the requirements of the security system.

2) We have found a susceptibility to influence which could have serious implications for the security interests of the country.

3) We find his conduct in the hydrogen bomb program sufficiently disturbing as to raise a doubt as to whether his future participation, if characterized by the same attitudes in a government program relating to the national defense, would be clearly consistent with the best interests of security.

4) We have regretfully concluded that Dr. Oppenheimer has been less than candid in several instances in his testimony before this board.[59]

There is considerable indication that Oppenheimer's policy views on the hydrogen bomb were the determining factor in the Board's judgment to deny his security clearance. Oppenheimer had indeed argued against an early rush to develop the H-bomb, but once the government made its commitment to a thermonuclear program, he did not oppose it, did not decline to cooperate in it, and did not attempt to dissuade others from working on it. The AEC Board acknowledged this but, astonishingly, identified Oppenheimer's degree of enthusiasm as a security criterion. "The Board finds that if Dr. Oppenheimer had enthusiastically supported the thermonuclear program either before or after the determination of national policy, the H-bomb project would have been pursued with considerably more vigor, thus increasing the possibility of earlier success in this field."[60] The Board concluded that "enthusiastic support on his part would *perhaps* have encouraged other leading scientists to work on the program."[61]

In discussing the Board's "criterion of enthusiasm," Dael Wolfle wrote: "Its implications are too grave and frightening to have the basic issue clouded. It has been pointed out by a variety of writers that adherence to such a doctrine will dampen free discussion—not only in public but in secret councils. Who wants to risk such drastic punishment, years after a decision was made, for having honestly opposed the decision before it was made?"[62]

The lone dissenting view on the AEC Personnel Security Board came from its only scientist, Ward Evans. Evans noted that Oppenheimer had been cleared by earlier security investigations, the last in 1947, on virtually the same evidence used by the AEC Board to convict him. "To deny him clearance now...when we must know he is less of a security risk than he was then, seems hardly the procedure to be adopted in a free country." Not only did Evans see no risk to national security in Oppenheimer's continued government service, he feared that the Board's decision would have an adverse effect on the nation's scientific development.[63]

The AEC insisted that scientists were "ill-advised" to consider themselves under general attack by the Board's decision, but Oppenheimer's attorney had his doubts. Garrison said the AEC had avoided "the fundamental question as to what are the appropriate limits of a security inquiry under existing statutes and regulations and under a government of laws and not of men—a question of concern not merely to scientists and intellectuals but to all of our people."[64] Rather than appealing the Personnel Security Board's decision, Garrison requested permission to submit an additional brief and oral argument to the AEC itself. The AEC accepted the brief but refused to hear an oral argument.

The five-man AEC, by a four to one vote, repeated the judgment of its Personnel Security Board that J. Robert Oppenheimer was a security risk who should be denied further government employment or atomic work in the national defense. But the basis for the Commission's judgment differed somewhat from that of its Security Board. The Commission dismissed the absurd claim that Oppenheimer was insufficiently enthusiastic about the H-bomb program, admitting that he was entitled to his opinion. Instead, the Commission faulted Oppenheimer for "fundamental defects in his character" and political associations that were judged to "have extended far beyond the tolerable limits of prudence and self-restraint." In particular, Oppenheimer was judged to be "disloyal" under a definition that required "exact fidelity" to the security regulations.[65]

As was the case with the Security Board, the dissenting opinion on the full Commission came from its lone scientist, Henry D. Smyth, who asserted that Oppenheimer's continued employment would not endanger the common defense and security, but would in fact "continue to strengthen the U.S." Smyth insisted that the only proper question for the Commission to consider was whether Dr. Oppenheimer might intentionally or unintentionally reveal secret information to unauthorized persons. Smyth concluded, "To me this is what is meant within our security system by the term 'security risk.' ... In my opinion the most important evidence in this record is the fact that there is no indication that Dr. Oppenheimer has ever divulged any secret information."[66]

But the paranoia surrounding atomic information reigned supreme, and the voice of the scientist remained irrelevant in the world of science. Scientists have always known that atomic secrets are secrets of nature. The natural phenomena that compose these secrets are the atomic and subatomic particles, which know no national boundaries and cannot be locked away in government vaults. Their secrets await any scientist with the talent and the freedom to search for them. Years before the AEC witch-hunt, Albert Einstein had rendered a critical judgment of atomic secrecy and an implicit rejection of the Atomic Energy Act:

> Through the release of atomic energy, our generation has brought into the world the most revolutionary force since prehistoric man's discovery of fire. This basic power of the universe cannot be fitted into the outmoded concept of narrow nationalism. For there is no secret and no defense; there is no possibility of control except through the aroused understanding and insistence of the peoples of the world. We scientists recognize our inescapable responsibility to carry to our fellow citizens an understanding of the simple facts of atomic energy and its implications for society. In this lies our only security and our only hope—we believe that an informed citizenry will act for life and not for death.[67]

PRIOR RESTRAINT

On March 14 and 20, 1950, the AEC sent telegrams to its managers describing broad new restraints to be applied to written or spoken communication of atomic information. The telegram demanded that AEC staff "avoid release of technical information which, even though itself unclassified, may be interpreted by virtue of the project connection of the speaker as reflecting the Commission's program with respect to thermonuclear weapons."[68] The Commission made it clear that these new restraints applied to all persons associated with the atomic energy project, past or present. This would include most of the nation's atomic physicists. The first application of this new policy came when Hans Bethe, a prominent physicist and consultant to the AEC, submitted an article on thermonuclear fusion for publication in the April issue of *Scientific American*. Bethe sent copies of his manuscript to some of his colleagues, including one who was a member of the AEC. All who read the manuscript agreed that the information contained in it had been widely published and had no "national security" implications.

On March 15, after the April issue of *Scientific American* containing Bethe's article, "The Hydrogen Bomb: II," went to press, the AEC sent a telegram to the publisher asking that the technical portions of the article be deleted. The presses were stopped to allow the Commission to specify the objectionable material. *Scientific American* reluctantly capitulated to the AEC's threat of an injunction. Publisher Gerard Piel recalls the humiliation: "We acceded to ritual cuts made by AEC agents on security grounds and published a mutilated article."[69] But even then the Commission was not satisfied. It demanded that *Scientific American* destroy all copies of the original article. An AEC security officer went to the printing plant to supervise the destruction of the type and printing plates and the burning of 3,000 copies of the original issue.

In assessing the AEC's action, publisher Piel concluded that the Atomic Energy Act confuses ignorance with secrecy. "In the thirty years since America lost its imagined monopoly on the atomic secret, we should have learned that there never was a secret that could keep another country from making a bomb. . . . The power of prior restraint of publication is not invoked to protect any other military secret in peacetime. It can only stifle public discussion of the awesome questions that confront Government officials every day."[70] Piel says, "We consider that the Commission's action with regard to the Bethe article and the sweeping subsequent prohibition issued to the nation's atomic scientists raises the question of whether the Commission is thus suppressing information which the American people need in order to form intelligent judgements on this major problem."[71]

The ease with which the AEC imposed prior restraint on *Scientific American* avoided a court test of that action, but the legal basis appears to be *Schenck v. United States* (249 US 47, 39 S.Ct. 247 [1919]), which found that restraints on freedom of speech "would appear to be a reasonable exercise of sovereign power . . . in the interest of the common defense and security." This assumed power to restrict the communication of privately owned information suggests that even if a publisher refused to comply with the AEC's censorship demands, the Atomic Energy Act would authorize a federal court to issue an injunction restraining the publication of such information. But such action, called prior restraint, must meet a severe constitutional test. In fact, the Supreme Court has construed the elimination of prior restraints on publications to be the "leading purpose" of the First Amendment.[72]

The judicial policy against prior restraints, like the common law doctrine, focuses principally on the *form* of governmental restraint. Prior restraint is not unconstitutional per se, but it is subject to exacting judicial scrutiny because, as Justice Harry Blackmun commented, "a free society prefers to punish the few who abuse rights of speech *after* they break the law than to throttle them and all others beforehand."[73] Alexander Bickel has pointed out that even if a prior restraint on speech is ultimately lifted, there is an irremediable loss in the immediacy and impact of speech. "A criminal statute chills, prior restraint freezes. Indeed it is the hypothesis of the First Amendment that injury is inflicted on society when we stifle the immediacy of speech."[74]

In *Near v. Minnesota* (283 US 697, 51 S.Ct. 625 [1931]), Chief Justice Charles Evans Hughes outlined circumstances under which prior restraint might be acceptable to the Court. The most significant example cited concerned the restriction of wartime information on "the sailing dates of transports or the number or location of troops." In more general terms, Hughes said that communication that had no essential part in the exposition of ideas could be subject to government control.

The Pentagon Papers case (*New York Times Co. v. United States*, 403 U.S. 713 [1971]) tested the Government's claim of an inherent power to seek injunctions against the publication of materials relating to both public affairs and national security. The Pentagon Papers contained classified technical information, but they were also political-historical studies of considerable general interest. In a 6–3 decision, the Supreme Court refused to enjoin the publication of the Pentagon Papers, but the Court's per curiam ruling, with nine separate concurring and dissenting opinions, failed to establish a precedent on the issue. A majority of the Court did agree on the following points:

1. The First Amendment does not provide absolute protection for the dissemination of all information.

2. The executive branch possesses no inherent right to impose a prior restraint on publications.

The majority in the *Pentagon Papers* case made it clear that any national security exception to the policy against prior restraint was extremely narrow, limited to situations where, in Justice Potter Stewart's words, "publication must inevitably, directly, and immediately cause the occurrence of an event kindred to imperiling the safety of a transport already at sea."[75]

Justice Thurgood Marshall claimed that, in the absence of authorization by Congress, the judiciary could not legitimately enforce prior restraints on communication. He noted: "It is not for this Court to fling itself into every breach perceived by some Government official nor is it for this Court to take on itself the burden of enacting law, especially law that Congress has refused to pass."[76] Marshall emphasized that the executive branch and judiciary may constitutionally enjoin publications that threaten the national security, but only when Congress has given explicit authorization. Prophetically, Marshall suggested that the Atomic Energy Act might be an example of such authorization.

UNITED STATES v. PROGRESSIVE

Surely the most spectacular legal challenge to the concept of "born classified" and the threat of prior restraint occurred in early 1979 when *The Progressive*, a popular political magazine, attempted to publish an article on the hydrogen bomb by a free-lance writer named Howard Morland. Morland's article, "The H-bomb Secret," was intended to stimulate public debate and understanding of the nuclear weapons industry while showing that the secrecy surrounding the bomb was a sham. In introducing the article, Morland wrote:

> What you are about to learn is a secret—a secret that the United States and four other nations, the makers of hydrogen weapons, have gone to extraordinary lengths to protect.... I discovered it by simply reading and asking questions, without the benefit of security clearance or access to classified materials.... I am telling the secret to make a basic point as forcefully as I can: Secrecy itself, especially the power of a few designated "experts" to declare some topics off limits, contributes to a political climate in which the nuclear establishment can conduct business as usual, protecting and perpetuating the production of these horror weapons.[77]

Indeed, the technical information in Morland's article, describing the nature, composition, and reaction processes of the hydrogen bomb, was derived from public sources like Dr. Edward Teller's 1975 article in the *Encyclopedia Americana*. Morland was moved to action when he observed the arrogance with which the Department of Energy (DOE) rebuffed Congressional attempts to monitor the nuclear weapons industry. One Congressman had asked DOE whether its projected shortcoming of plutonium was due to the scheduled construction of the neutron bomb. DOE refused to provide even an unclassified response to such questions, claiming that *the questions themselves* should be classified because they contained "secret restricted data," as defined in the Atomic Energy Act.

Morland concluded that not only could DOE officials withhold answers, they could confiscate the questions.

Sam Day, *The Progressive*'s managing editor, advanced Howard Morland $550 for the article, after considerable discussion of its substance. In a July 7, 1979, letter to *The Progressive*, Morland summarized his understanding of the assignment:

> We agreed that nuclear weapons production has prospered too long in an atmosphere of freedom from public scrutiny. *The Progressive* should raise the visibility of the nuclear warhead assembly line.... The Bomb should be described in sufficient detail to allow readers to see nuclear warheads as pieces of hardware rather than as score-points in a contest.... I hope to know as much as it is legal to know—and possible for a layman to understand—about thermonuclear warhead design. I will then trace each major component through its fabrication process, starting with the mineral ore and ending with final assembly of the warhead.... Some of the needed information is classified, of course, and holes in the story will have to be filled by educated speculation.[78]

Morland researched his article by reading encyclopedia and magazine articles, textbooks, and unclassified government reports. Then he met with Charles Gilbert, DOE's Deputy Director of Military Applications, to describe his intended article. Morland says, "[I]t was agreed that I would ask any question that I desired, and that it was up to the person who was talking to me to know whether the answer to my question is classified or not. He [Gilbert] agreed with that procedure and that was the principle upon which I operated during the entire course of my research."[79] Morland soon realized that there was no secret at all, that anyone with the most basic knowledge of physics could piece together an explanation of the workings of the hydrogen bomb.

In January 1979 Morland submitted a rough draft of his article, consisting of about 18 manuscript pages and 7 hand-drawn sketches, and *The Progressive* sent the draft to several reviewers to be checked for accuracy. Without the magazine's knowledge or consent, one of the reviewers sent a copy to George Rathjens, an MIT professor and government consultant. Rathjens called managing editor Sam Day at *The Progressive*, claiming that Morland's article contained "secrets" that should not be published. He added that he had sent a copy of the draft to the DOE. Day protested, but a First Amendment struggle had already been set in motion.

Duanne Sewell, DOE's Assistant Secretary of Energy for Defense Programs, showed the Morland article to Secretary of Energy James Schles-

inger and to other agency heads. Schlesinger took the article to Attorney
General Griffin Bell, telling him that the article could provide foreign
nations with a "map and shortcut" to the design of thermonuclear weapons. Schlesinger insisted that even though Morland had drawn only upon
information in the public domain, no one had previously published such
data in easy-to-understand language. Bell recalls, "No cabinet secretary
in my tenure ever pushed us harder to move in court."[80]

On March 1, shortly before the deadline for *The Progressive*'s April
issue, the DOE's general counsel called Sam Day, announcing that unless
he agreed to withdraw the Morland article, the government would take
legal action to prevent publication. The next day, the editors of *The
Progressive* met with four representatives from DOE and two from the
Justice Department. The DOE's Sewell read from the Atomic Energy
Act and claimed that all of Morland's sketches and about 20 percent of
his text were Restricted Data. Sewell said DOE would be willing to rewrite
the article to make it suitable for publication, but he could not identify
the secret part of the article without breaching security. After consultation with *The Progressive*'s staff, the magazine's attorney notified DOE
that the magazine intended to publish the article without changes, and
if the government planned court action, it should act with dispatch. The
same day, Attorney General Bell sent a memo to President Carter stating
that his office was negotiating with *The Progressive* to prevent publication
of Morland's article; if the negotiations failed, he recommended immediate legal action. "While we cannot assure you that we will prevail
in this suit," Bell wrote, "the potentially grave consequences to the security of the U.S. and the world itself resulting from the disclosure of
the data are obvious and frightening." President Carter responded with
a terse handwritten note: "Good move—proceed. J."[81]

Erwin Knoll, editor of *The Progressive*, soon came to understand the
Draconian measures of the Atomic Energy Act, which made every scrap
of information about atomic energy classified at birth. Knoll commented,
"That such language, which is, in our judgement and that of our attorneys, unconstitutionally broad and in clear violation of the First Amendment, should have stood unchallenged for decades is, in itself, evidence
of the oppressive secrecy that has surrounded the nuclear program."[82]
Morland's article was to appear in the April 1979 issue of *The Progressive*,
but in a Milwaukee court on March 9, Federal Judge Robert W. Warren
issued a temporary restraining order that he characterized as "the first
instance of prior restraint against a publication in this fashion in the
history of this country." Though he had not read Morland's article, Judge
Warren stated, "I want to think a long, hard time before I'd give a

hydrogen bomb to Idi Amin. It appears to me that is just what we're doing here." Warren's long, hard thought lasted until March 26, when he issued a preliminary injunction barring author Morland and all employees and attorneys of *The Progressive* from "publishing or otherwise communicating, transmitting or disclosing in any manner any information designated by the Secretary of Energy as Restricted Data contained in the Morland article."[83]

By the time of his injunction, Warren had learned enough to know that the Morland article would not give a hydrogen bomb to Idi Amin. He admitted: "Does the article provide a 'do-it-yourself' guide to the hydrogen bomb? Probably not. A number of affidavits make it quite clear that a *sine qua non* to thermonuclear capability is a large, sophisticated industrial capability coupled with a coterie of imaginative, resourceful scientists and technicians. One does not build a hydrogen bomb in the basement." Yet despite his newfound technological insight, Warren approved the government's request for an injunction that he admitted would "curtail defendants' First Amendment rights in a drastic and substantial fashion" and "infringe upon our right to know and to be informed as well." He justified his action by claiming that "a mistake in ruling against the United States could pave the way for nuclear annihilation for us all."[84]

The judge had accepted the government's national security arguments on faith, without bothering to read Morland's manuscript. Surprisingly, many of the liberal publishers who had defended the First Amendment in the *Pentagon Papers* case were unwilling to support *The Progressive*. The *Washington Post* called the case "a real First Amendment loser."[85] Even those who deplored the government's restraining order feared an adverse court decision, and therefore advised *The Progressive* to agree to voluntary censorship. The scientific community also showed the effects of intimidation. The Committee on Scientific Freedom and Responsibility of the American Association for the Advancement of Science seemed to betray its name by sending a telegram to *The Progressive* asking that it avoid litigation and recommending, "We would prefer to have these sensitive issues resolved by voluntary editorial changes by the publisher after discussions with the Government, if necessary."[86]

Still, spokespersons for 21 prominent publications and 5 national organizations released a statement in support of *The Progressive*, which read, in part:

> In a time when military policy is closely linked with technological capabilities, debate about military policy that uses technical information is part

of a vigorous system of freedom of expression under the First Amendment. The Government's tendency to hide widely known technical processes under a mantle of secrecy in the national interest and prevent press commentary on these matters can only result in stifling debate, not in protecting the physical security of Americans.[87]

The *New York Times* editorialized: "What the Government really aims to protect is a system of secrecy, which it seeks now to extend to the thought and discussion of scientists and writers outside Government. And Judge Warren has become its accomplice—in his reasoning, in his misguided request that the magazine let experts do the censoring and in his overreaching opinion that *The Progressive* had no reason to publish such an article." *In These Times* commented: "The Government's attempt to prohibit publication by *The Progressive* of a story on 'The H-bomb Secret' has less to do with anxiety over nuclear weapons proliferation than over the proliferation of legitimate information about the nuclear weapons industry among the American people." The *Charlotte Observer* said, "The day when safety was guaranteed by secrecy is long past. . . . The nuclear threat doesn't come from magazines but from governments, including ours."[88]

During Morland's trial, even the most trivial scientific statements were censored. A reporter commented, "[The] Justice [Department] declared that Dr. Teller's article in the *Encyclopedia Americana* was secret, the affidavits by which it was introduced were secret, and the court's opinion about these secrets was secret."[89] Morland's public sources, cited in his affidavit, included his elementary college physics textbook with some passages underlined. The government claimed that the textbook had to be kept secret until his underlining was erased. Morland tried to explain, to no avail, that he had done the underlining as a freshman preparing for an exam.

The government made things difficult for *The Progressive*'s attorneys, censoring briefs, affidavits, and exhibits, excluding them from the public record. Defense attorneys had to be "cleared" before they could examine these secret filings, and even then they were prohibited from discussing this "Restricted Data" with the defendants. When *The Progressive* asked Judge Warren to lift the injunction, he responded by issuing a secret opinion that the defendants were never allowed to read!

The affidavits for the plaintiff were led by statements from the Secretaries of State, Defense, and Energy, all citing the national security threat posed by Morland's article. On the other hand, *all* affidavits for the defense were from physicists, who were unanimous in declaring that the data in Morland's article were drawn from unclassified, public sources. Theodore Postol of the Argonne National Library stated that the article "contains no information or ideas that are not already common knowledge among scientists, including those who do not have access to classified information." Ray Kidder of the Lawrence Livermore Laboratory said, "The basic principles of operation of the hydrogen bomb as set forth in the Morland article are deductible from information widely available to the public by a person having an unexceptional knowledge of physics and without access to classified information."[90]

In his affidavit, Hugh DeWitt of the Livermore Lab said, "If this article by Morland is not published, I expect that it will be only a short time before another reporter working independently for a different publication will uncover the same information and write a very similar article. In short, after more than twenty-five years the H-bomb is not so secret anymore." Edward Cooperman of the University of California stated, "Such information has been published or otherwise disseminated in one form or another, or is otherwise known or available to so many people, that it is readily accessible to anyone interested in acquiring it. Governmental policy designed to preserve secrecy with respect to such matters not only is unsuccessful but inhibits research and obstructs the advancement of scientific knowledge."[91]

The only defense affidavit that expressed reservations about Morland's article showed no concern about its *content*, and may have revealed more about compulsive secrecy and paranoia than the prosecution's affidavits. As an afterthought, physicist Ralph Hager of Livermore stated, "I do not recommend publishing the Morland article because it unnecessarily draws attention to an issue which has not been demonstrated to be in the interest of national security."[92]

Judge Warren initially justified his restraining order on the claim that Morland's article contained scientific concepts not in the public realm that, if published, would result in direct, immediate, and irreparable damage to the United States by accelerating the capacity of certain nations to manufacture thermonuclear weapons. But Judge Warren's argument began to unravel when an American Civil Liberties Union investigator, seeking to demonstrate *The Progressive*'s claim that technical information on the H-bomb was publicly available, found highly technical H-bomb reports on the open shelves at the public library at Los Alamos Scientific Laboratory.

The government's argument that such information was not in the public realm, and would cause dire harm to the nation if it were, was clearly compromised. The government quickly claimed that the Los Alamos documents must have been declassified by mistake, and declared that the "clerical error" would be corrected. The DOE promptly classified the reports and closed the library. Many in the Justice Department wanted to drop the case at this point, but American intelligence agencies assured the Attorney General that the information in Morland's article had not yet reached hostile foreign powers. Therefore, despite clear evidence that the "secret" was out, Griffin Bell advised his staff that "some disclosure does not mandate full disclosure." Bell concluded, "The public interest and the Atomic Energy Act require that we do our best."[93]

By the time the case reached the Appeals Court in Chicago, the government had added a new wrinkle, claiming that "technical" information, unlike political expression, was not protected by the First Amendment. Unlike many nervous liberals in the mass media, the publishers and editors at *The Progressive* never doubted that they would win their case in court. In fact, they began to suspect that the Government would try to drop the case and declare the issue "moot," thus avoiding a ruling that might invalidate the secrecy provisions of the Atomic Energy Act. Indeed, on September 15, 1979, the government's case began to crumble when it became clear that articles similar to Morland's would soon be published elsewhere. Several physicists from the Argonne National Laboratory wrote a letter to Senator John Glenn (R-OH), claiming that Edward Teller's *Encyclopedia Americana* article and diagrams were the key to the H-bomb design. When officials at DOE became aware of the scientists' letter, they simply classified it as "secret/restricted data," but not before a "nuclear hobbyist" named Charles Hansen had acquired a copy and circulated it to numerous newspapers. A student newspaper in Berkeley, California, defied a DOE warning and printed the letter. Six other college newspapers soon did the same.

Hansen had written repeatedly to DOE officials challenging their suppression of Morland's article, and he infuriated them during the Spring of 1979 when he organized a nationwide "H-bomb Design Contest." The first entry that DOE felt compelled to classify would be declared the winner. But more important, Hansen wrote a lengthy letter to Senator Charles Percy (R-IL) in which he summarized the technical data from Morland's article and other sources. Hansen mailed copies of the letter to several newspapers and the DOE, which classified the letter as "secret/restricted data." When the same California college newspaper that had printed Hansen's earlier "restricted" letter threatened to do it again, the government went into court in San Francisco to obtain a restraining order.

But the genie was out of the bottle. On September 16, Hansen's letter to Senator Percy was published in a Madison, Wisconsin, newspaper. The next day the Justice Department announced that it would seek dismissal of its case against *The Progressive*, giving as its reason the publication of an article containing Restricted Data concerning thermonuclear weapons. Griffin Bell stated, "The printing of the Hansen letter by one publication, an action that was repeated throughout the world, made pointless any effort to restrain publication by others."[94] On September 28, the U.S. Seventh Circuit Court of Appeals vacated John Warren's injunction. *The Progressive* retrieved its cover design and reproduction proofs and Morland's article appeared in the November 1979 issue, without a word of the original manuscript changed.

The Progressive asked the Appeals Court to rule that Judge Warren had acted improperly in imposing prior restraint on grounds of national security and that the secrecy provisions of the Atomic Energy Act were so broad and vague as to be unconstitutional. The court was also asked to open the records of the case to public scrutiny, since they had been censored by the government throughout the trial. As feared, the Justice Department immediately moved to declare the case "moot," leaving the concept of "born classified" unchallenged. But *The Progressive* submitted a brief stating:

> This case clearly is capable of repetition both for these defendants and others. Yet it will continue to evade review until these defendants, another magazine, newspaper, or individual again forfeits—however temporarily—First Amendment rights to litigate the fundamental issues raised by the Atomic Energy Act.... These cases also have provided ample evidence of the potential for the arbitrary and discriminatory use of the Act. There are in the record of this case more than twenty-five publications and broadcasts that have stated one or more of the three concepts the Government sought to protect in the context of thermonuclear weapons, yet the Government sought no injunction or brought a criminal action.[95]

The arbitrariness referred to in *The Progressive*'s brief was underscored by the subsequent revelation that the government had deliberately ignored the publication of an article in *Fusion* magazine that contained considerably more "Restricted Data" than did Morland's article. In fact, the editors of *Fusion* had prefaced the March 1979 article with a note: "We fully expect that with the appearance of this issue of *Fusion* magazine, Energy Secretary James Schlesinger and his staff will begin circulating the story—if not attempting legal prosecution—that the information in 'The Secret of Laser Fusion' is classified. Therefore, we want to make it clear that this article is based on information made public by the Soviet Union and readily available in other international scientific circles."[96]

Even today, no one at *The Progressive* quite understands why the government chose to target the Morland article for suppression. Morland himself asks, "Why did the Government react so forcefully to my story? It is not because of any scientific or technical secrets I found. There are none. It was because I discovered the passwords.... The thousands who know the correct design concepts for thermonuclear weapons form a fraternity. It is a fraternity of people who are able to claim superior insight into nuclear matters by virtue of possessing accurate knowledge." Morland described the relative ease with which he himself entered the fraternity. "Insiders began to accept me. Once I knew the 'handshake,' people would discuss technical matters with little hesitation. Often I would be told that all my information had been previously published anyway. I knew that indeed it had been.... What they mind—and what gave them deep offense when they discovered it—was that I promised, once I had been admitted, to pass out membership cards to everyone. *The Progressive*'s intentions to publish the H-bomb secret amounted to a threat to flood the market with their currency—the currency of secrecy."[97]

THE LEGAL LEGACY OF *THE PROGRESSIVE* CASE

Some fear that Judge Warren's easy granting of a preliminary injunction against *The Progressive* opened the door to prior restraint. Others argue that in conjunction with the *Pentagon Papers* case, *United States v. Progressive* (467 F.Supp. 990 [W.D. Wis.], dismissed [Oct. 1, 1979]), showed the ultimate futility of prior restraint. In retrospect, Griffin Bell admits that in cases like *The Progressive*, "I don't think prior restraint does work."[98] But Bell still maintains that the government was correct in trying to stop publication, and he would do the same thing again in similar circumstances. On the other hand, publisher Erwin Knoll says he would do things quite differently. He would not obey a court's injunction to prevent publication, and he would not obey the court's orders of silence during the trial.

The consensus among legal experts is that in seeking to restrain publication of *The Progressive* article, the government pressed a hard case on weak facts. In seeking its injunction, the government initially relied upon the Atomic Energy Act of 1954, section 2014(y), defining Restricted Data, and sections 2274(b) and 2280, which describe the penalties for disclosure and the injunction proceedings available to the government.

Because the case against *The Progressive* was dismissed, no formal legal judgment was rendered on the constitutionality of the Atomic Energy Act and its concept of "born classified." But what of Justice Marshall's prophetic comment during the *Pentagon Papers* case that the Atomic Energy Act was precisely the kind of Congressional authorization under which the government and the courts might enjoin publication? The Atomic Energy Act does indeed authorize the government to seek, and the courts to provide, injunctions against dissemination of "Restricted Data." But although the Court in the Pentagon Papers case did anticipate this question, a majority agreed that the government may enjoin publication only when authorized by a *narrowly drawn statute*. Had the government not sought dismissal of its case against *The Progressive*, the courts might have found the Atomic Energy Act both vague and overly broad in authorizing prior restraint on *any* information concerning atomic weapons.

In order for Morland to have violated section 2774(b) of the Act, he must have had "reason to believe" that publication of his article would harm the United States. Since his article was derived from information in the public domain, Morland had no reason to believe it represented a threat to his country. In its brief, the government admitted that "if the data in question was already in the public domain and well known in the scientific community, it is difficult to see how the defendant could have reason to believe that the disclosure would injure the United States. ... [T]he government contends that the disputed article is unique because it combines the individual concepts synergistically for the first time."[99] The government was here applying the notorious "mosaic theory," which claims that public information, properly organized and combined, becomes classified information.

But this tendentious argument had been explicitly rejected by the courts in *United States v. Heine* (151 F.2d 813 [1945], 328 U.S. 833 [1946]), which reversed the conviction of a German American who had collated and synthesized public data on the aviation industry and sent it to Germany shortly before America entered World War II. Heine was initially convicted under the Espionage Act of 1917, under language strikingly similar to section 2274(b) of the Atomic Energy Act. But the Second Circuit reversed his conviction, with Justice Learned Hand writing: "[W]hen the information has once been made public, and thus becomes available in one way or another to any foreign government, the 'advantage' intended by the section cannot reside in facilitating its use by condensing and arranging it."[100]

After the collapse of its initial argument that Morland's article contained unique nuclear information (Restricted Data) not available to the public, the government felt compelled to introduce a new wrinkle when the case reached appeal: the claim that scientific information, unlike political expression, was unprotected speech. By taking this position the government hoped to avoid the very strict standards required to justify prior restraint. Whatever else Judge Warren's frightened and frightening legal pronouncements in *The Progressive* case may portend, the government's arguments represent the most explicit legal attempt to place scientific expression outside constitutional protections. By misreading the statute and granting a preliminary injunction on very weak grounds, Judge Warren severely diminished First Amendment guarantees, particularly with respect to scientific expression.

Legal experts Lawrence Tribe and David Remes noted: "[T]he government did seem to argue, amazingly, that scientific knowledge plays no vital role in discussions of current events and political choices, and for *that* reason deserves little or no First Amendment protection." Indeed, the government persuaded Judge Warren to treat Morland's article as a lower form of speech, subject to prior restraint on a mere showing that the government has a greater need for secrecy than the public has a right to know. If it had been sustained on appeal, this view of scientific expression would have had far-reaching consequences. Tribe and Remes ask: "What sort of information would the government next claim deserved no greater protection than this? Even if such claims were confined to information bearing only on matters of science and technology—a dubious prospect, at best—their sweep would be breathtakingly broad in an era when science and society, technology and culture, are pervasively and powerfully linked."[101]

NOTES

1. "Science Hush-Hushed," *Time*, 11 May 1942, 90.
2. Patrick S. Washburn, "The Office of Censorship's Attempt to Control Press Coverage of the Atomic Bomb During World War II," paper presented at the annual meeting of the Association for Education in Journalism and Mass Communication, Portland, Oregon, 2–5 July 1988, ERIC document ED295201, 8.
3. Ibid., 8–9.
4. Ibid., 9–10.
5. Ibid., 12.
6. Ibid., 14–15.
7. "Washington Memo," *Minneapolis Tribune*, 24 August 1944, 4.
8. Washburn, "The Office of Censorship's Attempt," 21.

9. Ralph McGill, "V-Bomb Attacks on This Nation?" *Atlanta Constitution*, 13 January 1945, 4.

10. Washburn, "The Office of Censorship's Attempt," 23–24.

11. "Superman," *Washington Post*, 14 April 1945, 7B.

12. Washburn, "The Office of Censorship's Attempt," 28, 39.

13. Ibid., 31.

14. Ibid., 37–38.

15. Ibid., 38.

16. Michael J. Yavenditti, "Atomic Scientists and Hollywood," *Film and History*, 8 (1978), 76.

17. Ibid., 77.

18. Nathan Reingold, *Science, American Style* (New Brunswick, NJ: Rutgers University Press, 1991), 336–340.

19. Yavenditti, "Atomic Scientists and Hollywood," 79–80.

20. Reingold, *Science American Style*, 338.

21. Yavenditti, "Atomic Scientists and Hollywood," 82.

22. Ibid., 83.

23. Ibid., 84.

24. Ibid.

25. Ibid., 85.

26. Ibid.

27. Ibid., 86.

28. Reingold, *Science American Style*, 346–347.

29. Richard G. Hewlett, "A Historian's View," *The Bulletin of Atomic Scientists*, December 1981, 20.

30. Ibid.

31. Ibid.

32. Ibid., 21.

33. *Science, Technology, and the First Amendment: Special Report* (Washington, DC: Office of Technology Assessment, 1988), 45.

34. Hewlett, "A Historian's View," 22.

35. Ibid., 23.

36. Ibid., 24–25.

37. Ibid., 25.

38. Ibid.

39. *In the Matter of J. Robert Oppenheimer: Transcript of Hearing Before Personnel Security Board, Washington, D.C., April 12, 1954 Through May 6, 1954* (Washington, DC: GPO, 1954), 837–838.

40. Joseph W. Alsop, "Witness to the Persecution," *Washington Post Magazine*, 2 February 1992, 29.

41. Dwight D. Eisenhower, *The White House Years: Mandate for Change* (Garden City, NY: Doubleday, 1963), 311.

42. Alsop, "Witness to the Persecution," 30.

43. John Mason Brown, *Through These Men* (New York: Harper & Bros., 1956), 242.

44. Richard Nixon, speech to editors, *New York Times*, 17 April 1954, p. 1.

45. *In the Matter of J. Robert Oppenheimer*, 22.

46. Ibid., 201.

47. U.S. Atomic Energy Commission, *In the Matter of J. Robert Oppenheimer: Transcript of Hearing Before Personnel Security Board and Texts of Principal Documents and Letters*, foreword by Philip M. Stern (Cambridge, MA: MIT Press, 1970), p. vii.

48. *In the Matter of J. Robert Oppenheimer*, 415.

49. Ibid., 735–736.

50. Ibid., 565, 567.

51. Ibid., 710, 722.

52. Ibid., 726.

53. Philip M. Stern, *The Oppenheimer Case: Security on Trial* (New York: Harper & Row, 1969), 349.

54. *In the Matter of J. Robert Oppenheimer*, 758–759.

55. Ibid., 974.

56. Ibid., 977, 990.

57. *In the Matter of J. Robert Oppenheimer: Texts of Principal Documents and Letters of Personnel Security Board, General Manager, Commissioners, Washington, D.C., May 27, 1954 Through June 29, 1954* (Washington, DC: GPO, 1954), 1.

58. "Science and the Citizen: Verdict," *Scientific American*, August 1954, 36.

59. Dael Wolfle, "The Trial of a Security System," *Science*, 18 June 1954, 7A.

60. *In the Matter of J. Robert Oppenheimer*, 886.

61. *The Oppenheimer Case*, p. 371.

62. Wolfle, "Trial of a Security System," p. 856.

63. "Science and the Citizen: Oppenheimer Decision," *Scientific American*, July 1954, 43.

64. Ibid., 43–44.

65. "Science and the Citizen: Verdict," *Scientific American*, August 1954, 36.

66. Ibid.

67. Howard Morland, "The H-Bomb Secret," *The Progressive*, November 1979, 17.

68. "Concerning H-Bomb Reactions," *Scientific American*, May 1950, 26.

69. Erwin Knoll, "Born Secret," *The Progressive*, May 1979, 17.

70. Gerard Piel, "Idi Amin and the H-bomb," *The Progressive*, May 1979, 17.

71. "Concerning H-Bomb Reactions," *Scientific American*, May 1950, 26.

72. *Lovell v. Griffin*, 303 U.S. 444, 451 (1938).

73. *Southeastern Promotions v. Conrad*, 420 U.S. 546, 559 (1975).

74. Alexander Bickel, *The Morality of Consent* (New Haven: Yale University Press, 1975), 61.

75. Ellen Alderman and Caroline Kennedy, *In Our Defense* (New York: Morrow, 1991), 48.

76. David M. O'Brien, *The Public's Right to Know: The Supreme Court and the First Amendment* (New York: Praeger, 1981), 162.

77. Howard Morland, "The H-Bomb Secret: To Know How Is to Ask Why?" *The Progressive*, November 1979, 3.

78. Knoll, "Born Secret," 13–14.

79. Ibid.

80. *In Our Defense*, 41.

81. Ibid., 45.

82. Knoll, "Born Secret," 16.

83. Ibid., 12, 18.

84. Ibid., 12, 18–19.

85. Erwin Knoll, "Wrestling with Leviathan," *The Progressive*, November 1979, 27.

86. Samuel H. Day, Jr., "Scientists of Conscience," *The Progressive*, May 1979, 32.

87. Knoll, "Born Secret," 15.

88. "The Way the Press Saw It," *The Progressive*, May 1979, 44–46.

89. *In Our Defense*, 51.

90. "*United States vs. The Progressive*; Excerpts from the Affidavits," *The Progressive*, May 1979, 36–38.

91. Ibid., 39–40.

92. Ibid., 39.

93. *In Our Defense*, 52.

94. Ibid., 53.

95. Knoll, "Wrestling with Leviathan," 28.

96. Samuel H. Day, Jr., "The Other Nuclear Weapons Club," *The Progressive*, November 1979, 32.

97. Erwin Knoll, "Born Classified: The Story Behind the H-Bomb Article We're Not Allowed to Print," *The Progressive*, May 1979, 27.

98. *In Our Defense*, 53.

99. "COMMENTS: *United States v. Progressive, Inc.*: The National Security and Free Speech Conflict," *William and Mary Law Review*, 22 (1980), 154.

100. Ibid., 153–154.

101. Ibid.

CHAPTER 4

Cryptography: A Government Monopoly in Science

BACKGROUND

Cryptography has been defined as the science of protecting the privacy and authenticity of information in a hostile environment. Some modern writers, like David Kahn, restrict the word "cryptography" to the making of codes and ciphers, and use the word "cryptology" to cover both making and breaking them. But most people know cryptography as the science of code-making and code-breaking. The word is derived from the Greek *kriptos*, meaning "hidden," and *graphos*, meaning "writing." The associated term "cryptology" derives from the Greek *logos*, meaning "word" or "speech."

For centuries the esoteric field of secret codes and ciphers has been a government monopoly, as nation-states have sought to protect their official communications while breaking the codes of other nations. "The problem, however, is that 'cryptography' doesn't just mean spy stuff," warns Robert Kuttner. "Any time secure data is transmitted over telephone lines, that is a form of encryption. When you use your bank card to get money out of an automatic-teller machine, you can be secure that you alone have access to the code, because a computer program has encrypted the date."[1] Kuttner concludes that "cryptography" is coming to mean the entire advanced end of telecommunications.

Indeed, since the end of World War II, various social and technological changes have generated a broad, economically motivated interest in cryptography outside the government. Mathematical and engineering journals began to publish articles on cryptography, and computer conferences began to feature the topic. Businessmen sought to protect the security of their databases and the privacy of their communications through encryption. Despite the government's heavy hand on cryptography, the know-how has spread rapidly throughout the scientific community. For example, a quick look at a few databases (indexes) to *unclassified* scientific literature shows the following amount of published research.

MathSci (Math Reviews): 1980–1987; 254 records under CRYPTOGRAPHY; 82 records under CRYPTOLOGY; 376 records under CRYPTO-. 1988–1991; 715 records under CRYPTOGRAPHY; 345 records under CRYPTOLOGY; 859 records under CRYPTO-.

NTIS Index: 1980–1984; 67 records under CRYPTOGRAPHY; 37 records under CRYPTOLOGY; 31 records under CRYPTOGRAPHIC; 29 records under CRYPTOSYSTEM(S). 1985–1989; 91 records under CRYPTOGRAPHY; 49 records under CRYPTOLOGY; 46 records under CRYPTOGRAPHIC; 20 records under CRYPTOSYSTEM(S). 1990–March 1992; 52 records under CRYPTOGRAPHY; 16 records under CRYPTOLOGY; 19 records under CRYPTOGRAPHIC; 8 records under CRYPTOSYSTEM(S).

Both indexes reveal a dramatic increase in cryptographic literature in the last few years. In addition to this direct research, work in areas like complexity theory (the study of what makes mathematical problems difficult) has provided the basis for strong ciphers that can survive public inspection. Yet, as private research grows, the government struggles more jealously to protect its cryptographic monopoly, through methods devious and occasionally illegal.

THE BLACK CHAMBER

The dark origins of American cryptography are best revealed in the life and works of one man, Herbert Osborne Yardley. In 1912 the 23-year-old Yardley took a $900-a-year job as a clerk and telegrapher at the State Department. As thousands of official telegraph messages flowed across his desk, Yardley began to reflect on whether they were in code and how they might be deciphered. He later wrote, "As I asked myself this question, I knew that I had the answer...to a purpose in life. I would devote my life to cryptography."[2] Indeed, Yardley began to educate himself in the subject, surreptitiously practicing on State Department messages. In 1916 he pulled off his greatest achievement, solving the complex code on a sensitive cable to President Woodrow Wilson.

Throughout the following year Yardley worked secretly on a treatise analyzing American cryptography and its vulnerabilities. Eventually he presented his paper, "Solution of American Diplomatic Codes," to his dumbfounded supervisor. To test Yardley's cryptographic skills, his supervisor gave him messages encoded in a previously guarded system. Several weeks later Yardley returned with the deciphered messages.

Yardley's growing confidence and ambition soon led him to leave the State Department and seek his fortune with the War Department, which he believed "would soon rule America." In 1917 he assumed command of Section Eight of Military Intelligence (MI–8), which had responsibility for all code and cipher work during World War I. In 1919 Yardley was called upon to assess the postwar need for MI–8 and its conversion to a peacetime operation. His proposal called for a bureau consisting of 25 code and cipher experts and 25 clerks. The total budget of $100,000 was to be borne jointly by the War Department and the State Department, with all expenditures kept confidential and not subject to review by the Comptroller General. Yardley's proposal was quickly approved, and on May 20, 1919, what came to be known as America's Black Chamber was born.

Each new member of the Black Chamber was given a memorandum specifying the organization's cover story: "Where you work and what you do are not matters for discussion, but rather than appear mysterious you may say that you are employed by the War Department in its translation department."[3]

Yardley had boasted that he would solve the Japanese code within a year or resign. On December 12, 1919, he succeeded, and his triumph was quickly put to use during the 1920 negotiations on a Five-Power Treaty involving the United States, Japan, Britain, France, and Italy. Having deciphered Japan's coded communications, Yardley likened America's position during the negotiations to that of a stud poker player who knew his opponent's hole card.

Under the internationally binding terms of the Radio Communication Act of 1912, the United States and most other countries guaranteed the confidentiality of all telecommunications, except as required by a court order. But the Black Chamber was intent on overcoming these restrictions by any means necessary. Yardley personally visited Western Union's president, Newcomb Carlton, asking that he secretly send the Black Chamber copies of all necessary telegrams, though this was in explicit violation of the law. Yardley later recalled that Carlton seemed anxious to do everything he could to assist the government's secret monitoring. Arrangements were made for a messenger to be sent from the Black

Chamber to Western Union's Washington office each morning to pick up telegrams, which would be returned before closing each day. Similar agreements were reached with the other major telegraph company, Postal Telegraph. In his book *The Puzzle Palace*, James Bamford says, "[B]y the end of 1920 the Black Chamber had the secret and illegal cooperation of almost the entire American cable industry. American cryptology had lost its virginity."[4]

When President Herbert Hoover was inaugurated in 1929, Yardley advised his liaison at the State Department not to reveal the existence of the Black Chamber to the new Secretary of State, Henry L. Stimson. But after Yardley succeeded in cracking the most recent Japanese codes, he felt the time was right to approach Stimson. Stimson, shocked and offended at the Black Chamber's activities, announced, "Gentlemen do not read each other's mail."[5] He immediately directed that all State Department funds be cut off. Because the Chamber was receiving almost its entire support from the State Department, that meant instant doom. At midnight on October 31, 1929, the Black Chamber officially closed, as quietly as it had opened.

Yardley, now without a job, began work on a book describing his exploits in the Black Chamber. The *Saturday Evening Post* contracted to serialize the book in three issues, and Bobbs-Merrill agreed to publish the full book. The nervous publisher first contacted the War Department, which quickly convinced him that publishing Yardley's book would not be in the best interests of the United States. Officers from the War Department then visited Yardley and advised him that if he published his book, it might cause considerable international unpleasantness.

Nonetheless, despite threats of prosecution by the government, Yardley's *Saturday Evening Post* articles appeared between April 4 and May 9, 1931, arousing immediate popular interest and whetting the public's appetite for the book, which was published on June 1. One critic characterized the book as "the most sensational contribution to the secret history of the war, as well as the immediate post-war period, which has yet been written by an American."[6] The book sold about 18,000 copies, and Yardley quickly began a second book, *Japanese Diplomatic Secrets: 1921–22*. But Yardley was now too hot to handle, and when he offered his new manuscript to Bobbs-Merrill, the company's president immediately contacted Stanley K. Hornbeck in the State Department. Hornbeck warned, "I cannot too strongly urge that, in view of the state of excitement which apparently prevails in Japanese public opinion now, characterized by fear of or enmity toward the United States, every possible effort should be made to prevent the appearance of this book."[7]

An officer from the War Department, accompanied by two witnesses, then called on Yardley at his home. The officer read Yardley a prepared order that charged him with having in his possession certain documents acquired when he was an employee of the U.S. government, documents reproduced in *The American Black Chamber*. The statement went on to describe "diverse other documents" under Yardley's control, and concluded: "It is, therefore, demanded of you that you deliver to the Adjutant General...all such documents or copies of documents hereinabove described by reason of the relation of such documents and copies of documents to the National Defense."[8]

Yardley assured the officer that he had no documents that would threaten U.S. national security, and he refused to give up his manuscript or source documents to his visitors. Within a few days of this visit, Yardley, having been turned down by Bobbs-Merrill, delivered his manuscript to Macmillan. At this point a young assistant in the U.S. Attorney's Office, Thomas E. Dewey, interceded to suppress the book. Dewey, destined for subsequent national political prominence, contacted Macmillan's president, who quickly agreed not to publish the book: "I can readily see why the government should object to the publication of that book. Not only is it in very bad taste, but it seems to me that it reveals information which never should be revealed to the public."[9]

Dewey eventually decided to seize the manuscript as a threat to national security, an unprecedented action by the American government. He sent a U.S. marshal to the Macmillan office; he asked the company's cooperative president to bring the manuscript to the Federal Building, where it was instantly impounded by a grand jury. Dewey personally telephoned the news media, requesting that they withhold mention of the seizure, and the compliant media obliged. The *New York Times* actually agreed to remove an article that had already been prepared.

Yardley was summoned to Dewey's office, where he was told that his manuscript had been seized pursuant to the Espionage Act. Dewey said that if Yardley continued to pursue publication of his book, he would face prosecution; if he would agree to desist, all action against him would be stopped. A dejected Yardley reluctantly accepted Dewey's offer. (Yardley's manuscript remained impounded for almost 50 years. It was finally declassified on March 2, 1979.)

The State Department still feared that Yardley would return to the typewriter and produce yet another book to challenge the government's censors. Therefore, work began immediately to create legislation that would make it a crime punishable by up to ten years in prison to write or publish information on government codes. On March 27, 1933, the

Chairman of the House Judiciary Committee, Senator Hatton Sumners (D-TX), introduced H.R. 4220, which went far beyond the State Department's intentions by making it a crime for any government employee to "sell, furnish to another, publish, or offer for sale" *any* government document, even one unclassified or unrelated to codes, so long as the release of the information could be shown to be "prejudicial to the safety or interest of the United States." In a legal tautology, the bill concluded that "proof of the commission of any of the acts described herein shall be *prima facie* evidence of a purpose prejudicial to the safety or interest of the United States." H.R. 4220 was quietly passed without opposition, but when the press learned of the bill, there were charges that it violated the First Amendment and denied freedom of the press.

As the result of growing public opposition to the bill, a Senate subcommittee removed some of the more extreme provisions, but many in the Senate remained confused and concerned. Senator Arthur R. Robinson (R-IN) complained: "We cannot get the truth from the State Department up until this minute! Nobody knows why they want this bill passed—not even the Senator from Texas. We did our best to get them to tell us. We asked them to tell us how they got hold of the manuscript of Yardley. 'Did you steal it? Where did you get it?' Not a word."[10]

Eventually H.R. 4220 passed. The final version, signed by President Franklin D. Roosevelt, read as follows:

> [W]hosoever, by virtue of his employment of the United States, shall obtain from another or shall have custody of or access to, any official diplomatic code or any matter prepared in such code, and shall willfully, without authorization or competent authority, publish or furnish to another any such code or matter, or any matter which was obtained while in the process of transmission between any foreign government and its diplomatic mission in the United States, shall be fined not more than $10,000 or imprisoned not more than ten years, or both.

With minor changes, the law remains today as Section 952 of Title 18 of the United States Code.

SIGINT, COMINT, AND BEYOND

The closing of the Black Chamber in 1929 may have brought Yardley's government career to a halt, but it did not reduce the government's obsession with cryptography. The Chamber's operation simply shifted from Military Intelligence to the Army Signal Corps, where the new organization was called the Signal Intelligence Service (SIS). The chief of this new signal intelligence (SIGINT) service was William F. Friedman. The SIS quickly found itself in violation not only of the Communications Act of 1934, which set severe penalties for intercepting communications, but also of Secretary of State Stimson's stern prohibition of such activities. Like Yardley before him, Friedman chose to pursue his profession outside the law and beyond the scrutiny of government officials. He set up communications intercept stations in Virginia, New Jersey, Texas, California, Panama, Hawaii, and the Philippines. Friedman was sent the intercepted messages by secret registered mail.

By the time Germany invaded Poland in 1939, the SIS had increased its staff from 7 to 19, and by the time of Pearl Harbor it had reached 331. By the end of World War II the size of the SIS staff exceeded 10,000. A former SIS staff member recalled his colleagues as "young people who gave ourselves to cryptography with the same ascetic devotion with which young men enter a monastery."[11]

The same Henry Stimson who as Secretary of State had lectured Herbert Yardley that "Gentlemen do not read each other's mail" was now Secretary of War, and in that capacity he ironically became an aggressive supporter of cryptography and message interception. Shortly after Pearl Harbor, Stimson ordered increased support for the Army's SIS and its communications intelligence (COMINT) function. Throughout the war SIS underwent frequent reorganization and change of identity; by the end of the war it was named the Army Security Agency. The first COMINT "charter" was promulgated in National Security Council Intelligence Directive (NSCID) No. 9, which ominously described the uniquely secret status of COMINT within the government:

> The special nature of Communications Intelligence activities requires that they be treated in all respects as being outside the framework of other or general intelligence activities. Orders, directives, policies, or recommendations of any authority of the Executive branch relating to the collection ... of intelligence shall not be applicable to Communications Intelligence activities, unless specifically so stated and issued by competent departmental or agency authority represented on the [U.S. Communications Intelligence] Board. Other National Security Council Intelligence Directives... shall be construed as non-applicable to Communications Intelligence unless the National Security Council has made its directive specifically applicable to COMINT.[12]

According to these ultrasecret guidelines, any restraints on, say, electronic surveillance that might be announced publicly by the Attorney

General or even the President would not apply to the secret COMINT community, because they were not "specifically so stated." Definitions in NSCID No. 9 were so broad as to allow the COMINT community to eavesdrop on the entire U.S. international telecommunications system—clearly in violation of the Communications Act of 1934.

At the conclusion of World War II, President Truman issued Executive Order 9031, instructing the Director of Censorship to declare an end to most SIGINT activities. But like Yardley's Black Chamber after World War I, the modern SIGINT operation was unwilling to close shop. Just as the Black Chamber had arranged for the illegal complicity of almost the entire cable industry 25 years earlier, Brig. Gen. W. Preston Corderman, chief of the Signal Security Agency (SSA), sent his representatives to New York City on August 18, 1945, to make "the necessary contacts with the heads of the commercial communications companies in New York, secure their approval of the interception of all Government traffic entering the United States, leaving the United States, or transiting the United States, and make the necessary arrangements for this photographic intercept work."[13]

The first overture was made to an official of ITT Communications, but it failed to produce agreement. On the other hand, Western Union Telegraph Company agreed to cooperate, so long as the Attorney General did not prohibit such intercepts. Armed with the Western Union agreement, the SSA representatives went back to ITT and suggested that it would not want to be the only uncooperative company. ITT reversed itself and joined the project. With two-thirds of America's cable industry in its pocket, the SSA officers went to RCA's president and asked him to join the "patriotic" effort. RCA agreed, again on the assumption that the Attorney General would look the other way.

Despite warnings from their legal advisers, all three companies began turning their cables over to the Army Security Agency (ASA), as the former SSA was now known. As part of this secret program, now codenamed Operation Shamrock, ASA officers arrived at the companies each morning to sort through the communications traffic. Soon all restrictions were waived, and ASA began receiving complete copies of every telegram, regardless of whether it was to or from an American citizen, a corporation, or an embassy. Operation Shamrock was extended beyond New York to Washington, San Francisco, and San Antonio.

Nervous company executives eventually requested legal assurances, not just from the Attorney General but from President Truman himself. Truman arranged a meeting between the company executives and his Secretary of Defense, James Forrestal, who assured the executives that he was speaking for the President. Forrestal also promised that Congress would consider legislation to make their activity legal. In fact, such legislation never passed, and Shamrock continued secretly and illegally.

In 1949, the Secretary of Defense issued a top-secret directive creating the Armed Forces Security Agency (AFSA), placing it under the direction and control of the Joint Chiefs of Staff. Its mission was to provide for the conduct of communications intelligence and communications security activities. Because the very existence of AFSA was considered top secret, no announcement was made when Rear Admiral Earl Everett Stone was appointed as AFSA's first chief. President Truman was unsatisfied with AFSA's performance during the Korean War, and in 1951 he established a committee headed by George Abbott Brownell to recommend corrective action. For six months the Brownell Committee interviewed witnesses, held executive hearings, and looked more deeply into the secret communications intelligence community than had ever been done before.

THE NATIONAL SECURITY AGENCY

On October 24, 1952, after considering the Brownell Committee's report, President Harry S. Truman signed a top-secret presidential memorandum to the Secretaries of Defense and State authorizing virtually every recommendation of the Committee. On December 29 President Truman secretly incorporated those recommendations into a revised NSCID No. 9, which created a new organization—the National Security Agency (NSA). The typical fanfare that accompanies the creation of major governmental agencies was absent. There was no news coverage or Congressional debate, not even the whisper of a rumor. The new agency's director, its physical plant, and its 10,000 employees remained invisible. No statute established the NSA or defined the permissible scope of its responsibilities. There were only laws preventing the release of information about the NSA. Even today, President Truman's authorizing memorandum remains one of Washington's most closely guarded secrets, though it is the foundation upon which all past and current communications intelligence activities of the U.S. government are based.

In 1959 the NSA quietly arranged to have Congress pass a unique statute forever hiding the Agency's organizational structure. Section 6 of Public Law 86–36 provides: "Nothing in this Act or any other law . . . shall be construed to require the disclosure of the organization or any function of the National Security Agency, or any information with respect to the activities thereof, or of the names, titles, salaries, or number of the persons employed by such Agency." Thus, the NSA has the authority to deny its own existence. Despite this law, James Bamford, in his book *The Puzzle Palace*, has given a rough picture of the NSA structure and personnel.

The NSA employs hordes of linguists, computer scientists, and engineers, and is the nation's leading employer of mathematicians. Its Office of Signals Intelligence, also known as the Office of Production (PROD), is the centerpiece of NSA's organization. PROD employs a legion of eavesdroppers and code breakers in the esoteric craft of signals analysis. The Office of Communications Security protects the entire range of American telecommunications. The Office of Research and Engineering develops technological wonders ranging from microscopic electronic components to a dish-shaped antenna the size of two football fields.

The NSA's massive headquarters on the grounds of Fort Meade, in Maryland's Anne Arundel County, is that county's largest employer, with over 20,000 workers. The number is closer to 45,000 if one includes the NSA satellite offices nearby. Indeed, the NSA has more staff than all the other intelligence agencies combined, but the total number has only been estimated. For example, one county demographer tried counting parking spaces in aerial photographs and the number of NSA employees who joined the credit union. Indeed, some have claimed that the Agency's initials stand for No Such Agency or Never Say Anything.

Few outside the inner circles of the intelligence community are familiar with NSA's classification system, which goes beyond the standard Confidential, Secret, and Top Secret designations. The keystone of this system is the warning HANDLE VIA COMINT CHANNELS ONLY. Few messages, letters, or reports leave the NSA without this injunction, and once so marked, a document is elevated to a classification status higher than Top Secret. There are still more levels of classification, indicated by code words like TOP SECRET UMBRA, which imposes the highest SIGINT sensitivity, or SECRET SPOKE, which is one step below. The code GAMMA was reserved for important Soviet intercepts but, starting in 1969, it was used to monitor the conversations of Jane Fonda and Dr. Benjamin Spock.

The Government Accounting Office (GAO) has reported that the NSA classifies somewhere between 50 million and 100 million documents a year. "That means," concluded the GAO, "that its classification activity is probably greater than the combined total activity of all components and agencies of the Government"—more secrets than all of the armed forces and government agencies combined. Finding storage space for all of these secrets is a problem, but disposing of them after they have been shredded is proving even more difficult. The NSA produces about *40 tons* of classified waste each day, 200 tons in an average week. After considering such statistics, one Senator asked an NSA assistant director, "Is the National Security Agency lit erally burying itself in classified material?" The NSA official answered, "It would seem that way."[14]

When Gordon Aylesworth Blake became director of the NSA in 1962, he found himself involved in a typical NSA attempt at prior restraint. Journalist and amateur cryptologist David Kahn had signed a contract with Macmillan to write a book on cryptology, the subject over which the NSA claimed exclusive control. To make things worse, Kahn planned to include a chapter on the NSA. The Agency began a frantic effort to stop publication of Kahn's book, eventually titled *The Codebreakers*. The highest levels of the Agency, including the director, devised an elaborate set of options, including (1) have the government employ Kahn, thus making him subject to prepublication review and criminal statutes; (2) purchase the copyright of Kahn's book; (3) undertake "clandestine service applications," including a "black bag" job; (4) surreptitiously enter Kahn's Long Island home.[15] The director also suggested planting disparaging reviews of the book in the press, and such a review was actually drafted. In any case, Kahn's name was placed on the NSA "watch list," enabling the Agency to search the airwaves for his phone calls and telegrams.

In 1964, NSA director Blake brought the problem before the U.S. Intelligence Board, which he chaired. The Board issued a report recommending joint action by the intelligence agencies to discourage Kahn or his publisher from releasing the book. John McCone, director of the CIA, was to consider CIA actions to prevent publication of the book or at least allow NSA to review the manuscript. Just what action the CIA took to halt publication or procure the manuscript remains unknown, but somehow Macmillan was persuaded to turn the entire manuscript over to the Pentagon, without the author's permission. Ironically, Macmillan had agreed to do the same thing in the 1930s with Herbert Yardley's cryptographic manuscript.

After receiving Kahn's manuscript on March 4, 1966, the Pentagon sent it to the NSA. The Pentagon also wrote to Macmillan's chairman of the board, Lee Deighton, advising him that the Defense Department deplored the book and that it would not be in the national interest to publish it. Deighton was told that if Macmillan insisted on publication, it would be necessary to delete certain sections. After a month passed with no response from Deighton, it was decided that NSA's new director, Marshall Carter, should journey to New York to make a personal appeal to the publisher.

Carter first went to Defense Secretary Robert McNamara, seeking a letter of introduction to Deighton. As drafted by Carter, the letter read: "This will serve to introduce Lt. Gen. Marshall S. Carter, USA, who has a matter to discuss with you. I am aware of what Gen. Carter has to say and his remarks have my endorsement and approval."[16] Secretary McNamara did indeed approve of Carter's plan, but he refused to sign the letter, claiming it was too risky to put anything on paper. At their July 22, 1966, meeting in New York, Carter told Deighton that under no circumstances would the NSA give security clearance to the book. Deighton said that any changes in the manuscript would require the author's permission. Deighton agreed to approach Kahn with the suggested deletions, and that no record would be kept of the meeting with Carter. Eventually Kahn reluctantly acceded to the requested deletions, but he may have had the last laugh. Buried in the notes in the back of the book, overlooked by the censors, were the references to the deleted material, most of which could be obtained in any good library.

Operation Shamrock, begun by the ASA after World War II, was continued by successor agencies, the AFSA and the NSA. With no laws or legislative charter to restrain it, NSA began to routinely include American names and organizations on its "watch lists." NSA was vacuuming a massive amount of telecommunications, screening it through the enormous filter of "trigger words." Phone calls, telegrams, and telex messages to and from thousands of innocent Americans were analyzed. On July 1, 1969, a separate civil disturbance watch list was developed at NSA, so secret and compartmented that it received its own code word, MINARET, and its own charter. The charter described its purpose as to spy on organizations or individuals who might "format civil disturbance," and it added: "An equally important aspect of MINARET will be to restrict the knowledge that information is being collected and processed by the National Security Agency. . . . Further, although MINARET will be handled as SIGINT and distributed to SIGINT recipients, it will not . . . be identified with the National Security Agency."[17]

Though the science of code-breaking had undergone dramatic technological changes, one principle remained constant: it is always easier and cheaper to steal a code than to break it. For this reason, the NSA had long used the "black bag" experts of the FBI to assist its cryptologic efforts. In 1967, however, J. Edgar Hoover issued a memo stating that requests for "black bag" jobs would no longer meet with his approval.

He insisted that break-ins would be conducted only if ordered by the President or the Attorney General. NSA Deputy Director Louis Tordella says, "I couldn't go to the chief law enforcement figure in the country and ask him to approve something that was illegal." As for the President, Tordella said this was "not a topic with which he should soil his hands."[18]

When Richard Nixon was sworn in as President on January 20, 1969, he appointed an ad hoc Interagency Committee on Intelligence, which recommended a program for coverage by NSA of the communications of U.S. citizens using international facilities. In particular, it requested broader approval for electronic surveillance, mail coverage, and surreptitious entry. J. Edgar Hoover complained: "It is becoming more and more dangerous and we are apt to get caught. I am not opposed to doing this. I'm not opposed to continuing the burglaries and the opening of mail and the other similar activities, providing somebody higher than myself approves of it."[19] The Nixon Administration quickly provided that approval by recommending:

> Present restrictions [on surreptitious entry] should be modified to permit procurement of vitally needed foreign cryptographic material.... Use of this technique is clearly illegal: it amounts to burglary. It is also highly risky and could result in great embarrassment if exposed. However, it is also the most fruitful tool and can produce the type of intelligence which cannot be obtained in any other fashion.... NSA has a particular interest since it is possible by this technique to secure materials with which NSA can break foreign cryptographic codes. We spend millions of dollars trying to break these codes by machine. One successful surreptitious entry can do the job successfully at no dollar cost.[20]

LIFTING THE VEIL

For decades the NSA had eluded Congressional or media scrutiny by claiming that any inquiry into its fragile cryptologic efforts would jeopardize national security. The wall of anonymity remained almost without cracks until June 13, 1971, when the *New York Times* began publication of the Pentagon Papers. Scattered throughout the documents were numerous verbatim copies of classified and previously encrypted messages, including the numbers identifying the times and dates the messages were sent. NSA feared that an adversary might be able to compare these messages with an intercepted encrypted version, and thereby break the code. The matter was finally resolved during the Pentagon Papers trial when Vice Admiral Francis J. Blouin, Deputy Chief of Naval Operations and one of the government's three main witnesses, rose in court to say,

"Judge Gurfein, you and I are probably the only people in this room old enough to remember when verbatim texts comprised a code."[21]

On June 19, 1971, Judge Gurfein decided the historic case in favor of the *Times*, proclaiming: "The security of the Nation is not at the ramparts alone. Security also lies in the value of our free institutions. A cantankerous press, an ubiquitous press must be suffered by those in authority in order to preserve the even greater values of freedom of expression and the right of the people to know."[22]

The NSA was disappointed but not deterred. A high Agency official named Milton Zaslow contacted the *Times* and requested a meeting to discuss certain national security matters. Zaslow asked the *Times* to delete anything from the Pentagon Papers that might alert foreign governments to the fact that their communications systems had been penetrated. This could be accomplished, Zaslow said, by removing any reference to specific intercepts. Vice Chairman Harding Bancroft agreed to such deletions, and the Pentagon Papers were edited with NSA's concerns in mind.

No sooner had the Pentagon Papers been disposed of than another court challenge faced the NSA. *United States v. United States District Court* held that the President's duty to protect the government against subversion by domestic organizations did not extend to warrantless electronic surveillance. Attorney General Elliot Richardson then wrote to NSA Director Lew Allen, Jr., saying he considered the Agency's "watch list" to be of questionable legality and asking that the NSA "immediately curtail the further dissemination" of watch list information. Allen did terminate MINARET, but he did not bother to mention that that the Agency was continuing Operation Shamrock, which was almost certainly illegal. Finally, on May 12, 1975, fearing further exposure by Congress and the press, NSA Director Allen prepared a secret, handwritten memorandum for the record, ending Operation Shamrock: "I have been informed that the Secretary of Defense has decided that we must terminate the operation known as Shamrock. Effective 15 May 1975 no data from this source will be processed and all activities will cease as soon as possible. . . . Personnel who have been briefed or who otherwise know of the operation will be debriefed and reminded of their continuing obligation regarding protection of the compartmented source."[23]

In early October 1975, Sen. Frank Church (D-ID) announced that his committee would hold two days of public hearings on NSA improprieties and abuses. NSA Director Allen gave the Senators, and the world, their first look at the Agency's SIGINT operation. He admitted to the Agency's "watch list" and its Operation MINARET, estimating that between 1967 and 1973 the Agency had issued about 3,900 reports covering the approximately 1,680 watch-listed Americans. Sen. Walter Mondale (D-MN) asked NSA Deputy Director Benson K. Buffham if he had ever been concerned about the legality of monitoring Americans. "Legality?" Buffham asked, perplexed. "That particular aspect didn't enter into the discussion."[24]

The House Government Information Subcommittee, chaired by Rep. Bella Abzug (D-NY), was also interested in Shamrock, but that committee chose to bypass NSA and instead quiz the executives from the communications companies involved in the operation. These officials would presumably be unable to hide behind the shields of classification and executive privilege, as had the NSA. Just two days before the public hearing, RCA and ITT suddenly informed the Subcommittee that they would refuse to send officials unless so ordered by a subpoena. On February 4, 1976, the Subcommittee issued subpoenas to four FBI agents, one NSA employee, and executives of ITT, RCA, and Western Union. Two weeks later, in an unprecedented claim of the doctrine of executive privilege, President Gerald Ford instructed the Secretary of Defense and the Attorney General to notify the subpoenaed parties that they should "decline to comply." For the first time in history, executive privilege was extended to private corporations. Attorney General Edward Levi wrote to Western Union: "On behalf of the President, I hereby request that Western Union International honor this invocation of executive privilege."[25]

When the Subcommittee reconvened on February 25, the four FBI agents and the NSA employee all declined to testify, claiming they had been so instructed by the government. The Subcommittee voted to cite all five witnesses for contempt of Congress. On March 3, Thomas Greenish, Executive Vice President of Western Union International, and Howard Hawkins, CEO of RCA Global Communications, defied the President and the Attorney General by testifying before the Subcommittee and turning over a list of NSA targets. A week later, George Knapp, President of ITT World Communications, testified about Operation Shamrock.

Although the Subcommittee spared NSA the embarrassment of a public report on Shamrock, the Agency had one more investigation to survive. Attorney General Levi felt compelled to establish a top-secret task force to determine whether any other questionable surveillance was being conducted by NSA. The final report, classified TOP SECRET UMBRA/HANDLE VIA COMINT CHANNELS ONLY, was considered so sensitive that only two copies were printed. Despite the fact that the task force uncovered 24 categories of questionable electronic surveillance, the report recommended that the inquiry be terminated for lack of prosecutable potential.

By the time Bobby Ray Inman became Director of NSA in 1977, the Agency had recognized that it could no longer remain in total secrecy, free from the gaze of Congress or the press. Inman divided his tenure between trying to maintain NSA's monopoly on cryptography and lobbying Congress for protective legislation for NSA's SIGINT operations. In his efforts to eliminate outside competition in cryptography, Inman used public lectures and interviews in a way unprecedented for the secretive NSA. More recently, NSA has edged even closer to a public identity, murky though it may be. For years, NSA had shielded its facilities from the public and prohibited its employees from revealing the name of their employer. But on March 9, 1991, without fanfare, the NSA headquarters at Fort Meade, Maryland, suddenly decided to acknowledge its 37 years in residence by displaying a simple blue-on-black-granite sign bearing the words "National Security Agency" alongside the Agency seal.

The Agency now allows many of its employees to say where they work and what, in general, they do. "I can say I'm an NSA engineer, for instance,"said one employee, "but I still can't tell you what I'm working on." The chief of NSA's Office of Mathematical Research, Richard J. Shaker, proudly characterizes himself as a "cryptology chauvinist." He is typical of the new breed of NSA scientists who aggressively play the public relations game while withholding the particulars of their work from the public at large. In a 1992 article in *Chronicle of Higher Education*, Shaker said, "I work for a wonderful agency that does marvelous things I cannot tell you about."[26] Still, the Agency is making a powerful pitch to the broader educational community. When Shaker and his colleagues recently invited over 100 university mathematicians to visit the Agency, the visitors received only a cursory security check by NSA's standards.

There is an increasing number of NSA exchanges with academic mathematicians, and the Agency provides regular financial support for mathematical research at universities. Since 1987 the Agency has been giving academics an average of $2.5 million a year in peer-reviewed grants for theoretical mathematical research conducted at universities. It supports unclassified mathematical studies at Princeton University and the University of California, San Diego. The Agency has also been inviting faculty members to spend their sabbaticals at NSA headquarters. But academics at NSA do not publish their research; rather, they focus on classified problems central to the Agency's mission. Undergraduate students are now brought to the Agency each summer to work on classified mathematical problems under the tutelage of NSA staff. The staffers who conduct the security checks give the undergrads special handling and try to persuade them to come to work for the Agency.

The NSA has created a speakers' bureau that sends its mathematicians to elementary and secondary schools and holds workshops for mathematics teachers. To accommodate this explosion of NSA's public relations, it was necessary in 1990 for the agency's lawyers to work with Congressional staff to rewrite the NSA's Congressional authorization to include an educational component. In 1992, Agency mathematicians gave 12 talks at a Baltimore meeting of academic mathematical societies. At that meeting, Richard Shaker addressed an audience of over 400 mathematicians in a talk entitled "The Agency That Came in from the Cold."

Cryptologist Shaker says that neither the end of the Cold War nor budgetary austerity will halt the hiring of new NSA cryptologists. "The world remains a dangerous place," he says. Ezra Brown, a professor of mathematics at Virginia Polytechnic Institute completing his sabbatical at NSA, endorses the Agency's public relations approach. Though he will be unable to discuss his NSA research with his academic colleagues, he believes he can inspire his students with dramatic tales of secret science: "So many students get the impression the only thing they can do with mathematics is teach. As an educator I can go back and say it isn't so. I can't tell them what they would be doing here, but I can say there are a lot of opportunities to solve very hard, interesting problems."[27]

CRYPTOGRAPHY, ITAR, AND THE LAW

In August 1977 the Institute of Electrical and Electronics Engineers (IEEE) received a letter from an NSA employee threatening IEEE scientists with federal punishment should they publish or otherwise communicate their research in cryptology. The incident was precipitated when the IEEE innocently scheduled a symposium on cryptology for October 10, 1977. The symposium was to be open to the public, and a number of foreign guests and participants were expected to attend. In fact, there were plans to send reprints of the talks to the Soviet Union under a joint agreement made earlier.

As the IEEE Information Theory Group was preparing for the symposium, they received the mysterious letter warning them that publishing in the field of cryptology or exporting such information could violate the 1954 Munitions Control Act, the Arms Export Control Act, and the

International Traffic in Arms Regulations (ITAR), by which these Acts are implemented. The letter claimed that several of IEEE's past, present, and future activities violated the ITAR. As examples, the letter cited the scheduled symposium, a past symposium, several publications, and the plan to send reprints to the Soviet Union.

In warning the IEEE scientists, the letter stated: "I assume the IEEE groups are unfamiliar with the ITAR, which apply to the publication and export of unclassified as well as classified technical data." After claiming that atomic weapons and cryptology were "covered by special secrecy laws," the letter concluded ominously: "Superficially, it appears that a small number of authors are providing most of the papers and most of the motivation. They may not be aware of the full burden of government controls.... Unless clearances or export licenses are obtained ... or there is some special exemption, the IEEE could find itself in possible technical violation of the ITAR ... I suggest that the IEEE might wish to review this situation, for these modern weapons technologies, uncontrollably disseminated, could have more than academic effect."[28]

An NSA spokesman subsequently revealed that the letter was written by Joseph A. Meyer, but the Agency claimed that it was not an official communication. The spokesman would not comment on whether he had seen the letter or whether Meyer was employed by NSA. A reporter at *Science* magazine located Meyer in an NSA directory, but when called at his office, Meyer refused to admit he worked at NSA. The magazine then commented: "If Meyer is acting as an NSA agent and not as a private citizen, the incident seems to reveal that the NSA has no coherent policy to deal with research whose public dissemination may hinder national security.... Meyer's threats to the cryptologists seem even more misdirected since it is already too late to prevent information on the new code-making techniques from becoming widely disseminated." *Science* concluded that the ITAR may be useless in suppressing cryptographic publications, "not because it is unenforceable but because no one, not even the generously funded NSA, can have the foresight to decide which ideas should be kept under wraps."[29]

Still, the IEEE's Director of Technical Activities appeared to accept the letter's chilling interpretation, for he wrote to IEEE's scientists urging them to clear their papers with their companies or refer them to the Department of State's Office of Munitions Control for ruling. But Munitions Control officials at the State Department told IEEE scientists that any inquiries about publications on encryption or cryptographic devices are automatically referred to the NSA. Thus, Meyer's letter was proposing an NSA-administered censorship system over private crypto-graphic research.

The scientists were understandably disturbed by the sudden revelation that they could not publish in their field without prior approval from the State Department, that is, the NSA. The Information Theory Group's president, Fred Jellinek, responded, "I don't believe a law can say such a thing, because it would make scientists guilty until proven innocent."[30] Such is the essence of prior restraint.

The NSA's application of the ITAR to cryptographic research had thus restrained related information from publication in American journals or from discussion at scholarly symposia where foreigners might be present. The ITAR (discussed in detail in Chapter 5) con-trols the export of unclassified "technical data," very broadly defined. It defines "export" to have occurred whenever technical data is com-municated outside the United States or disclosed to foreign nationals in the United States.

ITAR controls over cryptography bear a remarkable similarity to the federal controls over atomic energy research, and development in both fields has been dominated by the federal government. The re-sults of government-created or -sponsored research have automati-cally been classified on national security grounds. Nonetheless, private research in both fields is substantial, supporting significant nongov-ernmental uses in atomic energy and cryptography. One principal difference between the two fields is that researchers in atomic energy often must depend on the government for radioactive source mate-rials, while cryptographers need little more than an adequate com-puter.

Under the Atomic Energy Act of 1954, all atomic energy informa-tion, whether developed by the government or private researchers, is "born classified" and subject to strict controls. Though the Atomic Energy Act does not specifically authorize prior review of publications on atomic energy, the Atomic Energy Commission is empowered to control such publications through the threat of injunction or severe criminal penalties. On the other hand, the authority and constitution-ality of ITAR restrictions on communications in public cryptography can only be inferred from Supreme Court decisions on general First Amendment principles.

Even the Justice Department has admitted that "the existing provisions of ITAR are unconstitutional insofar as they establish a prior restraint on disclosure of cryptographic ideas and information developed by sci-entists and mathematicians in the private sector."[31] In a 1978 memo to the President's science adviser titled "Constitutionality Under the First Amendment of ITAR Restrictions on Public Cryptography," the Justice Department's Assistant Attorney General, John M. Harmon, commented on the use of the Mutual Security Act of 1954 and the Arms Export Control Act of 1977: "It is by no means clear from the language or legislative history of either statute that Congress intended that the President regulate noncommercial dissemination of information, or considered the problems such regulation would engender. We therefore have some doubt whether [section] 38 of the Arms Export Control Act provides adequate authorization for the broad controls over public cryptography which the ITAR imposes."[32]

In his 1978 memo to the President's science adviser, Harmon analyzed the applicability of ITAR to cryptographic information developed by scientists and mathematicians in the private sector, independent of government supervision or support. The memo advised: "Even if it is assumed that the government's interest in regulating the flow of cryptographic information is sufficient to justify some form of prior review process, the existing prior review provisions we think fall short of satisfying the strictures necessary to survive close scrutiny under the First Amendment."[33]

Harmon claimed that the standards under which the government issued or denied licenses were not sufficiently precise to guard against arbitrary and inconsistent administrative action. In addition, he noted that there was no mechanism to provide prompt judicial review of State Department decisions to bar disclosure. "For these reasons it is our conclusion that the present ITAR licensing scheme does not meet constitutional standards. There remains the more difficult question whether a licensing scheme covering either exports of or even purely domestic publications of cryptographic information might be devised consistent with the First Amendment."[34]

Harmon suggested that a licensing scheme requiring prepublication submission of cryptographic information might overcome the strong constitutional presumption against prior restraint. However, he warned, "Before imposing a prior restraint on exports of public cryptographic information, we believe that a more clear-cut indication of Congressional judgement concerning the need for such a measure is in order.... Second, further Congressional authorization would obviously be necessary in order to extend governmental controls to domestic as well as foreign disclosures of public cryptographic information.... Third, no final restraint on disclosure may be imposed without a judicial determination."[35] In that regard, Harmon's analysis of recent Supreme Court decisions led him to doubt whether a generalized claim of threat to national security from publication of cryptographic information would constitute an adequate basis for prior restraint.

Harmon concluded that "the existing provisions of the ITAR are unconstitutional insofar as they establish a prior restraint on disclosure of cryptographic ideas and information developed by scientists and mathematicians in the private sector. We believe, however, that a prepublication review requirement for cryptographic information might meet First Amendment standards if it provided necessary procedural safeguards and precisely drawn guidelines."[36]

THE NSA/NSF CONNECTION

The NSA has recognized that the major difficulty in protecting its cryptographic hegemony against private encroachment lies in the relative independence of university researchers. But the common Achilles' heel of these researchers turned out to be the National Science Foundation (NSF). Because most nongovernmental cryptologists are funded through NSF grants and contracts, the NSA concluded that it could control private cryptographic research by controlling NSF grants in the field. An unfortunate gentlemen's agreement between NSF and NSA can be traced to a series of communications between 1975 and 1978. On June 13, 1975, Dr. Fred Weingarten, NSF's special projects director in the Division of Computer Research, wrote to his General Counsel, stating: "A DCR grantee who also works with the National Security Agency tells me that NSA has sole statutory authority to fund research in cryptography; and, in fact, other agencies are specifically enjoined from supporting that type of work." Weingarten noted that because his program and others were currently supporting work in cryptography, it was important to know if they were "acting counter to federal law." He concluded: "I'll hold up making any new grant in this field until you let me know."[37]

On June 19, 1975, the assistant to NSF's General Counsel responded: "We have been unable to locate any statute of the nature described in your memorandum of June 18, 1975. We also contacted NSA's legal office which knew of no such statute. NSA may have primary or exclusive authority pursuant to executive orders in connection with certain phases of cryptographic transmissions within the Government, but this has nothing to do with support of research."[38]

Despite this seemingly definitive resolution of the dispute, the matter arose again on April 20, 1977, when NSA's Assistant Deputy Director for COMSEC, Cecil Corry, approached Dr. Weingarten. Corry, one of COMSEC's founding fathers, told Weingarten that an unspecified Presidential directive gave the NSA "control" over all cryptographic work and that the NSF was straying outside that directive. When Weingarten told Corry that the NSA's claims had been previously examined and found to be baseless, Corry dropped the matter, stating that if no such law existed, it would have to be passed. In the meantime, Corry's strategy was to propose that NSF and NSA "coordinate" the review process for all cryptographic grant proposals. Weingarten agreed to send such proposals to NSA, but only to receive NSA's expert opinion on the technical merits of the work. He told Corry that the NSF would continue to openly consider proposals in the field of cryptography, and would decline proposals only for documented scientific reasons. He would not permit any "secret reviews—reviews of the form 'Don't support this, but I can't tell you why.' "[39]

Several days after the meeting, Weingarten recorded his views in an internal memorandum: "NSA is worried, of course, that public domain security research will compromise some of their work. However, even further, they seem to want to maintain their control and corner a bureaucratic expertise in the field. They point out that the government is asking NSA help in issues of computer security. However, unquotable sources at OMB tell me that they turned to NSA only for the short-term, pragmatic reason that the expertise was there, not as an expression of policy that NSA should have any actual authority."[40] Weingarten concluded: "It seems clear that turning [over] such a huge domestic responsibility, potentially involving such activities as banking, the US mail, and cable television, to an organization such as NSA should be done only after the most serious debate at higher levels of government than represented by peanuts like me."[41]

Corry decided to move up in NSF's peanut gallery, writing to Weingarten's boss, Dr. John Pasta, director of NSF's Division of Mathematical and Computer Sciences. In a May 11, 1977, letter to Pasta, Corry said, "NSA remains concerned about heightened interest and activity relating to cryptography and cryptanalysis in the private sector, and we are grateful for your willingness to cooperate with us in considering the security implications of grant applications in this field." Corry said NSA would be pleased to review NSF proposals which "directly relate to, or seem to impinge on, cryptographic matters."[42]

Pasta responded that NSF would submit research proposals "which bear explicitly on cryptography" to NSF, but only "for information purposes." After all, said Pasta, this was "publicly releasable information."[43]

Pasta claimed that though he agreed to use NSA people as reviewers, he did not agree to "cooperate" with NSA in the manner suggested by Corry. Again the negotiations were bumped upstairs, with Pasta suggesting that NSA monitoring of NSF research "be pursued at some appropriately higher level."[44]

Soon NSA Director Bobby Inman began briefings with NSF Director Richard Atkinson. On September 7, 1978, Atkinson wrote to Inman, suggesting that NSA take over funding of some university research in cryptography. "It seems to me that a small unclassified research support program at universities ($2–3 million, say) sponsored by NSA would help prevent future problems.... Thus, you could support the work liable to be of interest to you and NSF support would undoubtedly be shifted." Atkinson offered NSF resources to help set up such an operation. By assuming responsibility for funding private, unclassified research in cryptography, NSA would acquire arbitrary control over such work. Inman responded promptly and positively to the proposal, saying it would give NSA the opportunity to manage the sponsorship of basic research. He suggested similar arrangements "with other agencies involved in public sector cryptography." On December 27, 1978, Atkinson wrote to Inman to formalize the transfer of funding responsibilities in cryptography. "[M]y offer to provide assistance to effect such a transition is hereby renewed, not only in the spirit of cooperation but also because it is perceived to be in the public interest with respect to our respective missions."[45]

On August 14, 1980, Leonard Adleman, a theoretical computer scientist at MIT and one of the fathers of public-key cryptography, was notified by the NSF that it had decided not to fund his grant proposal because of an "interagency matter." The following day, Adleman received a call from NSA director Inman, who offered to fund the proposal. Adleman would have nothing to do with the offer, stating, "It's a very frightening collusion between agencies."[46]

Following the Adleman incident, Inman met with Donald Langenberg, the new Deputy Director of the NSF, and Frank Press, the White House science adviser. It was decided that all proposals for cryptographic research would go first to the NSF and then to the NSA for technical review. Should the NSA find a proposal it wished to fund, it would notify the NSF, which would offer the researcher a choice of accepting funds from either agency.

A Congressional committee examined the relationship between NSA and NSF and concluded that it was "not that of two agencies at loggerheads, but of the mission-oriented NSA having sent the NSF a message in bureaucratic code that the latter is still struggling to decipher. The record leaves little doubt about NSA's intentions."[47]

VOLUNTARY PRIOR RESTRAINT

The NSA wanted a "gentlemen's agreement" with the scientific community. If scientists would agree to submit their cryptographic research to NSA for review, NSA would censor such materials with a light hand. Otherwise, NSA threatened total censorship. In the spring of 1980, under heavy pressure from the NSA, the American Council of Education formed the Public Cryptography Study Group (PCSG) to examine the issue of prepublication review of papers in cryptography. Along with some prominent scientists, the nine-member group included NSA's General Counsel. NSA Director Bobby Inman proposed that the Study Group consider the feasibility of a statute permitting the NSA to exercise prepublication censorship over a "central core" of nongovernmental cryptologic information. Such a statute would either make it a crime to disseminate cryptologic information or require prepublication review by a government agency such as the NSA. In the first case, NSA would monitor almost all published literature and recommend criminal prosecution for inappropriate publication. In the second case, *anyone* publishing cryptologic information without first having it cleared by NSA would face a jail sentence.

Because the constitutionality of either form of the statute was highly questionable, the Study Group chose instead to consider a system of voluntary censorship, under which the NSA would reserve the right to notify anyone working on cryptology of its desire to review such information before publication. The Agency could then request that the author voluntarily refrain from publishing the work. If the author disagreed, a five-member advisory committee appointed by the Director of the NSA and the President's science adviser would make the final recommendation.

Attending the first meeting of the Study Group on May 31, 1980, as an "authorized observer" was Richard Leibler, former head of NSA's important think tank, IDA-CRD. Leibler remarked that "NSA would take over the funding of cryptographic research grants from the NSF, assuming there are no legal impediments to such transfer and the study group produces worthwhile recommendations on how to effect it."[48]

On February 7, 1981, the PCSG completed its final report, which claimed that the NSF "has responsibility under routine executive orders to refer information developed in NSA-supported cryptologic research it believes may be classifiable to NSA for possible classification." The report also quoted from the NSF form "Potentially Classifiable Research," which stated that NSF grantees must allow NSF to review such work "prior to dissemination or publication of potentially classifiable research results." If the review results in classification, the grantee must "cooperate with NSF or other U.S. agencies [e.g., NSA] in securing all related notes and papers."[49]

The PCSG report recommended a voluntary system of review of papers in cryptography. No author or publisher would be required to participate in this process, but the PCSG believed that most authors would cooperate. The Association for Computing Machinery (ACM), one of the scholarly organizations represented on PCSG, suggested a review process under which ACM editors would include a special note in their acknowledgment of submitted papers, asking the authors to voluntarily send their papers to NSA for review. The author's willingness to cooperate would not be a condition of publication.

The final PCSG report included a minority opinion by Dr. George Davida of the University of Wisconsin, titled "The Case Against Restraints on Non-Governmental Research in Cryptography." Davida analyzed NSA's claims that open research and publication in cryptography could be used by foreign governments to secure their data against NSA intelligence gathering and to compromise the security of NSA-designed cryptosystems. Davida argued that restraints, even if desirable or possible, would be ineffective in achieving NSA's objectives, primarily because cryptography is not hardware intensive. This means that the restraints would have to be placed on the intellectual activity of designing and analyzing algorithms, thereby seriously handicapping American researchers. Researchers in other countries were unlikely to suffer such restraints, and would be quite capable of designing their own algorithms. Davida also noted that because cryptanalysis, the science of breaking codes, was *not* an intellectually attractive area for scientists, it would be unlikely to produce public research that would compromise the government's cryptosystems.

Davida was generally critical of PCSG's procedures, saying that by recommending restraints (initially mandatory, then voluntary) it had exceeded its original charge to consider model legislation. He also complained that the PCSG refused to address the question of whether the broader interests of the country, including privacy protection, would outweigh the risks (*if any*) of the NSA's mission. "The need for a nongovernmental effort in this area is crystal clear in view of the remarkable insensitivity of the common carriers to the public's concern about privacy," concluded Davida. "I find NSA's effort to control cryptography to be unnecessary, divisive, wasteful, and chilling. The NSA can perform its mission in the old-fashioned way: STAY AHEAD OF OTHERS."[50]

Davida was particularly concerned about the misuse or misinterpretation of the Study Group's report: "It is easy to imagine the NSA offering the decision of our study group to Congress as evidence that academicians do indeed agree with the NSA—that our work could compromise the national security.... One gets the impression that the NSA is struggling to stand still, and to keep American research standing still with it, while the rest of the world races ahead."[51]

Peter Denning, ACM's President, gave initial reluctant support to the PCSG deliberations, but he became increasingly concerned about NSA's attempts to extend its control to public cryptography through its funding of private research in that field. He also feared the overly broad export control regulations and the extension of the "born classified" concept to cryptography. Denning concluded: "I believe very strongly that scientists have responsibilities to use knowledge wisely. Their freedom to publish and exchange scientific data is not absolute. I believe, however, that the balance now tilts toward restraints imposed by government. It is time to even that balance. There's a chill in the wind: Icebergs loom in the fog."[52]

The PCSG report recommended that the voluntary system of prior review of cryptographic manuscripts be instituted "on an experimental basis." Yet NSA's prepublication review of cryptography, set in motion by the PCSG in 1981, has continued unabated. This is not to say that the voluntary review system has been a success, because most of the member societies of the Study Group ignore the system altogether. Many follow the approach of IEEE, which leaves it entirely to the individual researcher whether to submit papers for review. When NSA Director Bobby Inman noted the lack of cooperation, he proclaimed that "the tides are moving, and moving fast, toward legislated solutions that in fact are likely to be much more restrictive, not less restrictive, than the voluntary" censorship system.[53] Thus far, Inman's tidal wave has yet to emerge.

In 1985, Lincoln D. Faurer, Director of NSA, wrote to a past president of the ACM, saying he considered the prepublication review program a success:

Since our invitation to receive papers in mid–1981, we have reviewed over 200 papers. We are sure this is not the total number of papers written during that time which are related to cryptography. However, we view this volume of papers as a display of good faith on the part of the public cryptography community, and we applaud their cooperation.... To date, we have asked six authors not to publish their papers. All six have cooperated fully.... NSA would like the program to continue and would welcome seeing, for prepublication review, all papers or conference presentations related to cryptography.[54]

Simultaneous with the Study Group's voluntary review system, the NSA introduced its Computer Security Technical Evaluation Center. On September 15, 1981, NSA Director Faurer invited industry, on a voluntary basis, to submit computer products to the Center for an evaluation of their vulnerability to hostile penetration. But Faurer left little doubt that if companies failed to do so, they would risk the loss of lucrative government contracts. "Frankly," Faurer warned, "our intention is to significantly reward those DOD suppliers who produce the computer security products that we need." Former NSA Director Bobby Inman justified this approach by claiming that a lack of cooperation with the Center "might lead to a highly undesirable situation where private-sector users (e.g., banks, insurance companies) have higher integrity systems than the government."[55]

PUBLIC CRYPTOGRAPHY AND INDIVIDUAL PRIVACY

Though the PCSG acceded to NSA demands for prepublication review of cryptological research, it recognized that private research in the field could benefit broader government interests, and should therefore be expanded, not discouraged. The PCSG report noted: "In an era of instantaneous communication and pervasive computer data bases, it is becoming increasingly important to protect the privacy of both individuals and corporations, often using the tools previously used only by national governments." Citing the need for increased security of personal records and commercial, proprietary, or financial data sorted or transmitted electronically, the report concluded: "In many of these areas, cryptography is one of the most effective ways for providing the requisite security. Restriction of public research and development in cryptography might have an adverse effect on the ability of American industry to compete in world telecommunications and data-processing markets."[56]

In his minority report for the PCSG, George Davida spoke even more anxiously of the "electronic windows" proliferating in modern society, windows that work like one-way mirrors that prevent us from knowing who is looking into the most intimate details of our lives. He suggested: "Encryption can serve as a curtain. Therefore the need for a civilian (or non-governmental) effort in cryptography is a strong one."[57]

For decades, scientists have grappled with the growing electronic threats to privacy in American society. When confronted with evidence of routine eavesdropping by U.S. intelligence agencies on private telephone conversations and data communications, most scientists have concluded that the government is part of the problem, not the solution. For example, some American banks have acquired a special waiver allowing them to design secure money transfer systems, but the associated encryption was required to contain "trapdoors" through which NSA could enter the system at will. Even so, waivers allowing private research into advanced coding technology are seldom granted by NSA, presumably out of fear that the technology might fall into the hands of adversaries.

In 1976, university scientists began to challenge NSA's monopoly over cryptography by opening the door to private research into "public-key systems." Public-key systems can be compared to mailboxes with two different keys, one for locking and one for unlocking. The locking combination, or public key, is used to encrypt messages and can be given out freely to anyone who wishes to put messages in your mailbox. But the unlocking combination, or decryption key, is kept secret, allowing only the owner of the mailbox to remove messages. In this way, individuals could allow friends, businesses, or even strangers to encrypt messages to them. Public keys could be listed in directories like phone numbers, and both individuals and institutions could use them to secure phone calls, electronic mail, and telecommunications in general.

In 1977, two scientists wrote in *Science* magazine: "If everyone—governments, corporations, even private citizens—had the capability to encode their communications absolutely, all these threats to privacy would at least abate, and might just go away. In this context, the NSA's interest in denying access to the research seems rather narrow."[58]

Tom Athanasiou wrote in *Technology Review*: "The possibilities are enormous and the main point is clear: this approach doesn't require citizens to trust institutions any more than institutions are required to trust citizens."[59] He noted with concern the ease with which large organizations, governmental and private, amass extensive electronic dossiers on individuals. He pointed out that public-key systems would employ "digital pseudonyms" to short-circuit the collection of dossiers while still allowing the routine transactions of an information economy, such as electronic purchases and credit verification.

During Congressional hearings in 1980, cryptography expert David Kahn asked, "Why is the Government concerned about this whole issue of whether or not people outside the Government should do work in cryptology?" The answer, he claimed, lies in the government's fear that as scientists publish their research on cryptosystems, foreign countries will learn to create better codes, harder for the United States to crack. Kahn told how the NSA directed the U.S. Patent Office to impose secrecy orders on applications for patents on cipher devices, but claimed, "[T]he issue really is the Government's attempt to abate or even to suppress non-governmental research in cryptology. It applies to more people than [patent] secrecy orders, and it raises problems more fundamental than those thrown up by secrecy orders."[60]

Not only does David Kahn deny that public research in cryptography poses a threat to national security, he believes it brings major benefits to the nation. It improves America's overall cryptographic skills; it produces spin-off advances in fields like communications, mathematics, and computer science; and it provides database security for the most computerized nation in the world. Kahn concludes: "For all of these reasons, then, I feel that no limitation should be placed on the study of cryptology. Besides all of these reasons, it seems to me that something more fundamental will in the end prevent any restrictions anyway. It is called the First Amendment."[61]

One privately produced public-key encryption algorithm, called RSA, is based on the difficulty of factoring large numbers into prime numbers. An RSA-based cipher would require factoring an enormous number into "cryptographic primes," which can be hundreds of digits long. The very large number that would be embedded in the public key effectively resists factorization into primes, the process necessary to break the cipher. However, once the user is provided the cryptographic primes, the other operations necessary to generate the keys are relatively simple and require no centralized authority such as the NSA. Some claim that public-key cryptography is not practical because NSA will never agree to a public-key standard outside of its control. But the International Standards Organization, with many European members, has international authority to legitimate systems, and it is ready to give RSA its official seal of approval.

INVENTION SECRECY IN CRYPTOGRAPHY

The Invention Secrecy Act of 1951, described in detail in Chapter 5, allows the government to issue a "secrecy order" on a patent application if *any* federal defense agency believes public disclosure of the invention would threaten national security. In 1981, NSA had seven secrecy orders in effect, six of them concerning inventions made before World War II. For example, in October 1977, inventor Carl Nicolai submitted a patent application for a new type of voice scrambler he called the Phasor-phone. In April 1978, Nicolai received a letter from the Patent Office, but instead of a patent, he found a form with the words SECRECY ORDER across the top. Nicolai's secrecy order told him he faced two years in jail and a $10,000 fine if he disclosed any aspect of his device "in any way to any person not cognizant of the invention prior to the date of the order." The order did not say who ordered the action or why. In fact, Nicolai's initial patent application had traveled through the Patent Office's Special Laws Administration Group, where patents are screened to determine whether they contain any national security information. Applications that are suspect are passed on to the Armed Services Patent Advisory Board (ASPAB), which requests an opinion from the appropriate defense agency. When Nicolai's Phasorphone reached the ASPAB, the NSA official on the Board requested a secrecy order. The Army representative saw no need for such action, so the matter was referred to NSA Director Bobby Inman for a final decision. Inman affirmed the secrecy order.

Most patent secrecy orders are placed on inventions owned by or associated with the government, but Nicolai's device was a private invention. NSA was concerned that the private sector was now moving into the field of "transmission security," once an exclusive NSA domain. For years the Agency had combined cryptography and transmission security to protect its communications with clandestine agents. Now Nicolai wanted to market his Phasorphone at an affordable price of about $100, thus increasing public interest in the technology.

On the very day that Nicolai's secrecy order was issued, another inventor received an NSA-instigated secrecy order on yet another *private* device. Dr. George Davida, a professor of electrical engineering and computer science at the University of Wisconsin, had submitted a patent application for a cryptographic device that, like Nicolai's invention, threatened NSA's hegemony. The Dean of Wisconsin' College of Engineering and Applied Science immediately arranged a meeting with Chancellor Werner Baum and other University officials. Baum expressed concern about the chilling effect the secrecy order would have on academic freedom and research, and he said he would contact the NSF to try to resolve the matter. Baum wrote to the Director of the NSF, which had sponsored Davida's project, denouncing the secrecy order and demanding "minimal due process guarantees." He told *Science* magazine that he regarded the order as an invasion of academic freedom reminiscent of McCarthy-era tactics. Nicolai joined the fray, claiming that the secrecy order against Davida "appears to be part of a general plan by the NSA to limit the privacy of the American people." He said, "They've been bugging people's telephones for years, and now someone comes along with a device that makes this a little harder to do and they oppose this under the guise of national security."[62]

Davida notes: "The university environment is not one in which secrets can be kept. The first time I knew anything about the Secrecy Order was in a telephone conversation, with several students waiting to see me and who couldn't help but listen to the conversation." Davida was concerned about his responsibility to keep the material secret and the threat of a $10,000 fine and a two-year jail term for noncompliance. The technical report describing his device had already been sent to anyone who requested it, including the NSF. Davida says, "Thus, many people whom I didn't know may have had access to the material. Yet, there was a requirement that I report the names of individuals that I had sent the report to. . . . I was worried about having to prove that I did not leak the report."[63]

Davida was concerned that his colleagues were being drawn into the secrecy order: "As a matter of fact one colleague of mine would not open letters from me for a while." There were also questions about a graduate student who had assisted Davida. Would the student be denied his degree because of the secrecy?[64] Davida recalls, "The order vaguely referred to other material related to the patent application. Questions arose as to whether I could continue working in data security at all. Things didn't look good. The 'chilling effect' that the Chancellor had talked about had already been felt."[65]

After news of the secrecy order appeared in the press, the Chancellor was able to get in touch with the Secretary of Commerce, Juanita Kreps, and NSA Director Bobby Inman, and the order was lifted on June 13, 1978. Shortly thereafter, the Nicolai secrecy order was also withdrawn. But Inman felt the NSA had received a "bum rap" from the media on the controversy, and he initiated his own public relations blitz. For the first time in history, an incumbent NSA Director granted an interview to the press. In *Science* magazine, Inman said it would be necessary to find a middle ground between classified information and academic freedom. He complained, "[A]s we moved into burgeoning public interest in public cryptography, a substantial volume of unfavorable publicity has occurred with no counterbalance . . . to point out that there are valid national security concerns." Inman claimed that Davida's secrecy order had been a "bureaucratic error, because, as it turned out, the material had already appeared in the open literature and so could not be classified." In Nicolai's case, Inman admitted that there was disagreement among the reviewers and that he had opted to "err on the side of national security."[66] Inman concluded that he would like to have NSA given the same authority over cryptology that the Department of Energy has over atomic energy research, making all research related to cryptology "born classified."

After his interview in *Science* magazine, Inman spoke in January 1979 before a symposium of the Armed Forces Communications Electronics Association, where he warned of the dangers of "unrestrained public discussion of cryptologic matters." He claimed:

> Application of the genius of the American scholarly community to cryptographic and cryptanalytic problems, and widespread dissemination of resulting discoveries, carry the clear risk that some of NSA's cryptanalytic successes will be duplicated, with a consequent improvement of cryptography by foreign targets. No less significant is the risk that cryptographic principles embodied in communications security devices developed by NSA will be rendered ineffective by parallel nongovernmental cryptologic activity and publication.... All of this poses clear risks to the national security [and places the mission of the NSA] in peril.... While some people outside NSA express concern that the government has too much power to control nongovernmental cryptologic activities, in candor, my concern is that the government has too little.[67]

NSA AND THE DATA ENCRYPTION STANDARD

In 1971, IBM responded to the growing market potential for computer security devices by setting up a cryptology research group. The group soon developed a cipher named Lucifer, which was immediately used with IBM's cash-dispensing system. After further strengthening of the cipher, Lucifer was marketed for commercial use. At about the same time that IBM was turning its attention to cryptography, the National Bureau of Standards (NBS) began a study of the government's needs for computer security. NBS proposed a national civilian encryption system, to be called the Data Encryption Standard (DES). IBM submitted its Lucifer cipher for consideration as the nation's standard, but it first weakened the cipher by reducing its key size.

From the beginning, NSA had shown enormous interest in Lucifer. "IBM was involved with the NSA on an ongoing basis," admitted Alan Konheim, former manager of IBM's Lucifer project. "They [NSA employees] came up every couple of months to find out what IBM was doing."[68] NSA's code breakers were concerned that an economical and highly secure data encryption device would eventually challenge their ability to decipher the world's communications. The cryptographers in NSA's COMSEC feared that the commercial cryptography industry would learn NSA's methods, thus compromising the Agency's codes. Concerned that its preeminence in cryptography was at risk, NSA insisted that NBS modify Lucifer in ways that would make DES far more vulnerable. Lucifer's key size was reduced from 128 bits to 56 bits, reducing the number of possible keys by *millions* of times and thus making it substantially less secure. IBM's Alan Konheim recalls, "If they [NSA] had had their way, they would have had 32 bits."[69]

In addition to shortening Lucifer's key, NSA redesigned its numerical tables, called "substitution boxes" or S-boxes, then classified the associated data. Because the design of these boxes, so crucial to the strength of DES, was classified, many critics believed that NSA's changes concealed a trapdoor, a secret numerical pattern that would allow NSA to decipher, without the key, any DES-encrypted message. Because of such suspicions, a number of foreign countries that have been offered DES have chosen to use other systems. Nonetheless, NSA recommended the weakened Lucifer as the best candidate for the nation's encryption standard. On July 15, 1977, DES became the official government cipher, the only unclassified code approved by NSA, and a number of firms began producing it for private industry. DES quickly took over the encryption market, becoming the code provided by 99 percent of the companies selling encryption equipment.

Scientists have analyzed the DES strength against a "brute force" attack, which would match deciphered messages against intercepted, encrypted versions. It was calculated that by using a high-speed computer with a million special-purpose chips, the 56-bit DES key could be broken in 24 hours. The cost to do this was estimated at $5,000 per solution. But what if IBM had ignored NSA and stayed with its 128-bit key? The cost per solution would then have been *$200 septillion.*

In response to scientific criticism, NBS sponsored two workshops on the DES, at which it defended its choice. Yet the makeup of NBS's DES team raised doubts about its impartiality. The leader of the NBS computer security project was a former NSA employee, and an NBS consultant on the project had been one of the NSA's senior code breakers.

Suddenly, in 1985 NSA abandoned the DES system, after years of assurances to American businesses and foreign governments. NSA's deputy director, Walter Deeley, went so far as to state that he "wouldn't bet a plugged nickel on the Soviet Union not breaking it [DES]."[70] People throughout the information industry felt betrayed, but bankers were particularly upset, since they were committed to the use of DES to en-

crypt electronic fund transfers. In response to complaints, NSA agreed
that DES would remain certified for bank fund transfers. DES products
for use in telecommunications equipment and systems are no longer
being endorsed by NSA, but federal agencies may still purchase products
that have not been validated under the NSA endorsement program
without processing a waiver.

U.S. government users of DES products that have been endorsed by
NSA may obtain DES cryptographic keys for these products from NSA
at no cost. Alternatively, users of DES, including federal organizations,
may generate their own cryptographic keys. Hardware and software
implementations of DES are subject to federal export controls, as specified in the ITAR and administered by the Office of Munitions Control.
License requests for products to be shipped to "prohibited" countries
are denied for foreign policy reasons by the Department of State. More
routinely, the Department of Commerce's Bureau of Export Administration is responsible for export licenses for cryptographic products,
including DES, that relate to functions like authentication, access control,
proprietary software protection, and automatic teller devices.

Why did NSA abandon DES? Was there evidence of successful cryptanalytic attacks on DES? If so, why allow banks to continue using it? If
the inadequate number of variations within the DES key was the problem, why not restore the key length to its original 128 bits? Because NSA
has refused to declassify the relevant evidence, these questions remain
unanswered.

Even greater secrecy surrounds NSA's new line of codes, being
dumped on the public marketplace as alternatives to DES. Citing its
communications security obligation to protect the United States from
foreign spying, NSA has marketed a new family of encryption systems, to be sold as tamper-resistant integrated circuits. But NSA has
classified the encryption algorithm contained within the chip, keeping
it hidden from those who use the system as a security device on their
computers or telephones. Once again, many private businesses and
institutions are reluctant to acquire the system NSA is offering because they believe NSA has built a "trapdoor" into it, allowing NSA to
decipher the seemingly secure messages. Herb Bright, an officer with
the data-security firm Computation Planning Associates, warns: "With
a hardware black box you can describe several schemes that would be
almost impossible to test for from the outside and could, in effect,
constitute a hardware Trojan Horse." Cryptology expert Tom Athanasiou says cryptologists are trained to be dubious and will never have
confidence in a classified cipher: "A cipher will be trusted if it is open

to independent evaluation and if breaking it is shown to require solving a very difficult numerical problem. Such ciphers do in fact exist and they enjoy a freedom from suspicion that NSA's new ciphers can never hope to share."[71]

NSA decided that it would supply codes not just to government agencies but to anyone in the private sector who needed them. In fact, Michael Fleming, the head of NSA's new Industrial Relations Group, says NSA will become a "service agency," providing code-making algorithms to U.S. companies with appropriate security clearances. These trusted companies will produce the new codes in the form of small chips and sell them to other U.S. companies or to government agencies. NSA will *tell* government agencies which codes to purchase, but it will only *advise* the private sector. In addition, NSA will provide individualized encoding/decoding keys to all government agencies using the new codes. The private sector, including banks and businesses, will have the choice of purchasing the keys from NSA or from one of its "trusted" companies. In 1985 the NSA's Michael Fleming discussed the new codes with industry groups, after which he proclaimed, "There is a lot of interest, a lot of companies are calling us. We're on our way."[72]

But NSA's continuing secrecy and increasing influence in the field of public cryptography make critics uneasy. Allan Adler of the ACLU says, "Putting the NSA in charge ensures a one-dimensional approach. The NSA operates largely in secret and has no feeling for the protection of individual privacy or access to the government's information." Adler is also concerned with NSA's desire to encode any unclassified information that it considers "sensitive." He asks, "Just what kind of information doesn't have a national security element to it?"[73]

NSA's authority to develop new encryption standards for unclassified government data and to promote new standards for the private sector derives from National Security Decision Directive 145 (NSDD 145), signed by President Ronald Reagan in 1984 (see Chapter 4). IBM's Harry DeMaio said that beginning in 1988, any encryption devices endorsed by NSA incorporate NSA's new algorithms, but products endorsed by NSA prior to 1988 may be sold and used beyond 1988. DeMaio added, "For IBM's part, we have no plan to discontinue support for the algorithm [DES], especially in banking."[74] DeMaio expressed doubts about the ability to export NSA's new devices, pointing out that encryption devices developed and endorsed by NSA's Commercial Communications Security Endorsement Program (CCEP) are subject to export restrictions. "This makes planning difficult for multinational companies intending to use a single encryption method throughout worldwide networks....

It is also unclear how those CCEP devices approved for export will be accepted by foreign governments."[75]

Geoffrey Turner of Bank of America says, "I talked with one NSA official recently and outlined our problems. I told him they had been underhanded and had leaked statements. I asked him to state in public just what NSA's position was on these new algorithms. He said, 'No, we don't want to get into a political firestorm.' " Turner concedes, "I will try to work under NSDD 145.... But in essence, I am saying to the NSA, 'Tell government agencies to use your CCEP gear, but don't mess with my DES.' "[76]

Indeed, despite its critics, DES seems to be holding its own. It has been reviewed and reaffirmed twice, most recently in 1988, at which time it was affirmed until 1993. The use of DES is mandatory for all federal agencies, including defense agencies, for the protection of sensitive unclassified information requiring cryptographic protection. In addition, DES may be used by private-sector individuals or organizations at their discretion. The head of a federal department or agency may waive the use of DES for the protection of unclassified information for a variety of reasons. Waivers will be considered for alternative devices certified by NSA as complying with the CCEP when such devices offer equivalent cost/performance features.

Even the fears of built-in NSA trapdoors seem to have abated. Robert Courtney, IBM's former data security specialist, says, "Forget about those trap-door-in-DES allegations. We weren't smart enough to build a trap door." Courtney believes DES will survive NSA's attempt to corner the market, but only "after a fight behind closed doors, and NSA will end up as confused as ever. They have shot themselves in the foot over NSDD 145."[77]

The Computer Security Act of 1987 and the July 1990 classified Presidential directive, "National Policy for the Security of National Security Telecommunications and Information Systems," clarified the division of responsibility between the National Institute of Standards and Technology (NIST) and the NSA. Among the services now provided by NIST to federal departments and agencies are security planning, risk management, encryption, and virus detection. However, in accordance with the Computer Security Act, NIST draws upon the technical expertise of NSA as appropriate.

NIST was assigned the responsibility for the development and promulgation of computer standards and guidelines for *unclassified* federal systems. The Presidential directive assigns to the NSA the responsibility for the security of systems and telecommunications involving classified and Warner Amendment systems, collectively known as "national security systems." These are the systems operated by the U.S. government, its contractors, or its agents, that contain classified information or involve intelligence activities, cryptologic activities related to national security, command and control of military forces, equipment related to weapons systems, or equipment critical to military or intelligence missions. NSA offers a wide range of services for these systems, and at the request of federal agencies or contractors, it assesses the vulnerabilities of information systems to hostile exploitation or disruption, and recommends countermeasures.

GOVERNMENT ACCOUNTABILITY

The NSA has always claimed that its right to eavesdrop on foreign or domestic communications derived from no law but from "inherent presidential authority." The extralegal nature of the Agency's power was challenged in 1976 when President Ford gave his blessing to a Senate bill that would have required the NSA to submit to judicial review before initiating certain surveillances. The Foreign Intelligence Surveillance Act (FISA) was introduced by Senator Edward Kennedy (D-MA) after closed-door negotiations with the Justice Department. After two years of legislative struggle that compromised the original desire for judicial review, a weakened bill was signed into law by Ford's successor, Jimmy Carter.

The FISA introduced a complex authorization procedure to control the use and distribution of communications inadvertently intercepted by Americans. If an American's telephone call or message falls within the broad area providing for the "national security, defense, or foreign policy of the United States," the NSA is authorized to pass along the communication.

The FISA also established a supersecret federal court, hidden behind a door with a coded lock in a windowless room on the top floor of the Justice Department Building. This Foreign Intelligence Surveillance Court was surely the strangest creation in the history of the federal judiciary. A request to conduct surveillance originates with the NSA General Counsel, then goes to the NSA Director, the Secretary of Defense, the Justice Department's Office of Intelligence Policy and Review, and then to the Attorney General for final approval. If the request is granted, the attorneys, accompanied by an official from NSA's SIGINT Office, enter the Foreign Intelligence Surveillance Court to argue the case before a properly cleared judge. The Court sits in secret session, holds no adversary hearings, and rarely issues a public opinion. It is listed in neither the *Government Organization Manual* nor the *District Court Directory.* "On its face," said one legal authority, "it is an affront to the traditional American concept of justice."[78]

If the government's claim that the requested surveillance meets FISA requirements is not shown to be "clearly erroneous," the judge *must* issue a warrant authorizing the intercept. The judge does not examine the necessity or propriety of the surveillance. So long as he finds that the target is "foreign" and that the application procedures have been followed, he has no choice but to approve the surveillance. It is no surprise that the federal government has *never* lost a case before this secret court. The closest it came was when Reagan Administration lawyers requested warrants for surreptitious entries—black-bag jobs—and the Court rejected the applications on the grounds that the authority for black-bag jobs was vested not in the Court but in the Presidency itself. As a result, the rejected break-in and all subsequent surreptitious entries needed no Court authorization.

The secret FISA Court appears to have become a rubber stamp for surveillance. Indeed, testimony before the Senate Intelligence Committee suggests that surveillance requests were examined far more critically *before* the FISA than after it. Under a 1981 Reagan Executive Order, the NSA is apparently authorized to lend its full cryptanalytic support—both analysts and computers—to "any department or agency" in the federal government, and even to local police departments "when lives are endangered."[79] Within the United States, the NSA is free to pull into its massive surveillance system every telephone call and message entering, leaving, or transiting the country, so long as it is done by microwave interception. Indeed, microwaves and satellites have so transformed telecommunications that the wire has become almost obsolete.

In 1975, Sen. Frank Church (D-ID) led a valiant, though ultimately unsuccessful, foray against the entrenched secrecy of America's intelligence agencies and their increasing intrusion on the privacy of American citizens. He warned particularly of the NSA's growing SIGINT powers:

> [T]he technological capacity that the intelligence community has given the government could enable it to impose total tyranny, and there would be no way to fight back, because the most careful effort to combine together in resistance to the government, no matter how privately it was done, is within the reach of the government to know. Such is the capability of this technology.... [W]e must see to it that this agency and all agencies that possess this technology operate within the law and under proper supervision, so that we never cross over that abyss. That is the abyss from which there is no return.[80]

In his definitive book on the NSA, James Bamford responded to Senator Church's warning: "If there are defenses to such technotyranny, it would appear, at least from past experience, that they will not come from Congress. Rather, they will most likely come from academe and industry in the form of secure cryptographic applications to private and commercial telecommunications equipment. The same technology that is used against free speech could be used to protect it, for without protection the future may be grim."[81]

In the spring of 1992, the struggle between government and industry over the technology of free speech was highlighted in Congressional hearings on the Threat of Foreign Espionage to U.S. Corporations. In his opening statement, subcommittee chairman Jack Brooks described advances in encryption technology offering protection against unauthorized access to sensitive business information. He noted that U.S. intelligence and law enforcement agencies feared that if encryption technology became readily available, it would be used by our adversaries to cover illegal activities.

> Apparently these agencies believe that the federal government must restrict the use of this technology to ensure that they will be able to listen in or intercept electronic communications involving these type of activities. Leaders of U.S. industry, on the other hand, believe that the intelligence and law enforcement agencies are misguided in their attempts to stop the inevitable progress of encryption technology, especially since it is already available today worldwide. They argue that the use of this technology is crucial to U.S. corporations if they are to be able to protect their trade secrets and remain competitive in the world marketplace.[82]

The NSA and FBI argued that publicly available technology to secure telephone transmission was outpacing the government's ability to monitor such communications for intelligence and law enforcement purposes. Phone companies were installing digital equipment that converts conversations into computerized code, which is sent at high speed over transmission lines and turned back into voice at the other end. This digital technology would not only frustrate the FBI's phone-tapping efforts but also improve the security of data transmissions in ways that are almost impossible for intelligence agencies, including U.S. agencies, to penetrate.

The FBI pressed for legislation that would require telephone companies to install equipment to facilitate wiretaps, with the cost to be reflected in the public's phone bills. The American Civil Liberties Union and a long list of companies, including IBM, AT&T, and Microsoft

Corp., signed a letter expressing "grave concern" over the FBI's proposed legislation. "The proposal would not only impede development of digital communications technology, but prohibit American businesses from installing secure communications lines," the letter said. "We firmly believe that any otherwise secure system which is made open to FBI surveillance would be vulnerable to others." FBI Director William Sessions disagreed. "I don't look at [the FBI proposal] as impeding technology," testified Sessions. "There is a burden on the private sector... a price of doing business."[83]

As expected, the National Security Agency's spokesperson, Dr. James J. Hearn, told Congress that private industry did not really need additional cryptographic or communications security technology because all NSA-documented penetrations of unclassified systems were simply the result of bad security practices or failure to correct known operating system flaws. The NSA's intentions are believed to go beyond the FBI's proposals, requiring that all government computers use security technology that is weak enough to allow NSA to continue surveilling overseas computer data transmissions. For this reason, when the government introduced a new "signature" encryption standard, it became the focus of debate between government and business. The new Digital Signal Standard (DSS) was proposed by the NIST as a way to electrically sign and verify government messages. DSS would generate the equivalent of a written signature in electronic form, calculating a digital value based on the content of the message and the person signing the message. This digital value could then be appended to the message or document, allowing appropriate personnel to verify that the document had not been altered and that it was approved by the signer. Like the government's DES, discussed earlier in this chapter, DSS is cryptographic based, but it can only sign documents, not encrypt them.

Much of the criticism of DSS comes from private corporations like RSA Data Security, Inc., which has a competing algorithm licensed for general use. D. James Bidzos, RSA's president, sees no justification for the government's attempts to impede the private sector's development of data security technology. "In industry's quest to provide [data] security, we have a new adversary, the Justice Department," said Bidzos. "It's like saying that we shouldn't build cars because criminals will use them to get away." NIST, a branch of the Commerce Department that has worked closely with NSA, has the legal authority to certify federal computer security standards, and it claims that DSS is virtually unbreakable. But Milton Socolar, special assistant for the General Accounting

Office, stated that DSS "is much weaker technology for the protection of electronic transmissions and is an added burden to U.S. industry."[84]

Socolar told the House Subcommittee on Economic and Commercial Law that cryptographic technology to protect sensitive industrial information is readily available under internationally accepted industry standards, but the intelligence community is insisting on a different standard for electronic communications between U.S. industry and the government. "This separate standard is weaker than what is commercially available, is an added burden on commercial activities, and raises the question as to whether any practical purpose would be served by the requirement." Socolar concluded, "We need to examine openly the extent to which the government should be hampering industry's use of generally available cryptographic technology that would better protect electronic business communications."[85] Socolar joined business representatives in predicting that if DSS becomes the government's signature encryption standard, companies and banks would feel compelled to pay for two separate computer security systems: DSS for government-related work and a genuinely secure system for everything else.

Marshall Phelps, Jr., IBM Vice President, testified that businesses increasingly use electronic signatures instead of exchanging paper documents, yet he complained, "The recent draft DSS issued by the U.S. government unfortunately uses a different and unproven methodology, rather than relying on an internationally accepted standard for digital signature encryption. The result of this approach will require vendors to design multiple devices to meet both the international standard and the DSS. Moreover, users will be forced to use multiple products to implement the differing encryption methodologies." Phelps explained that IBM customers around the world needed to ensure the security and integrity of transmitted information through the use of encryption. "[I]n formulating policy in this important area, it is essential that the government recognize the lawful uses of encryption technologies as well as the offerings of comparable products by non-U.S. firms on the global market."[86]

NIST claims that because DSS is intended to be royalty-free, RSA is fighting it tooth and nail. In fact, because the RSA algorithm can be used to encrypt *and* sign data, it is a competitor to *both* NIST-certified algorithms, DES and DSS. There are also some unresolved patent issues arising from RSA's claims that NIST has infringed its patents. NIST admits that final approval of DSS as a new government standard may be slow in coming, because all of the criticisms generated by the April 1992 hearings will have to be answered.

The 1992 hearings produced an ironic confrontation between government and business when the CIA testified that increasing international economic espionage required the CIA and NSA to improve their surveillance of America's electronic transmissions. But American business executives cited that very threat as justification for their demand for more and better public encryption devices to scramble the voices and data they send on telephone lines. When Director of Central Intelligence Robert Gates warned American business executives not to leave sensitive documents unattended in foreign hotel rooms, James Riesbeck, Executive Vice President of Corning, Inc., replied that American executives would have less need to travel with such documents if they could depend on secure video teleconferences without worrying about eavesdropping by foreign agents. In other words, let the private sector develop their own genuine transmissions security technology.

Riesbeck told Congress of the need for more secure corporate communications. "Encryption devices and other security measures must be implemented globally to be effective," said Riesbeck. "Domestic or foreign barriers to expanded use of security devices should be identified and eliminated. Our international agencies of the government must become full participants in, not obstacles to, this public-private partnership. . . . Adoption of inflexible government regulations which inhibit technological progress will be damaging to U.S. competitiveness."[87]

Congress is beginning to show some willingness to reduce such regulations. In November 1991, when the House of Representatives passed legislation to renew the Export Administration Act, the bill contained an amendment to prevent government controls on the export of mass market software, including software with encryption capability. In the summer of 1992, as the legislation went into conference between the House and Senate, the Bush administration threatened to veto the bill if the final version contained the amendment.

Many in business and government point out the impossibility of controlling cryptographic software. Indeed, the United States has agreed to let its allies decontrol mass market software with encryption features, and foreign companies, unencumbered by munition-type restrictions, are bringing encrypted software and related services to the international market. The British have stated publicly that they are permitting the uncontrolled export of such software, but U.S. software manufacturers are prevented from selling their products abroad. Even the Moscow-based Askri company offers a software encryption package called Cryptos for $100. The package is based on the Data Encryption Standard, America's own national standard. How, then, can we expect our export controls to keep encrypted software out of the hands of adversaries or competitors?

Eric Hirschhorn, an export control official in the Carter and Reagan administrations, and David Peyton, a policy analyst with the Information Technology Association of America, explained why the federal government insists on these unrealistic controls: "The reason is that when it comes to encryption, the Department of Defense won't yield to common sense unless compelled to do so. It fears that the availability of encryption-capable software will complicate its mission of listening in on foreign communications." Hirschhorn and Peyton say the executive branch has failed to keep pace with the new role of cryptography on the international marketplace. "Unfortunately, the U.S. government, clinging to the futile hopes that it can stem the tide of technology, refuses to acknowledge this sea change. With the exception of personal identification numbers and authentication messages, the U.S. government treats all encryption-capable computer software as munitions and tightly restricts its export. The restrictions apply even to 'mass market' software, which can be purchased at thousands of retail outlets."[88]

Philip S. Gutis, a spokesman for the ACLU, said, "It's just a question of how far our Government goes in making it easier for them to invade our privacy." Rep. Dan Glickman (D-KA) concluded, "Our Government is impeding the private sector in developing modern cryptographic techniques because they don't want those techniques to get too sophisticated."[89]

NOTES

1. Robert Kuttner, "Spooks and Science: An American Dilemma," *Washington Post*, 20 August 1989, B7.

2. Herbert O. Yardley, *The American Black Chamber* (Indianapolis: Bobbs-Merrill, 1931), 20.

3. Theodore W. Richards, *Historical Background of the Signal Security Agency* (Washington, DC: Army Security Agency, 1946), vol. III, 47.

4. James Bamford, *The Puzzle Palace: A Report on America's Most Secret Agency* (Boston: Houghton Mifflin, 1982), 12.

5. Henry L. Stimson and McGeorge Bundy, *On Active Service in Peace and War* (New York: Harper & Brothers, 1947), 188.

6. Bamford, *The Puzzle Palace*, 19.

7. Ibid., 20.

8. Ibid., 21.

9. Ibid., 22.

10. *Congressional Record*, 77, 10 May 1933, 3129.

11. David Kahn, *The Codebreakers* (New York: Macmillan, 1967), 387–388.

12. Department of Justice, "Prosecutive Summary," 4 March 1977 (as quoted in *Puzzle Palace*, p. 46).

13. U.S. Senate, Select Committee on Intelligence, *Supplementary Detailed Staff Reports on Intelligence and the Rights of Americans, Final Report* (Washington, DC: GPO, 1976), 767–768.

14. U.S. House of Representatives, Committee on Appropriations, *Military Construction Appropriations*, Hearings, 93rd Cong. 1st Sess. (Washington, DC: GPO, 1974), 461.

15. Bamford, *The Puzzle Palace*, 126–127.

16. Ibid., 128.

17. U.S. Senate, Select Committee to Study Governmental Operations with Respect to Intelligence Activities, *The National Security Agency and Fourth Amendment Rights*, Hearings, Vol. 5, 94th Cong. 1st Sess. (Washington, DC: GPO, 1976), 150.

18. U.S. Senate, Select Committee on Intelligence, *Supplementary Detailed Staff Reports*, 932.

19. Ibid., 942.

20. U.S. Senate, Select Committee to Study Governmental Operations with Respect to Intelligence Activities, *Huston Plan*, Hearings, Vol. 2, 94th Cong., 1st Sess. (Washington, DC: GPO, 1976), 193–197.

21. David Wise, *The Politics of Lying: Government Deception, Secrecy, and Power* (New York: Vintage Books, 1973), 233–235.

22. *United States v. New York Times*, (1971) 328 F. Supp. 324.

23. Bamford, *The Puzzle Palace*, 236.

24. U.S. Senate, Select Committee to Study Governmental Operations, *The National Security Agency and Fourth Amendment Rights*, 45–46.

25. U.S. House of Representatives, Committee on Government Operations, Subcommittee on Government Information and Individual Rights, *Interception of Nonverbal Communications by Federal Intelligence Agencies*, Hearings, 94th Cong., 1st and 2nd Sess. (Washington, DC: GPO, 1976), 99.

26. David Wheeler, "Long-Secretive Agency Begins to Come in from the Cold," *Chronicle of Higher Education*, 29 January 1992, A17.

27. Ibid., A20.

28. Deborah Shapley and Gina Bari Kolata, "Cryptology: Scientists Puzzle over Threat to Open Research, Publication," *Science*, 30 September 1977, 1345–1346.

29. Ibid., 1349.

30. Ibid.

31. Stephen H. Unger, "The Growing Threat of Government Secrecy," *Technology Review*, February/March 1982, 38.

32. *The Government's Classification of Private Ideas*, Hearings, 96th Cong., 28 February, 20 March, 21 August 1980 (Washington, DC: U.S. GPO, 1981), 271.

33. Ibid., 277.

34. Ibid., 278.

35. Ibid., 282–283.

36. Ibid., 284.

37. Ibid., 762.

38. Ibid., 763.

39. Bamford, *The Puzzle Palace*, 352.

40. Ibid.

41. *The Government's Classification of Private Ideas*, 764–765.

42. Ibid., 767.

43. Ibid., 768.

44. Ibid., 766.

45. Ibid., 770, 773.

46. Gina Bari Kolata, "Cryptography: A New Clash Between Academic Freedom and National Security," *Science*, 29 August 1980, 995–996.

47. Bamford, *The Puzzle Palace*, 362.

48. Ibid., 361.

49. "Report of the Public Cryptographic Study Group," *Communications of the ACM*, July 1981, 440.

50. Ibid., 447, 450.

51. Bamford, *The Puzzle Palace*, 360–361.

52. Peter J. Denning, "Government Classification of Private Ideas," *Communications of the ACM*, March 1981, 105.

53. Bamford, *The Puzzle Palace*, 363.

54. Letter from Lincoln D. Faurer, Director, NSA/Chief CSS, to David H. Brandin, *Communications of the ACM*, March 1985, 236.

55. Bamford, *The Puzzle Palace*, 362–363.

56. "Report of the Public Cryptographic Study Group," 437.

57. Ibid., 446.

58. "Cryptology: Scientists Puzzle Over Threat to Open Research, Publication," *Science*, 30 September 1977, 1348.

59. "Encryption Technology, Privacy, and National Security," *Technology Review*, August/September 1986, 58.

60. *The Government's Classification of Private Ideas*, 406.

61. Ibid., 410.

62. David Kahn, "Cryptology Goes Public," *Foreign Affairs*, Fall 1979, 155.

63. *The Government's Classification of Private Ideas*, 420.

64. Ibid., 417.

65. Ibid., 449.

66. Deborah Shapley, "Intelligence Agency Chief Seeks 'Dialogue' with Academics," *Science*, 27 October 1978, 407–410.

67. *The Government's Classification of Private Ideas*, 359.

68. Ibid., 346.

69. "Encryption Technology, Privacy, and National Security," 60.

70. Ibid., 61.

71. Ibid.

72. "NSA to Provide Secret Codes," *Science*, October 1985, 46.

73. Ibid., 45–46.

74. Charles Howe, "Into the Night," *Datamation*, June 1986, 22.

75. Ibid., 23.

76. Ibid., 24.

77. "Busting DES," *Datamation*, June 1986, 24.

78. Bamford, *The Puzzle Palace*, 370.

79. Ibid., 376.

80. NBC, "Meet the Press," transcript of August 17, 1975, broadcast (Washington, DC: Merkle Press, 1975), 6.

81. Bamford, *The Puzzle Palace*, 379.

82. Opening statement of Congressman Jack Brooks before the House Subcommittee on Economic and Commercial Law, House Committee on the Judiciary, April 29, 1992, 2.

83. "Intelligence Community in Breach with Business," *Washington Post*, 30 April 1992, A8.

84. Ibid.

85. Statement of Milton J. Socolar, Special Assistant to the Comptroller General, before the House Subcommittee on Economic and Commercial Law, House Committee on the Judiciary, April 29, 1992, 6.

86. Statement of Marshall C. Phelps, Jr., IBM Vice President, Commercial and Industrial Relations, before the House Subcommittee on Economic and Commercial Law, House Committee on the Judiciary, April 29, 1992, 8–9.

87. Statement of J. E. Riesbeck, Executive Vice President, Corning, Inc., before the House Subcommittee on Economic and Commercial Law, House Committee on the Judiciary, April 29, 1992, 4–5.

88. Eric Hirschhorn and David Peyton, "Uncle Sam's Secret Decoder Ring," *Washington Post*, 25 June 1992, A23.

89. "U.S. Warns on Advances in Encoding," *New York Times*, 30 April 1992, D1, D5.

CHAPTER 5

Not Quite Classified

SENSITIVE BUT UNCLASSIFIED

Even the federal government has come to recognize that the vast overclassification of information is damaging the credibility of appropriate
access restrictions. Unfortunately, the government's response to this unmanageable mountain of formal secrecy has not been to pursue a declassification program; instead, it has created new categories of
information control outside the classification system. A 1982 National
Academy of Science (NAS) report, *Scientific Communication and National
Security*, attempted to reassure academia that "security by accomplishment" rather than "security by secrecy" would be recommended as the
best approach for the nation's universities and scientific laboratories. But
the NAS panel, financed in part by the Defense Department (DoD),
acknowledged the existence of technological "gray areas" within which
the government might reasonably impose some controls through contract restrictions rather than export regulations or security classification.
The presidents of Stanford, Caltech, and MIT warned that it would be
impossible for the majority of American universities to accept contracts
that would require government approval of scientific publication. Even
Under Secretary of Defense Richard DeLauer found unworkable the
NAS panel's notion of gray areas for "sensitive but unclassified" research.
He preferred a clear-cut decision, with research labeled either Classified
or Unclassified at the time a government agency issued a funding grant.
   In an initially secret 1982 report, *The Exploitation of Western Data Bases*,

the government claimed popular acceptance of the need to protect unclassified information on privacy or proprietary grounds, but admitted,
"The case for withholding unclassified information which is 'militarily
critical' is not as readily accepted, partly because the 'unclassified but
sensitive' designator sounds like a contradiction in terms."[1] Indeed, Herbert S. White, Dean of the School of Library and Information Science
at Indiana University, has written: "If things are unclassified then they
are presumably available to anyone, and everything in the general collections of public and academic libraries is unclassified. Phrases such as
'unclassified but sensitive' are oxymorons comparable to George Carlin's
giant shrimp, or perhaps in our field to library administration."[2]

In 1984, without the laughter that accompanied George Carlin's oxy-
moron, President Reagan quietly signed National Security Decision Directive 145 (NSDD–145), officially designating a category of information
called "sensitive but unclassified." Initially described as "unclassified but
sensitive national security-related information," this category was subsequently described by DoD to include anything from crop forecasts to
personnel records. The NSDD–145 Systems Security Steering Group
recommended restricting access to any information that might adversely
affect federal government interests, but the precise determination of
what was "sensitive" was to be left to agency heads, thereby ensuring
unpredictable and contradictory interpretations. Among the more ominous aspects of NSDD–145 was its assignment of enforcement authority
to the military, by way of the highly secretive National Security Agency
(NSA). NSDD–145 extended NSA's authority to include "all computers
and communications security for the Federal Government and private
industry . . . including non-national security sensitive information." Jerry
Berman of the ACLU warned: "With NSA in the lead, we are on the
verge of militarizing our information systems. . . . And—full circle—limited access to heretofore openly accessed government and private data
base systems."[3]

Public awareness of NSDD–145 was heightened as the result of the
resignation of former National Security Adviser John Poindexter for his
role in the Iran-Contra scandal. During the investigation of Poindexter's
last days at the National Security Council, attention was drawn to various
of his orders and directives, including his memo outlining the implementation of NSDD–145. In October 1986, Poindexter had issued National Telecommunications and Information Systems Security Policy No.
2 (NTISSP–2), a memo that attempted to provide a definition of the
"sensitive but unclassified" category of information, but did so in dan-
gerously broad terms.

Poindexter defined sensitive but unclassified information to include "information the disclosure, loss, misuse, alteration, or destruction of which would adversely affect national security or other Federal government interests.... Other government interests are those related, but not limited, to the wide range of government or government-derived economic, human, financial, industrial, agricultural, technological, and law enforcement information, as well as the privacy or confidentiality of personal or commercial proprietary information provided to the U.S. Government by its citizens."[4] Upon considering Poindexter's comprehensive list of "government interests," the Office of Technology Assessment concluded, "It now appears that the definition of 'sensitive' could be applied to almost any information, or at least a very broad range of information, even if it is already published or available."[5]

According to Kenneth de Graffenreid, who was then Director for Intelligence Programs at the National Security Council, the concern behind the directive was the protection of U.S. government systems from intrusion by hostile foreign powers. But on June 27, 1985, in testimony before the House Science and Technology Committee, Chairman Jack Brooks described NSDD–145 as "one of the most ill-advised and potentially troublesome directives ever issued by a President. It seeks to vest in the Department of Defense...the authority to...govern the access to and processing of all computerized information which it deems to be critical to the national security of the United States. This would include not only classified information but any other information within...civilian agencies which the Department considers 'sensitive.' "[6]

Early in 1987, hearings were held before the House Government Operations subcommittee to examine the implications of the Administration's new security policy. On February 25, physicist Robert L. Park expressed his concern about the Poindexter Memorandum's broad restrictions on "other government interests": "Now I don't know what 'other Federal Government interests' Admiral Poindexter has in mind, but language like that makes me very uncomfortable. Moreover, the directive specifically applies to government contractors that 'electronically store, process, or communicate sensitive but unclassified information.' Since almost all university research receives some federal funds, it would seem that this could be applied to almost any university scientist with a word processor."[7]

On March 17, 1987, Admiral Poindexter appeared before the same Government Operations subcommittee but refused to testify, invoking his Fifth Amendment protection against self-incrimination, exactly as he had done before the House Foreign Affairs Committee as a key player

146   SECRET SCIENCE

in the Iran-Contra scandal. Chairman Brooks asked Poindexter four
questions about NTISSP–2, the now notorious Poindexter Memorandum, but Poindexter refused to answer each time. This exploitation of
the Fifth Amendment was outside any judicial context.

Subsequently, in a stunning reversal of policy, Frank Carlucci, who
had replaced Poindexter as National Security Adviser, submitted a con-
ciliatory letter to Chairman Brooks, announcing that the Reagan Administration was rescinding the Poindexter Memorandum. Carlucci
indicated that NSDD–145, the broad directive that had created, in Chairman Brooks's words, a "shadow government," was being reviewed. But
Congressional sources made it clear that the retrenchment was only
temporary, "intended to disassociate the plan from Poindexter's name
in the wake of the Iran-Contra arms scandal." Senator Patrick Leahy
(D-VT) complained that there was no real change of thinking on the
issue. "The administration is so enthralled by the idea of secrecy they
won't give up their attempts to control the flow of information."[8]

On May 28, 1987, the National Commission on Libraries and Information Science (NCLIS) held its "Hearing on Sensitive but Not Classified
Information," offering the library and information community an opportunity to speak against this ominous concept. Unfortunately, far from
being a watchdog, NCLIS had earned a reputation as an apologist for
government secrecy. Presiding over the NCLIS hearings was banker
Gerald C. Newman, who subsequently organized the secret 1988 FBI
briefing linking NCLIS to the FBI's notorious Library Awareness Program.

In his written introduction to the transcript of the NCLIS hearing,
chairman Newman endorsed the government's belief that "in order to
slow up the flow of valuable technological and other information to the
East Bloc," the library and information communities must exercise judgment before releasing unclassified scientific data to foreign nationals.[9]
Newman claimed that the difference of opinion among those who testified at the hearing was over the means, not the desirability, of restricting
access to sensitive information. He stated, "In general, the library and
information science communities felt that sensitive materials should be
classified in order to relieve these communities of the burden of limiting
access to information and determining which information should not be
made available to foreign nationals or governments." Quite to the contrary, the transcript reveals a consensus in the scholarly community that
the arbitrary and ill-defined category called "sensitive but unclassified"
should have unrestricted public access. Librarians and scientists con-

ceded only that if the government felt compelled to restrict such information, the formal classification process was the appropriate method.

The first government witness at the NCLIS hearings, James Dearlove
of the Defense Intelligence Agency, warned against giving away our
sensitive technology. When asked why the government did not simply
classify such information, Dearlove responded, "They don't want to classify everything because I don't think they have that many safes." David
E. Whitman, from the Office of the Deputy Under Secretary of Defense
for Policy, then testified that just a few years earlier the DoD had not
felt that unclassified information was a security concern. He added,
"Over the years that position has changed. We now view the matter of
unclassified information, technology transfer, and related issues as having grave security potentials, if not actual problems, not only for DoD
but for the Government, and, indeed this country as a whole." When
asked what percentage of the total "document universe" might fall within
the category of "sensitive but unclassified," Whitman responded, "If I
had to take a guess, . . . and only within the DoD realm, that could be a
very, very substantial part of the information load within the Department." Whitman concluded gravely and ominously, "Ladies and gentlemen, we are simply giving the store away and the silver tray." In his
impassioned defense of the "sensitive but unclassified" concept, Whitman
blamed bad press for its poor public reception. "In my estimation, bad
media or misguided media stampeded the government into the situation
we now have where, in fact, we caused the withdrawal by Mr. Carlucci
of that policy implementing [NSDD] 145."[10]

Miriam Drake, representing the Association for Research Libraries,
testified that the traditional classification system was preferable to "a
muddy, imprecise, almost whimsical definition of sensitive." When Drake
was asked by NCLIS Commissioners if she would be willing to act as "an
additional filter" between unclassified information and the public, she
unequivocally rejected such a function, stating that she and other librarians would find it offensive. Sandra Peterson of the American Library Association (ALA) took a similar position: "The purpose of public
and academic libraries is to support the free and open exchange of
information, and the idea of restricting access to information that is
unclassified is contrary to the library's very existence." Peterson described
library visits by the FBI, CIA, and DoD in which they attempted to block
database access by foreign customers. She emphasized that once the
government has released information to the public, it is inappropriate
for vendors or libraries to monitor or restrict access to it. The ALA's

Christie Vernon also warned NCLIS of the efforts of the Pentagon and certain intelligence agencies to control and limit access to "virtually the entire information universe." She described the disinformation programs of the DoD and the CIA, through which "deliberately false, incomplete and misleading information, including altered technical information, would be released to impede the accurate transfer of technical information to the Soviet Union." Vernon noted, "We might reasonably inquire what will happen to the rest of us if we don't know what information in our scientific databases is disinformation."[11]

Kenneth Allen of the Information Industry Association warned NCLIS that the threat posed by notions like "sensitive but unclassified" must be evaluated in the context of other government actions, including federal control over commercial database systems, intelligence agency visits to private information companies, government requests for private-sector customer lists, and an Administration proposal to exempt technical data from the Freedom of Information Act. Allen concluded, "When viewed together, a pattern emerges of which NSDD–145 is only one piece. . . . I believe that there is a clear philosophy within certain elements of the government which believes that too much information is available to too many people, and that some sort of restrictions or controls should be placed on that information."[12]

Subsequent to the NCLIS hearings, Congress expressed its concern over NSDD–145's proposed military control of civilian information by passing the Computer Security Act of 1987 (H.R. 145), making the civilian National Institute of Standards and Technology (NIST), rather than the National Security Agency (NSA), responsible for the security standards within unclassified federal computer systems. The Act restricted the "Big Brother" activities of the DoD and NSA while simultaneously providing a statutory mandate for a national computer security system. H.R. 145 somewhat narrows Admiral Poindexter's definition of "sensitive" information as follows:

> The term "sensitive" information means any information, the loss, misuse, or unauthorized access to or modification of which could adversely affect the national interest or the conduct of Federal programs, or the privacy to which individuals are entitled . . . , but which has not specifically been authorized under criteria established by an Executive order or an act of Congress to be kept secret in the interest of national defense or foreign policy. . . . Nothing in this Act, or in any amendment made by the Act, shall be construed . . . to authorize any Federal agency to limit, restrict, regulate, or control the collection, maintenance, disclosure, use, transfer, or sale of any information (regardless of the medium in which the information may

be maintained) that is—(A) privately owned information; (B) discloseable under section 552 of title 5, United States Code, or other law requiring or authorizing the public disclosure of information; or (C) public domain information.[13]

The House report on H.R. 145 emphasized that the Act was designed to *protect* and not to *restrict* access to government information, and that the designation of information as "sensitive" under the Act had no bearing on its disclosure. This is in contrast to the role assigned to DoD and NSA by NSDD–145. Computer security consultant Robert H. Courtney said,

[W]e rarely see within DOD adequate appreciation of the need to protect data against illicit modification, whether it be accidental or intentional, as opposed to the problem of disclosure.... It is important that those developing security measures for Federal agencies understand that the security problems of many agencies more closely resemble those of J.C. Penny than they do those in C3I [command, control, communications, intelligence].[14]

During the hearings on H.R. 145, Congressman Glenn English (D-OK) stated:

I do not believe that the national security bureaucracy has done such an exemplary job of protecting national security information that it should be assigned any responsibility over unclassified, privately owned information. Further, I do not know where the government derives authority to regulate privately owned, unclassified information. Doesn't the First Amendment to the Constitution prevent such activity by the government? ...The apparently insatiable desire of the military for controlling information—whether classified or unclassified, whether government or private,—is the most convincing argument for H.R. 145. One only has to examine the record to understand the need for a legislative rejection of the National Security Decision Directive (NSDD–145) and for preserving civilian agency management of civilian information.[15]

H.R. 145 was a legislative attempt to halt, if not reverse, the repressive momentum of NSDD–145; but to date NSDD–145 remains dormant, not dead. On May 4, 1989, during Congressional hearings on the implementation of the Computer Security Act of 1987, Miriam Drake expressed the ALA's concern over the Memorandum of Understanding (MOU) between NIST and NSA:

By inserting the phrase "sensitive unclassified" into the MOU, NSA and NIST wanted to establish control over a broad universe of sensitive but unclassified information. It is our understanding that by enacting the Computer Security Act, Congress wanted to prevent the withholding of unclassified information and the abuses resulting from NSDD–145.... We continue to urge, as we did two years ago, that NSDD–145 be rescinded.[16]

MISINFORMATION AND DISINFORMATION

Author Sissela Bok defines disinformation as "a neologism that stands for the spreading of false information to hurt adversaries." Formerly common only in wartime, disinformation is now used in peacetime by contending secret service networks, as governments try to influence public opinion against other nations and against domestic adversaries. Disinformation often goes unnoticed by the public and the media alike, but when conflicting stories circulate and accusations of disinformation are voiced, suspicions arise. Such stories could not achieve their effect without secrecy—about their falsity, but above all about their source. Bok doubts that any real national benefit results from disinformation, and she reminds us that deceptive news stories can seldom be controlled, because "once they are planted, they take on a life of their own and reverberate back, as often as not, to embarrass the originators."[17]

Loch Johnson has described the great tide of disinformation flowing secretly into hundreds of hidden channels around the world. Johnson says 70 to 80 covert media insertions are made each day. Once released, this information cannot be bottled up or directed to only one spot on the globe, as one might apply antiseptic to a sore. Rather, the propaganda is free to drift here and there, even back to the United States. This can lead to "blow back" or "replay," whereby information directed toward America's adversaries abroad finds its way back home to deceive U.S. citizens.

The scientific disinformation program described by Christie Vernon during the 1987 NCLIS hearings was first revealed in 1986 in the authoritative journal *Aviation Week and Space Technology*. The article told how the DoD, in conjunction with the CIA, had initiated "a disinformation program that it is applying to a number of its aircraft and weapons development projects to impede the transfer of accurate technological information to the Soviet Union."

Government officials involved in the program acknowledged that the decision to pursue the use of disinformation was made during President Reagan's first term, with the CIA coordinating the release, through various channels, of deliberately false, incomplete, and misleading information. The government's disinformation policy covered about 20 military programs, including the Air Force's special mission aircraft and its Advanced Technology Bomber, the Navy's Advanced Tactical Aircraft, and the Strategic Defense Initiative (SDI).

One government official admitted: "There has been discussion on establishing a disinformation, or counterintelligence, program of deception for years." He claimed that after seeing the Soviet Union use disinformation, "the U.S. decided it would benefit by creating a similar program." The purpose of the program was to cause the Soviet Union to make decisions based on false perceptions. "The active part of the disinformation program has been going on for a time," said the official, "but it has not been until very recently that there has been an increased emphasis on this type of approach to program management."

Written instructions for the DoD's disinformation activities involved all operational levels and were provided to many of the armed services' offices and departments. The six-inch-thick instructional document provided false or misleading information to be given at press interviews, including inaccurate performance figures for aircraft and weapons systems, and other altered technical information. These disinformation guidelines were to be applied to technical data such as specific project documents related to development schedules, prototype performance, test results, production schedules, and operational achievements.

A DoD official stated, "Disinformation can be injected at every stage of a weapon program from documentation and the test envelope, to the actual operation of the system." He said the range of deception could apply to everything from the release of inaccurate performance data to the apparent creation of a weapon system that does not exist. In the latter case, funds appropriated for the system would be spent elsewhere. "The most dangerous technique in supplying deliberately false information is a mixture of truth and fiction," claimed the official. "The most difficult decision in carrying out disinformation activity of this type is to determine what to convey and why. An active disinformation policy can cover international, national, strategic, regional and tactical deceptions."

Most of the funding for this particular disinformation plan came from individual program budgets. The responsibility and chain of command at DoD are compartmental, with no single person in charge of disinformation, although a number of top government officials are aware that deception is being used in their programs. A DoD official gave the lame assurance: "If some of the results of the disinformation activity on a particular program get passed to Congress through hearings or other means, there are channels on the Hill that can be used to get the correct information to the people who need to know." But Congress was particularly disturbed when Lt. Col. Simon P. Worden, assistant to the director of the Star Wars Program (SDI), revealed that the Reagan Administration had provided a "classified briefing" on SDI to the Soviet Union even as it channeled *disinformation* on the program to Congress and the American public. Another SDI spokesman claimed that Worden "misspoke," but when a transcript of Worden's remarks verified that classified information is sometimes provided to the Soviet Union but kept secret in the United States, he explained:

> Because the SDI deals with nuclear weapons and defenses against them, that comes under an entirely different set of rules and regulations, and Congress has mandated that certain of that information must remain classified at that level. In some cases, it is useful for the U.S. to tell the Soviets what we know about them and it is not useful to tell, to have the debate publicly [on] how we get that information.[18]

David Wise has written: "The excuse for secrecy and deception most frequently given by those in power is that the American people must sometimes be misled in order to mislead the enemy. This justification is unacceptable on moral and philosophical grounds, and often it simply isn't true. Frequently the 'enemy' knows what is going on, but the American public does not."[19] Roy Godson, associate professor of government at Georgetown University, has warned that such government disinformation programs set a dangerous precedent by knowingly misleading the American people. A special adviser to the DoD expressed guarded agreement with Godson's concern, but insisted: "Our embarking on disinformation activity raises many difficult and emotional problems, that still need to be overcome. But we need to do it."[20]

Another U.S. scientific disinformation program was the "Yellow Rain" fiasco. In September 1981 Secretary of State Alexander Haig made a speech in West Berlin charging the Soviet Union with the manufacture of a highly toxic new poison, allegedly used against villagers in Laos, Cambodia, and Afghanistan. Assistant Secretary of State Richard Burt had urged Haig to make the charge, though the State Department's chief scientific adviser warned against it. Subsequently released government documents revealed that the Reagan Administration's scientific advisers had no evidence of the existence of this mysterious poison, and the State Department's own investigators conducted a fruitless three-year search for nonexistent corroboration. These negative findings were kept secret by the government until they were pried loose by Dr. Matthew Meselson through a Freedom of Information Act request. Dr. Meselson has published his own research showing the "poison" to be nothing more than bee excrement.

Eventually the media caught up with the facts, and one published account concluded: "The poison, which supposedly fell from the sky, was called Yellow Rain. Its composition: one part bee excrement, plus many parts State Department disinformation, the combination mixed with a high level of media gullibility. Recently released State Department documents demonstrate that the administration invented the Yellow Rain scare."[21] Despite Dr. Meselson's authoritative research and the revelations of government deception, the government has never formally retracted its disinformation, and it remains the silent but official State Department explanation to this day.

Even if the disinformation and misinformation presented to the American public is eventually corrected, the truth is often given less media coverage than the original falsehood. Even then, the truth seldom emerges in time to effectively revise and influence public opinion and government policy. The many recent examples of official U.S. disinformation support Sissela Bok's belief that the secrecy with which disinformation is manufactured and planted adds to the likelihood that governments will resort to it. Because government disinformation brings the least benefit to individual societies and the greatest danger to nations collectively, Bok advocates a deescalation of such activities along with increased public oversight.

TECHNOLOGY TRANSFER

In the past, the FBI has claimed that "sensitive but unclassified information . . . provides the Soviet Union with the tools necessary to keep pace with America's scientific and technical achievements."[22] Indeed, the American government seems to subscribe to the oft-quoted view of Nikita Khrushchev that the buttons on a soldier's pants represent critical military technology because they free his hands to hold a rifle. These reiterated fears of Soviet advantage from "technology transfer" were in conflict with the 1982 National Academy of Sciences study that concluded that very little of the transfer of significant U.S. technology to the Soviet Union came from open scientific communication.

In 1982, Arthur Van Cook, DoD's Director for Information Security, told Congress: "The Department of Defense has been concerned for some time about the virtual unremitting flow of unclassified defense information to our adversaries. This hemorrhage of information to hostile nations ... is one of the more serious problems confronting the Department."[23] Lawrence J. Brady, then Assistant Secretary of Commerce, described the Soviet Intelligence Services as a "gigantic vacuum cleaner, sucking up formulas, patents, blueprints and know-how with frightening precision." Claiming that this vacuuming allowed the Soviets to develop their industry and technology far more rapidly than otherwise, Brady condemned the "strong belief in the academic community that they have an inherent right to ... conduct research free of government review or oversight." Brady said our adversaries were exploiting America's "soft underbelly," which he defined to be our traditions of an open press, unrestricted access to knowledge, and the desire of academia to preserve its prerogatives free of government regulations.

Bobby Ray Inman, then Deputy Director of the CIA, echoed Brady's view, claiming, "In terms of harm to the national interest, it makes little difference whether the data is copied from technical journals in a library or given away ... to an agent of a foreign power."[24] He warned the American Association for the Advancement of Science (AAAS) that if scientists did not voluntarily submit to prepublication review of their research, a "tidal wave" of public outrage at the hemorrhage of the country's technology would impose legislative restrictions on them. The AAAS characterized such threats as more compatible with a dictatorship than a democracy.

A DoD 1981 report, *Soviet Military Power*, blamed the openly published American technical and professional literature for the Soviets' ability to keep pace with American industry. William D. Carey of the AAAS wrote to Frank Carlucci, then the Deputy Secretary of Defense, criticizing the report. In particular, Carey stated that blaming the openness of American society for Soviet military strength "strikes in a deadly way at the dependence of science programs on open communication and shared information. Our own military power will be diminished, not enhanced, if the wellheads of scientific communication are sealed and new knowledge confined in silos of secrecy and prior restraint." Carlucci rejected Carey's concerns, repeating the claim that the Soviets were conducting a "highly orchestrated, centrally directed effort aimed at gathering the technological information required to enhance their military posture," an effort Carlucci said could not be stopped "without infringing on legitimate scientific discourse."[25]

The most frequently cited documentation of the government's need to restrict access to unclassified technical information is the report *Soviet*

Acquisition of Militarily Significant Western Technology: An Update. Since it was first issued in 1982, this unclassified report has been surrounded with an odd atmosphere of secrecy and publicity. On September 18, 1988, Defense Secretary Caspar Weinberger and Assistant Secretary Richard Perle publicized the updated version of the report at a news conference. Weinberger claimed that Soviet acquisition of American technology was a far more serious problem than our government had previously realized. Perle said that the purpose of issuing the report was

> to sensitize the scientific and technical community to the fact that there is a very large and well-organized Soviet apparatus that has targeted scientists and engineers and universities and the like for military purposes. And with an awareness on their part, without intervention by the government, we think they may be more circumspect in the kind of material that they publish and the circumstances in which it's made available in general.[26]

Despite the authoritative public status of the report, it is difficult to get anyone to admit authorship. Nowhere in the report itself is there any indication of a personal or corporate author. Both the Library of Congress and the CIA cataloged the report with no verifiable author, while the U.S. Army and NASA attributed authorship to the DoD. The authoritative military journal *Signal* claims that the report was authored by the Technology Transfer Intelligence Committee (TTIC), a 22-member group headed by the CIA and including representatives of other intelligence agencies like the FBI. When I called the Pentagon's Office of Technology Control to pin down the source of this report, the spokesperson firmly denied that the DoD had authored it. "That's a CIA publication," he said. So, of course, I called the CIA's Department of Science and Technology. The person who returned my call said that when she posed my question to the CIA staff, they laughed and insisted that the DoD was at least the nominal source of the report. Both the Pentagon and CIA spokesperson tiptoed around the mysterious TTIC, but since both agencies are members of TTIC, it seems reasonable to accept that committee as the report's corporate author.

In its 1985 review of the report, the authoritative Armed Forces Communications and Electronics Association stated:

> The report by the Technology Transfer Intelligence Committee called on the West to better organize and protect its military, industrial, commercial and scientific communities from Soviet agents in search of technological innovation. This has been the call of many in the current administration to close down Soviet avenues of collection opportunities through the close

review of open technical publications, conferences, symposia, academic exchanges and export control policies.[27]

EXPORT CONTROL

The growing practice of restricting information without formally classifying it is encouraged by the Arms Export Control Act (1976) and the Export Administration Act (1979), which provide the authority to prevent foreign dissemination of scientific and technical data as described in the Export Administration Regulations (EAR), the Military Critical Technologies List, and the International Traffic in Arms Regulations (ITAR). In addition, the Defense Authorization Act of 1984 permits the DoD to impose restrictions on domestic dissemination or export of DoD-funded or DoD-generated technical data. Through the years, the network of export controls has been extended to the point where the National Academy of Sciences warns: "Such restrictions have the effect of creating de facto a new category of unclassified but restricted information. These new, more comprehensive technical data restrictions have had a chilling effect on some professional scientific and engineering societies."[28]

The Arms Export Control Act of 1976, via the ITAR, requires that articles designated on the U.S. Munitions List as "arms, ammunition, and implements of war" must be licensed by the State Department. But the ITAR also restricts the dissemination of unclassified "technical data," defined broadly to include any information that could be used in the design, production, manufacture, repair, overhaul, processing, engineering, development, operation, or maintenance of arms, ammunition, and implements of war on the U.S. Munitions List. In describing the Arms Export Control Act, a Justice Department memo admitted that unless there were "special circumstances posing a grave threat to national security, this law could not be enforced as written."[29] Its implementational rules, the ITAR, define the terms "technical data" and "export" so broadly that one court held that "An expansive definition of technical data could seriously impede scientific research and publishing and the international scientific exchange."[30] Even the DoD admitted that "the ITAR, if enforced to the letter, would cover virtually everything done in the United States."[31]

The ITAR was drafted so broadly that it would extend not only to private commercial transactions across national boundaries but also to noncommercial expression or communication of technical information in public settings such as scientific symposia. "Export" is defined to have occurred "whenever technical data is inter alia, mailed or shipped outside the United States, carried by hand outside the United States, disclosed through visits abroad by American citizens (including briefings and symposia) and disclosed to foreign nationals in the United States (including plant visits and participation in briefings and symposia)." In one instance, the State Department's Office of Munitions Control refused to "license" a group of scientists preparing to address an unclassified conference in Madrid on space technology. Even after the scientists arrived in Spain, they were refused permission to deliver their papers at the symposium.[32]

Most of the provisions of the ITAR were originally promulgated in the Mutual Security Act of 1954, which gave the President broad authority to identify and control implements of war and related technical data. In practice, the President delegates this authority to the Secretary of State and Secretary of Defense. Under the ITAR the Department of State may deny, revoke, suspend, or amend an export license in furtherance of (1) world peace; (2) the security of the United States; (3) the foreign policy of the United States; or (4) whenever the Department believes that the Mutual Security Act has been violated. The Arms Export Control Act of 1977 substituted the phrase "defense articles and defense services" for the phrase "arms, ammunition, and implements of war." The Department of Justice claimed that the revision was not intended to make any major substantive change in ITAR but, rather, to update and clarify the regulatory language.

The First Amendment implications of the ITAR have not been extensively analyzed in the courts. In *United States v. Danas-Botto* (1973), the defendants were charged with conspiracy to export technical data concerning a Munitions List article without an export license. The defendants moved to dismiss the indictment, claiming that the inclusion of technical knowledge within the ITAR restrictions violated the First Amendment. But the court disposed of that contention by stating: "[W]hen matters of foreign policy are involved the government has the constitutional authority to prohibit individuals from divulging 'technical data' relating to implements of war to foreign governments." The Sixth Circuit upheld the conviction of one of the defendants, relying upon two Espionage Act decisions.

Perhaps the most direct judicial challenge to the ITAR came in *United States v. Edler* (9th Cir., July 31, 1978), in which the defendant, Edler Industries, Inc., was charged with unlicensed export of technical data to a French aerospace firm. The government alleged that the defendant delivered information to the French both in France and in the United States. The defendant was tried before a jury and found guilty. On appeal Edler Industries contended that the Munitions Control Act and the ITAR were overly broad and imposed an unconstitutional prior restraint. The government claimed that the ITAR restrained *conduct*, not speech, and that any effect on First Amendment freedoms was merely incidental. The court, construing the statute and the regulations narrowly, held both to be constitutional so long as they "prohibit only the exportation of technical data significantly and directly related to specific articles on the Munitions List." The Ninth Circuit ruled that this construction did indeed focus only on the control of conduct, but cautioned that failure to comply with the ITAR's licensing scheme may be punished only when the violator *knowingly* aids and abets foreign concerns in the manufacture and use of certain items of war.[33] Both the Department of Justice and the Department of State claim they support this narrow interpretation of the ITAR.

In 1981, then Assistant Attorney General John M. Harmon commented: "The government's argument to the Ninth Circuit in *Edler*, that the impact of the ITAR upon protected communications is merely incidental, and that the ITAR should be viewed as a regulation of conduct not speech, deserves note.... Although that may be true with respect to certain portions of the ITAR, even a cursory reading of the technical data provisions reveals that those portions of the ITAR are directed at communication. A more stringent constitutional analysis ... is therefore mandated." Harmon saw two fundamental flaws in the ITAR. First, the standards governing the issuance or denial of licenses are not sufficiently precise to prevent arbitrary and inconsistent administrative action. Second, there is no mechanism to provide prompt judicial review of restraints on communication. With respect to the latter, Harmon stated:

> The cases make clear that before any restraint upon protected expression may become final it must be subjected to prompt judicial review in a proceeding in which the government will bear the burden of justifying its decisions. The burden of bringing a judicial proceeding cannot be imposed upon those desiring export licenses in these circumstances. The ITAR as presently written fails to contemplate this requirement.[34]

From *Edler* and other related cases, Harmon concluded: "The general principle we derive ... is that a prior restraint on disclosure of information generated by or obtained from the government is justifiable under the First Amendment only to the extent that the information is properly classified or classifiable.... [T]he existing ITAR provisions we think fall short of satisfying the strictures necessary to survive close scrutiny under the First Amendment."[35]

Harmon's views on the ITAR were reinforced in subsequent Congressional hearings when H. Miles Foy, a senior attorney and colleague of Harmon's at the Justice Department's Office of Legal Counsel (OLC), responded to questions from committee staff member Timothy Ingram.

Ingram: This seems pretty clear on its face. The OLC is stating that the regulation is unconstitutional under the narrow grounds you described.

Foy: It is still our view that if the regulation were applied in the broad class of cases that concerned us in that opinion, it would present very serious constitutional problems because in those cases it would impose a general licensing restriction on the dissemination of scientific ideas.

Ingram: . . . You have this 2-year-old opinion finding the regulations unconstitutional. There has been no change in the regulations. Is there any obligation on the Department at some point to go to the President to force the issue and to tell the President that one of his executive agencies is currently operating in violation of the Constitution?

Foy: Yes. I think there very well may be an obligation on the Department to go to the President, if we think that our opinion is not being complied with.[36]

But following Mr. Foy came the testimony of National Security Agency Director Bobby Ray Inman, who showed no inclination to accept the views of the Justice Department. "Early in my tenure," said Inman, "I was presented with an opinion by the Justice Department, that the ITAR was unenforceable. A brilliant new lawyer that I had persuaded to come to work for NSA and the General Counsel at the Defense Department strongly disagreed with that Justice interpretation." When asked if he felt that the OLC's decision was not binding on the NSA, Inman declared with a straight face: "You hire lawyers to give you opinions that will support the positions you have taken."[37]

Ruth Greenstein, former Associate General Counsel for the National Science Foundation, claims that export controls are deliberately written broadly to ensure that anything of importance can be controlled. As a result, they inevitably reach much information that is at best remotely or indirectly related to national security concerns. Greenstein says that a constitutional attack on the application of controls to such information would almost surely succeed. "The difficulty is increased by the nature of the current regulatory controls, which constitute a 'prior restraint' on communication. That is, current export controls seek not merely to punish offending communications, but also to prevent communications be-

fore they take place. Courts have long found prior restraint more ob-
noxious than other forms of regulation of speech."[38] The prior restraint
imposed by export controls is likely to be even less acceptable to the
courts than prior restraint by judicial injunction, because both the EAR
and ITAR place the power of restraint in the hands of executive branch
civil servants with little oversight by the government or the judicial system. The regulatory licensing decision is usually made by an administrative official whose job it is to suppress information, and who will be
held accountable for any harmful consequences of the communication
that he or she *approves*.

Perhaps the most dangerous aspect of the export control system is
that the government has no need to defend the imposition of its restraints. Instead, the burden of justifying communication is shifted to
the scientist. Greenstein warns: "This shift may have a 'chilling effect'
on protected speech. A system that requires scientists to become entan-
gled in government bureaucracies may discourage them from working
in controlled areas of research. The effect may be to suppress not only
the speech the controls are designed to suppress, but also speech beyond
the scope of controls. The fear of being called upon to defend one's
actions, precisely the position many scientists today believe they are in,
must necessarily [lead them to] steer far wider of the unlawful zone than
if the state must bear these burdens." Greenstein says the legal basis for
controls through the EAR is even weaker than for ITAR, because the
former applies to goods and data not limited to military uses and having
substantial legitimate civilian applications. "These civilian uses attenuate
the link to national security. . . . A court might well uphold the constitutionality of the ITAR (narrowly construed) while striking down the
EAR."[39]

The 600-page EAR define the term "technical data" broadly to include
information presented in papers at open scientific meetings. Such technical data need not be classified, being defined as "information of any
kind that can be used, or adapted for use in the design, production,
manufacture, utilization or reconstruction of articles or materials." This
export-controlled data may take a tangible form, such as a model, prototype, blueprint, or an operating manual, or an intangible form, such
as a technical service. The term "export" is defined to include communications overseas by "oral, visual or documentary means," such as "visits
abroad by American citizens."[40]

Similar restrictions are embodied in the 700-page Military Critical
Technologies List (MCTL), which, despite its name, has been described

by one DoD official as "really a list of modern technology."[41] The National Academy of Sciences (NAS) has advised Congress that the MCTL has been used inappropriately as a control list, restricting countless significant technologies without apparent prioritization. NAS recommended: "Congress should withdraw the statutory requirement for the integration of the Military Critical Technologies List into the U.S. Control List. The fundamentally different nature and functions of the two lists—the former an exhaustive list of all technologies with military utility and the latter a specific list of items requiring an export license—make this goal unattainable."[42]

The Export Administration Act of 1979 was officially scheduled to expire on September 30, 1983. When Congress prepared new export control legislation, it initially emphasized the right of scientists and other scholars "freely to communicate their research," but a floor amendment by Sen. Jesse Helms (R-NC) changed the wording to read, "freely to communicate their non-sensitive research." After a divisive floor debate, the 98th Congress failed to reach agreement, the major sticking point being the conflict between military security and international trade. In the absence of new export administration legislation, President Reagan invoked his Emergency Powers to extend the 1979 Act indefinitely.

Neither First Amendment advocates nor the scientific community has effectively challenged these heavy-handed controls. The pressure for change comes from the American business community, rallying around the demand to reclaim their international "competitiveness." American companies have come to realize that the export controls imposed on them are based not on national security grounds but on broad foreign policy objectives not shared by our allies. As a result of these unilateral restrictions, there is a significant and growing international shift away from the use of American products, described by former Commerce Secretary Malcolm Baldridge as "De-Americanization." "I have seen letters written by CEOs of major foreign companies instructing their managers to 'design out' U.S. parts from their product. This is being done to eliminate these companies from being bound by U.S. reexport regulations and other unilateral restrictions that accompany our products throughout the world."[43]

Ken Allen of the Information Industry Association has noted: "The on-line data base industry is one of the few places where there is a positive balance of trade. But now, in England and Australia in particular, editorials have been written that say: Don't depend on the Americans for information. At any moment their government may declare it sensitive."

Jack Biddle, of the Computer and Communications Industry Association, complained to Congress about the devastating effects of export controls on his industry:

> We have seen a level of paranoia develop in DOD to . . . the point where they would bar the export of paperclips because a terrorist might straighten one out and stick somebody in the eye with it. . . . Then we see NSDD–145. And with that background of DOD paranoia clearly in our minds, it's rather frightening, because we can foresee the possibility that our scientists will not be able to communicate with each other to maintain a leading edge in technology, while the Japanese scientists will be conversing with each other in open forums.[44]

Seeing their concerns ignored by Congress, major trade organizations formed the Industry Coalition on Technology Transfer to lobby for reform of export controls, and shortly thereafter the NAS undertook a major study on the impact of national security controls on technology transfer. The final NAS report, titled "Balancing the National Interest: U.S. National Security Export Controls and Global Economic Competition," was released in March 1987. The members of the panel that conducted the study included representatives from business and academia, but the panel's leadership was carefully chosen from former military and government officials. The Chairman, Lew Allen, was a former Air Force Chief of Staff; other members included former Secretary of Defense Melvin Laird and Bobby Ray Inman, former Director of the NSA. Inman had always been a prominent and aggressive proponent of strict government control of scientific communication. Still, the final NAS report recommended major reforms to existing controls.

The report warned:

> The extraterritorial reach of U.S. reexport controls is anathema to most U.S. trading partners. Moreover, many foreign governments do not agree that the United States has jurisdiction over the actions of their citizens outside U.S. territory. The extraterritorial extension of U.S. controls is viewed by these governments as a direct challenge to national sovereignty and a clear violation of international law. . . . The need for the unhindered exchange of large volumes of data in international commerce and research indicates that a strict system of control is neither feasible nor desirable.[45]

The multilateral cooperation recommended in the NAS report primarily concerned American activity within the Coordinating Committee on Multilateral Export Controls (COCOM). COCOM was organized after

World War II by the U.S. government and its West European allies to create an embargo policy against the Communist bloc. Under considerable secrecy, COCOM's organizational structure was completed in 1949, with little or no written documentation. Its initial membership consisted of the United States, England, France, Italy, the Netherlands, Belgium, and Luxembourg, with Norway, Denmark, Canada, West Germany, Portugal, Japan, Greece, and Turkey added by 1953. Though COCOM has no power of enforcement, its major activity is the development of lists of products and technologies to be embargoed, controlled, or monitored. There are three COCOM lists:

1. A munitions list that includes all military items
2. An atomic energy list that includes sources of fissionable materials, nuclear reactors, and their components
3. An industrial/commercial list.

It is this third list, containing "dual use" items such as computers and jet engines, that causes the most controversy within COCOM, and the United States is frequently at the heart of the dispute. The 1987 NAS report recommended that "because many of our COCOM allies continue to disagree profoundly with some unilateral U.S. foreign policy trade sanctions, the U.S. government should maintain the clearest possible distinction between the administration of national security and foreign policy controls." NAS recommended that COCOM reduce the overall scope of its controls, improve the procedures for decontrolling dual use items, and increase the transparency in COCOM decision making. It urged that "[T]he United States should actively seek to remove from both the U.S. Control List and the COCOM International List items whose control is no longer feasible because of their widespread production, distribution, and sale throughout the world." NAS advised the United States to maintain unilateral export controls only on a temporary basis and in limited, unique national security circumstances. Even then, it warned that such circumstances do not justify retaining the present U.S. unilateral Control List. "In the absence of appropriate corrective measures, these continuing problems will exact ever-higher tolls—on both Western economic vitality and innovative capacity and on the military security of the United States and its allies."[46]

Two Congressional bills offer some hope for a loosening of export controls through amendments to the Export Administration Act. During the 101st Congress, H.R. 4653 worked its way through the House and the Senate, and to conference, only to be vetoed by President Bush. In

February 1991, the Senate passed S. 320, a compromise that sought to remove any provisions from H.R. 4653 that the President found objectionable.

On September 24, 1991, Rep. Sam Gejdenson (D-CT) convened hearings on S. 320 before the House Subcommittee on International Economic Policy and Trade. He stated:

> At a time when the issue of aid to the Soviet Union is in the forefront of the American consciousness, the members of this subcommittee have a unique opportunity. We can help the Soviets to obtain technology that will upgrade the computers for their banking system, for their hotel and airline reservation networks and for their agriculture distribution system; and we can drastically increase their telecommunications capacity. And none of this will cost the American taxpayer a penny. We can do this by reducing some of the still burdensome export controls imposed on U.S. technology. Not only will this avoid the use of scarce tax dollars, but it will bring money and jobs into the United States.[47]

Richard Lehman, Public Affairs Director for IBM, testifying on behalf of the Emergency Committee on American Trade, said that the Bush Administration not only had failed to pursue previous commitments to export reform but also had retreated from the modest progress achieved in the Core List. Lehman warned, "We see serious signs that the 'new world order' will be characterized by unilateral controls on American business—controls with no benefit to U.S. national security."[48]

Many who testified before Gejdenson's subcommittee felt that the Bush Administration's initiatives earlier in 1991 had been unduly cautious. The development of a Core List that established "higher fences around fewer products" was particularly disappointing in the computer and telecommunications areas. Carleton S. Fiorina, AT&T's Vice President for Strategy and Market Development, testified that America's foreign competitors were establishing financial programs to ensure that the new Soviet telephone network would be built with French, German, and Japanese equipment. "Meanwhile," Fiorina said, "U.S. government policy remains focused almost exclusively on restricting Soviet access to basic telephone technology. Taken together, these events create the Soviet impression that American firms will be the last, not the first, to enter the market. Something must be done—and quickly." Fiorina proposed that the United States liberalize the "excessive" export controls on basic telecommunications technology and provide financial assistance to the Soviet Union to support this critical infrastructure element. In the absence of forward movement from the Administration, he said AT&T would support a move in Congress to initiate "sweeping reforms."[49]

Under pressure from Congress and the business community, the Bush Administration reversed itself in February 1992, allowing the former Soviet republics to buy state-of-the-art telecommunications equipment. The fiber-optic transmission lines included in the deal had been opposed by the NSA because they made eavesdropping on foreign phone conversations more difficult. Still, the United States agreed to sell the technology, but only after it discovered that a German firm had already sold fiber-optic transmission lines to Russia.[50]

In April 1992, President Bush further relaxed some of the Cold War restrictions on the sale of high technology to Western Europe, Japan, and Australia. He said the restrictions "served us well during the Cold War era but are no longer necessary in our new world." Under the new rules, special export licenses will no longer be required to sell semiconductor equipment, materials technology, aircraft, and certain computers to COCOM nations or nationals that follow COCOM export controls. Licenses will still be required for the export of supercomputers, high-speed cameras, cryptographic equipment, night-vision equipment, and missile technology.[51]

PATENT SECRECY

During World War I, Congress authorized the Patent and Trademark Office (PTO) to withhold patents important to the national defense. The publication, disclosure, or foreign filing of such patents was prohibited without the approval of the PTO Commissioner, and the penalty for violation was abandonment of the patent. This program of patent secrecy applied only for the duration of World War I, but in October 1941, before the U.S. entry into World War II, Congress reinstituted the provisions. The renewed authorization to impose patent secrecy orders was to remain effective for two years from July 1, 1940, during which time the filing of a patent application in a foreign country was also prohibited without a license. In 1942, Congress extended the secrecy provisions for the duration of World War II.

Only during the Cold War, with the enactment of the Invention Secrecy Act of 1951, was permanent, peacetime authority to impose secrecy orders introduced. The Act introduced broad statutory authority for controlling security-related patent applications, with the focus of controls predictably high technology. The majority of security-related applications are classified by a government agency or contractor *before* being filed, and such applications contain clearly visible security classification markings. But to assist the PTO in discovering unmarked applications that may contain aspects of "classifiable" technology, the defense agencies provide the Patent Office with "field of interest" lists. The primary guidance document is the classified Patent Security Category Review List (PSCRL), which describes the kinds of technical data and inventions that are of interest to each defense agency. The PSCRL is supplemented by the Militarily Critical Technologies List, the Commodity Control List, and the U.S. Munitions List contained in the ITAR.

By expanding or modifying the inspection scope of the screening lists supplied to the PTO, the defense agencies are able to control, as needed, the subject matter refused license. Any applications that "might be detrimental" to national security are referred by the PTO to appropriate defense agencies for their inspection. The opinion of the PTO Commissioner as to when disclosure of the invention might be detrimental to national security reflects the changing views of the defense agencies.

Under the guidance of the defense agencies, the PTO conducts security screening of all unclassified patent applications in which the government has no property interest. When questionable applications are found, the application is set aside for the attention of all interested defense agencies, any one of which may request the imposition of a secrecy order. The opinion of the defense agencies that publication or disclosure of the invention by the grant of a patent would be detrimental to the national security is *controlling* on the PTO Commissioner, who *shall* issue the secrecy order. The only discretion left to the Patent Office is to notify the agencies that the technical information in the patent application has already been published or otherwise made public. Though the Patent Office officially issues the secrecy order, it considers its role to be only "ministerial," responsive to the will of the defense agencies, which include the Army, Navy, Air Force, NSA, Department of Energy (DOE), NASA, and any agency so designated by the President. Even the Justice Department has been designated as a defense agency in the context of the Invention Secrecy Act.

The Invention Secrecy Act considers a government property interest to exist on any invention made by government employees or contractors. If there is *any* degree of government ownership, the issuance of a secrecy order requires only a recommendation to the Commissioner by a defense agency. A secrecy order withholds the grant of a patent, orders that the invention be kept in secrecy, restricts filing of foreign applications, and provides a security procedure to prevent technical data contained in a patent application from being disclosed in a manner that would be detrimental to the national security.[52] It prohibits any disclosure of the technical contents of a patent application or related information. Patent applications relating to atomic energy are considered particularly sensitive. The DOE has separate authority under the Atomic Energy Act to review *all* patent applications relating to "atomic energy" or "special nuclear materials."[53] The PTO makes such applications available to the DOE, which may withhold publication of the patent by recommending a secrecy order.

Once a secrecy order has been issued, the affected patent application is suspended, and no patent is granted until the secrecy order is rescinded and the application declassified. Violation of a secrecy order results in abandonment of the invention and criminal penalties. There exists an appeal process, but the applicant must pay an appeal fee and file a brief. In any case, further processing of the application must await the removal of the secrecy order. Except during war or national emergency, secrecy orders are issued for one year, though they may be renewed or the classification canceled upon defense agency notification to the PTO Commissioner.

Section 181 of the Invention Secrecy Act requires that during a national emergency or war, patent secrecy orders be issued for the duration of the emergency, and for a specified period thereafter. Unfortunately, the determination of what constitutes an "emergency" is left entirely to the President. For example, President Truman declared a national emergency in 1950, and if left to the judgment of the executive branch, it probably would have remained in effect to this day. But Congress passed the National Emergencies Act, which, effective September 14, 1978, terminated all existing "emergencies" as they affected the patent law's secrecy order provisions. The Patent Office was thereby required to apply the "peacetime" provisions of the Patent Secrecy Act, including annual review of all secrecy orders to verify that they serve the national interest. The transitional provisions of the National Emergencies Act required defense agencies to affirmatively determine whether existing secrecy orders should be continued. The review of these long-standing secrecy orders during the brief transition period resulted in 3,300 *renewals*.

The filing of a patent application in the United States is considered to include a petition for a foreign filing license, authorizing export of technical information *solely* for the purpose of preparing and/or filing a foreign patent application. Under the Invention Secrecy Act, licenses are granted only after completion of a national security review. The Act controls the disclosure of technology abroad by requiring a license for the filing of a foreign application on an invention made in the United States, unless a six-month period has elapsed since U.S. filing. The consent of the defense agencies that requested the secrecy order is needed before the PTO will grant a permit for foreign filing of a secrecy order application. When appropriate, defense agencies modify the secrecy order by permitting further disclosure to officials of other government agencies or their contractors or permitting foreign filing. In applications where national security concerns are present, applicants are notified in the filing receipt that prudent conduct is expected and conduct below that standard may result in the invalidation of the patent. If a patent under secrecy order is published, disclosed, or filed in a foreign country without the Commissioner's consent, the application will be abandoned. This prevents the filing abroad before the Commissioner or defense agencies have had an opportunity to examine the application during the six months after filing in the United States.

If one does not follow the foreign filing license requirements of the PTO, the invalidity stakes are very high. The Supreme Court has upheld the rejection of a patent application for failure to secure the needed foreign filing license. The Court emphasized that the purpose of the licensing statutes was to prevent exportation of information potentially detrimental to the security of the United States, requiring strict compliance by the individual inventor.

In recent years, three specialized secrecy orders have been established to handle the different sensitivity levels of technical information contained in patent applications. The Type 1 secrecy order applies to both private and government-owned inventions, and is used for applications containing unclassified technical data that is export controlled. Titled "Secrecy Order and Permit for Foreign Filing in Certain Countries," the order reads: "You are hereby notified that the above-identified patent application has been found to contain subject matter which discloses critical technology with military or space application. The unauthorized disclosure of such subject matter would be detrimental to the national security, and you are ordered to keep the subject matter secret (as provided in 35 U.S.C. 181) and you are further ordered NOT TO PUBLISH OR DISCLOSE the subject matter to any person except as specifically authorized herein." Because the publication of a U.S. patent effectively results in worldwide disclosure of the technical information therein, the government uses the Type 1 secrecy order to prevent publication of any patent containing information that could not otherwise be exported. The Type 1 Order sets forth the applicable export countrols for technical data in either the Commodity Control List or the Munitions List of the ITAR.

Type 1 secrecy orders are based upon the Department of Defense Authorization Act of 1984, which granted DoD authority to withhold from public disclosure unclassified technical data relating to militarily critical or space technology. Such restricted data would include any blueprints, drawings, plans, instructions, computer software and documentation, or other technical information that can be used, or adapted for use, to design, engineer, produce, manufacture, operate, repair, overhaul, or reproduce any military or space equipment or technology concerning such equipment. DoD's implementing regulations apply only to data in its possession or under its control, and they make no reference to secrecy orders, yet the procedures therein are being used by DoD to make secrecy order determinations on *all* patent applications, including those outside its possession or control.

Type 2 secrecy orders are applied to patent applications containing technical data that is either classified under E.O. 12356 (i.e., is marked Confidential, Secret, or Top Secret) or "classifiable" under a security guideline. Patent applications in which the government has no known property interest cannot be classified. The term "classifiable" here designates privately owned, unclassified subject matter that would warrant classification *if* a government property interest existed. The order itself reads: "You are hereby notified that the above-identified patent application has been found to contain subject matter which discloses classifiable information." Like the Type 1 secrecy order, it warns against the publication or disclosure of the subject matter, and adds: "The declassification, in whole or in part, of the subject matter of the above-identified application does not modify this secrecy order. The requirements of this secrecy order remain in effect until the secrecy order is rescinded by the Commissioner of Patents and Trademarks."

The Type 2 secret order is intended only for government-owned inventions or inventions whose owner has a current DoD Security Agreement obligating the owner to protect classified information in the manner prescribed in the Industrial Security Manual. The intent of the Type 2 secrecy order is to treat classified/classifiable information in a patent application in the same manner as any other classified material, allowing access only to persons with a proper security clearance and "need to know." Accordingly, such orders include notification of the classification level of the technical data in the application.

The imposition of a Type 2 secrecy order is based upon the facility clearance of the owner of the patent application. This may cause problems with the handling and/or disclosure of the application at different sites. As a result, some defense agencies recommend Type 2 secrecy orders only for government-owned and prosecuted cases. Another concern associated with Type 2 secrecy orders is that they specify a level of security classification without the classification authority, declassification instructions, or page markings. This creates substantial difficulties in classifying the related subject matter and in transmitting/disclosing the technical data itself. For example, without indication of which portions of the document are classified, the entire patent application must be treated as classified.

Type 3 secrecy orders cover privately owned, "classifiable" technology. They are imposed upon patent applications that contain technical data that would presumably be classified if the government had a known property interest in the invention, but cannot be placed under a Type 2 secrecy order due to the absence of such property interest. The Type 3 order is the remnant of the older secrecy order, which simply required that the patent application and related subject matter be kept secret because disclosure "might be detrimental to the national security." Information subject to a Type 3 secrecy order is not required to be protected as if classified, but since the information is of "classifiable" sensitivity, no further disclosure of the invention is allowed without the specific approval of the PTO.

It should be noted that all three types of secrecy orders cover *unclassified* information. Type 1 covers *only* unclassified information. Type 2 covers unclassified but "classifiable" information, as well as classified information. Type 3 covers only "classifiable" information. Indeed, the PTO admits that the vast majority of secrecy orders are being imposed on unclassified information. Type 1 orders alone represent 56 percent of the total imposed.

The number of patent applications referred by the PTO to defense agencies reached its highest level in 1990. Correspondingly, the number of secrecy orders issued during the Bush Administration has reached all-time record highs, and a concerned Congress is asking questions. Why not require the same security standard for a secrecy order as for classification, that is, "damage" to the national security? Why should the desire of defense agencies to impose peacetime secrecy outweigh the First Amendment rights of private inventors to publish/disclose their inventions? Why is privately owned information considered under "control" of the government, and thus "classifiable," simply because it is filed in a patent application?

The Office of Technology Assessment tells us: "Imposition of a secrecy order can be avoided simply by not seeking a patent. (The information may nevertheless be subject to control as Restricted Data or under export controls.) Nevertheless, imposition of a secrecy order does operate as a restriction on traditional freedom of scientific communication. This authority must therefore be considered as part of the total burden on the exercise of free speech."[54]

My own experience has taught me only too well how the Invention Secrecy Act reaches beyond the world of patents and into the nominally unclassified collections of university libraries. On June 15, 1989, Robert H. Swennes, Counsel for the Naval Research Laboratory (NRL), wrote to Dr. Peter Curtis at the University of Maryland's McKeldin Library to express NRL's concern over a master's thesis written by a student who was also an NRL employee. Swennes claimed that some of the student's work at NRL was reflected in the thesis, and though none of the information was classified, NRL had allegedly sought patent protection for the underlying process. Swennes said that due to a "secrecy order" regarding the technology involved, the patent would not be published at this time, and the associated information should not be discussed in a manner that might threaten the national technology base.

Swennes further specified that all copies of the disputed thesis be placed under restricted access in the University's libraries for at least one year, with any request to read the thesis cleared first with NRL. In short, an unclassified master's thesis, already a part of the libraries' collections, was to be withdrawn from the open shelves, sequestered, and made available only to persons authorized by the NRL. Curtis, the libraries' Marylandia Curator, placed his two copies of the thesis in a locked cage, and I was directed to remove the remaining copy from the Engineering and Physical Sciences Library. Shortly thereafter, Curtis was informed by NRL that still another University of Maryland, College Park, thesis was to have the same restrictions applied to it, and the implication was clear that this phenomenon might occur with increased frequency in the future.

In none of the communications from NRL was the legal basis for restricting the thesis revealed, causing some initial confusion at the University. But the use of the term "secrecy order" by NRL's counsel, and the reference to restricted access for one year led me to conclude that the Invention Secrecy Act was the statutory authority being invoked. These theses remained sequestered for almost three years, inaccessible to University scholars, except at the pleasure of the NRL. In 1992 I wrote to NRL's Patent Attorney, describing the secrecy order on one thesis and asking whether it was still in effect. The response from NRL was that "the MCTL [Militarily Critical Technology List] Secrecy Order ... has been recently rescinded. Consequently, the Department of the Navy no longer requests that this thesis be kept off the open library shelves at the University of Maryland."[55]

UNCLASSIFIED CONTROLLED NUCLEAR INFORMATION

A bizarre extension of the "restricted but not classified" approach to information control appeared on April Fool's Day, 1983, when the DOE, in response to earlier amendments to the Atomic Energy Act of 1954, proposed regulations to prohibit the unauthorized dissemination of what it called Unclassified Controlled Nuclear Information (UCNI). Sections 147 and 148 of the Atomic Energy Act had been added in 1980 and 1981 to give the Nuclear Regulatory Commission and DOE the authority to prohibit dissemination of certain unclassified information, and now the rules for defining and enforcing these prohibitions were being introduced. The DOE was directed to protect from unauthorized dissemination unclassified information pertaining to the following:

1. The design of nuclear production or utilization facilities
2. Security measures for the protection of such facilities or their nuclear material.
3. The design, manufacture, or utilization of any nuclear weapon or component.

UCNI was described very broadly in these regulations, even to the point of allowing that "Nothing in these regulations precludes the Secretary or his delegate from designating information not specifically described in these regulations as UCNI."[56] The justification for the UCNI regulations was the government's fear that unauthorized dissemination of such information could result in "significant adverse effect on the health and safety of the public or the common defense and security." Herman E. Roser, Assistant Secretary for Defense Programs, said the purpose of UCNI regulations was to protect the nation against terrorists. He assured the academic community that he understood their concerns and hoped to "achieve a balance between controlling the truly sensitive information without abridging the freedoms of the academic community and other members of the public-at-large."[57]

Daniel Steiner, then Vice President and General Counsel at Harvard

University, was not reassured. He complained: "Even read narrowly, the proposed rule would prevent dissemination of extensive nonsecret—indeed, published—information, and would likely chill or thwart academic or public discussion in the nuclear field." Anthony Lewis in the *New York Times* predicted, "It will be a case of prior restraint by uncertainty."[58] Hugh E. Dewitt, a nuclear scientist at the Lawrence Livermore National Laboratory, claimed that the notion of UCNI would "fit neatly into the mad world described by George Orwell in his book *1984*," allowing "government officials another very broad method to hide their own mistakes and keep information from the American people."[59]

Librarians were notified that once the proposed regulations were passed, all UCNI documents in their collections would have to be treated virtually as if they were classified. The movement of such materials would be closely controlled. Interlibrary loan would be rendered difficult by the required usage of registered mail to assure receipt only by authorized personnel. Access to UCNI documents would be restricted to U.S. citizens on an appointment basis only, with proper identification required and a "need to know" demonstrated. Librarians feared that important unclassified information would be denied to their libraries as the result of the UCNI regulations, but they were even more confused and concerned about the application of UCNI restrictions to existing library collections and to material they might continue to receive. UCNI material was to be marked with the warning:

UNCLASSIFIED CONTROLLED NUCLEAR INFORMATION. NOT FOR PUBLIC DISSEMINATION. UNAUTHORIZED DISSEMINATION SUBJECT TO BOTH CIVIL AND CRIMINAL SANCTIONS.

UCNI regulations specified that any person found in violation of any provision or order with respect to the unauthorized dissemination of UCNI shall be subject to a civil penalty not to exceed $100,000 for each such violation. In addition, any person who willfully violated, attempted to violate, or conspired to violate these regulations would be subject to a criminal penalty.

As a technical librarian at the University of Maryland, I had considerable apprehension about applying UCNI regulations to our library, particularly to our vast collection of DOE technical reports. In August 1984, in response to public hearings at which many librarians testified, revised regulations were issued and additional public comment solicited. In response to impassioned lobbying by the library and information science community, the DOE finally acknowledged the impossibility of controlling or gutting existing library collections, and it exempted from the regulations any material that a DOE reviewing official determines to have been widely disseminated in the public domain. These accommodations appeared in the final version of UCNI regulations, announced in the *Federal Register,* effective on May 22, 1985.

DOE's final assessment of the revised UCNI regulations stated, "Other than the fact that certain documents that, in the past, would have been released to libraries no longer will be released in the future, these regulations have no direct impact on the operation of public or university libraries."[60] UCNI regulations are nonetheless actively censoring material before it can reach libraries, with new research denied to universities and libraries on the basis of prior restraint by uncertainty. Though the concept of UCNI has receded from public view and concern, it continues alive and well behind the scenes, part of the growing pack of pseudo classifications that plague librarians and scientists alike.

MOSAIC THEORY

In his 1984 directive, NSDD–145, President Ronald Reagan likened intelligence data to a mosaic, saying innocuous bits of unclassified information "can reveal highly classified and other sensitive information when taken in the aggregate."[61] A similar concept appeared in the government's oft-cited 1985 report, *Soviet Acquisition of Militarily Significant Western Technology: An Update,* which claimed: "The individual abstracts or references in government or commercial data bases are unclassified, but some of the information, taken in the aggregate, may reveal sensitive information concerning US strategic capabilities and vulnerabilities."[62]

Dr. Robert Park of the American Physical Society spoke of the mosaic theory in his 1987 testimony on computer security before the House Committee on Government Operations. When asked what was behind all this high-level government concern about unclassified information, Park answered, "The concern has to do with the so-called 'aggregate' or 'mosaic' concept that argues that a collection of information, even if the individual items in the collection are unclassified, may reveal classified information when revealed as a whole." Dr. Park claimed that an Air Force report, *The Exploitation of Western Data Bases,* "carries the mosaic concept into another dimension. It reportedly argues that the KGB obtains information less by seducing embassy guards than by clipping items from public sources such as the *New York Times, Business Week, The Economist,* etc. and putting them all together to form a picture of classified programs."[63]

That 1986 Air Force report referred to by Dr. Park did more than carry the mosaic concept into another dimension. It carried it into the twilight zone. The heavily censored report, acquired in 1988 through a Freedom of Information Act request, documented in detail the work of the previously unknown Air Force Management Analysis Group (AF-MAG), established to determine the extent of the exploitation of commercial unclassified Western databases and to recommend methods to stem the transfer of technology through this means. In particular, AF-MAG was to slow the loss of sensitive technical information by using "regulations, directives, and classification guides to control unclassified or non-sensitive information that, when aggregated, can reveal highly sensitive data."

AFMAG claimed that "individual elements of non-sensitive scientific and technical information may, when combined with other non-sensitive information, yield MCT [militarily critical technology]." Throughout the report AFMAG referred to "aggregation theory information," suggesting that such ordinary, "non-sensitive" information required protection, because it could be aggregated to create "sensitive" information that could itself be aggregated to produce classified information.[64] Information *twice removed* from any level of classification should thus be restricted; not classified information, not even sensitive information, not anything. Just everything.

Kenneth Allen of the Information Industry Association has criticized the government's use of the mosaic theory to justify withholding unclassified information: "Ironically, much of the concern does not appear directed at information which now exists. Rather, the concern is about information which might be created at some point in the future from existing unclassified information. This is the mosaic theory. These same officials appear to believe that it is both possible to define this nonexistent body of information and technologically feasible to limit access to such information to . . . authorized individuals."[65]

The cumulative intellectual process described by the mosaic theory is neither esoteric nor dangerous; it is in fact a fundamental aspect of all scientific research and scholarly communication. But by applying a grand phrase like "mosaic theory" to a rather commonplace process, the government has reintroduced a simplistic and paranoid view that has been considered, and rejected, by scholars for many years. In 1950, Walter Gellhorn, in his book *Security, Loyalty, and Science*, warned against restraints on scientific information that could enhance the economic or physical well-being of the world: "It ought not be buried even if we can see that somehow it might conceivably be pieced together with other bits of information to the benefit of a potential enemy in wartime. For safety does not lie in secrecy. It lies in the purposeful utilization, stimulation, and encouragement of the nation's intellectual resources."[66] Gellhorn's early rejection of the mosaic theory not only predated today's furor by almost four decades; it came at the height of the Cold War as well as the hot war in Korea. Gellhorn would surely be disturbed by the imposition of the mosaic theory at a time when the Cold War has ended and Communist adversaries have become capitalist allies.

THE LIBRARY AWARENESS PROGRAM

Among the more dramatic attempts at federal control of scientific information are the FBI's various programs of surveillance of America's *unclassified* scientific and technical libraries. Described in detail in my 1991 book, *Surveillance in the Stacks*, these programs sought to recruit librarians around the country to restrict access to publicly available technical library collections and to report on those who tried to use them.

In a 1988 report, *The KGB and the Library Target*, the FBI warned that the KGB's "Line X" was utilizing America's "specialized and scientific libraries" to collect valuable information. The report claimed, "In all instances, Line X of the KGB is in search of sensitive but unclassified information which provides the Soviet Union with the necessary tools to keep pace with America's scientific and technical achievements." Without admitting the existence of its programs of library surveillance, the FBI revealed the broad rationalization for them. "By alerting potential targets to the KGB, Line X threat, the FBI seeks to diminish the severity of the threat while neutralizing the ability of Line X to selectively prowl America's specialized scientific and technical libraries, preying upon unsuspecting librarians, students, professors and scientists."[67]

The FBI has divided its library surveillance programs into two categories: proactive and reactive. The "proactive" surveillance programs have no particular counterintelligence targets. They follow no leads and pursue no suspects. Instead, they identify America's openly published scientific research as a national resource to be protected from foreign exploitation. These proactive programs have sought to use librarians to gather "positive intelligence," information about the scientific needs and interests of foreign nationals. Librarians are asked to determine the susceptibility of suspected foreign agents to being "turned" into double agents. The most infamous of the Bureau's proactive programs originated in New York City in 1973, and though the FBI's code name remains secret, it became known as the Library Awareness Program.

Librarians like myself were already familiar with similar FBI surveillance, but the details of the Library Awareness Program were first brought to national prominence in a September 18, 1987, front page story in the *New York Times*. The *Times* described an FBI visit to Columbia University's Mathematics and Science Library, during which the agents claimed to be conducting "a general 'library awareness program' in the city." The agents asked librarians "to be alert to the use of their libraries by persons from countries 'hostile to the United States, such as the Soviet Union' and to provide the FBI with information about these activities."[68]

During 1988 Congressional hearings on the Library Awareness Program, held before Rep. Don Edwards's (D-CA) Subcommittee on Civil and Constitutional Rights, FBI Assistant Director James Geer claimed that the Bureau had documented Soviet Intelligence Service (SIS) contacts with librarians in technical libraries. "In response to this effort," said Geer, "the New York Office [NYO] initiated an awareness program, which has come to be known as the Library Awareness Program." Chairman Edwards told Geer; "What disturbs some of us about this program is the FBI's apparent failure to recognize the special status of libraries in our society. . . . Going into libraries and asking librarians to report on suspicious users has ominous implications for freedom of speech and privacy."[69]

Simultaneous with the Congressional hearings, Freedom of Information Act requests by library organizations acquired a set of heavily excised documents from the FBI's NYO describing the origin of the Library Awareness Program in 1973. One document described FBI Headquarters' doubts about the program: "At those libraries where there is no classified material but where there is material of interest to the SIS, it is recognized that SIS may indeed acquire such data. In an open society, however, it is impractical to prevent all Soviet acquisition of such readily available material, and we must recognize realistic limitations in this regard."[70] Here the Bureau acknowledged only that *total* control of scientific information was impracticable.

Eventually, the FBI's NYO convinced Headquarters to approve its plan to surveil and control an unspecified number of technical libraries in New York City. Throughout New York City, the Bureau's tactics, and librarians' response to them, were consistent. Columbia University's Director of Academic Information Services, Paula Kaufman, described the behavior of FBI agents at Columbia's Mathematics and Science Library: "They asked us to report on who was reading what, and I refused to cooperate with them." Similar FBI intrusions at New York University were rebuffed by Nancy Kranich, NYU's Director of Library and Administrative Services, who commented: "We simply do not wish to have our readers feel that they may be under surveillance by intelligence agents." At the Brooklyn Public Library's Science and Industrial Division, an FBI agent told librarians "to look out for suspicious looking people who wanted to overthrow the government."[71]

The FBI agents visiting the New York Public Library (NYPL) apparently chose to monitor not just library users but library staff as well. One employee was secretly photographed and allegedly had his office phone called taped by the Bureau. NYPL Director Vartan Gregorian said the FBI's action "was an unwarranted intrusion into the private affairs of a member of our library." When the NYPL was asked to monitor and report on the use of its collections, Director Gregorian refused. "We consider reading a private act, an extension of freedom of thought. And our doors are open to all. We don't check IDs."[72]

The Library Awareness Program seems related to the notorious NSDD–145, described at the beginning of this chapter. According to that directive, the government shall "encourage, advise, and assist the private sector" to protect "sensitive non-government information." Dr. Robert Park of the American Physical Society warned, "Agents of the National Security Agency, the FBI, and the Department of Defense have therefore 'encouraged' commercial data base companies to supply lists of their subscribers. Such encouragement, however gentle, can seem to most citizens very much like intimidation." Dr. Park added, "Though without a clear legal basis, the Library Awareness Program is part of a larger government effort to restrict the use of electronic data bases by foreigners."[73]

The FBI's broad program of library surveillance is not an arbitrary initiative by an isolated federal agency. The Bureau's assumption that "sensitive but unclassified information" in America's technical libraries requires protection from foreign eyes is consistent with broader federal information policy and must be considered in the context of the many recent federal attempts to restrict information access. Miriam Drake of the American Library Association stated, "Although the FBI's activities received the most publicity, the pattern of attempts in the 1980s to restrict access to unclassified information suggests purposeful, pervasive and coordinated activities."[74] C. James Schmidt, Chairman of the American Library Association's Intellectual Freedom Committee, has described the "larger context" of the Library Awareness Program: "The FBI's visits to libraries are part of a systematic, coordinated interagency effort to prevent access to unclassified information. The effort is coordinated by the interagency Technology Transfer Intelligence Committee—a group representative of twenty-two agencies and hosted by the CIA."[75]

FBI Director William Sessions stated: "The active approach of the Library Awareness Program, which alerts librarians generally of the Soviet intelligence threat, should not be confused with reactive interviews of librarians in other areas of the United States which are in response to an investigative lead involving a specific Soviet national."[76] Sessions described the Bureau's nationwide program of "reactive" library surveillance as part of its general counterintelligence responsibilities, which, unlike the Library Awareness Program, have no assigned program name. Sessions told Congress: "In many cases the FBI will have already identified known or suspected hostile intelligence service officers and co-optees. When the FBI needs information about the activities of such persons, it will continue to contact anyone having that information, including librarians." Kathryn Bradford, a spokesperson in the FBI's Public Information Office, emphasizes the routine nature of these "investigative" contacts in libraries: "Those agents are just following logical leads, which might take them into a grocery store as often as a library. It's a misconception that the FBI is swarming around libraries."[77]

Perhaps. But the Bureau has intruded on technical libraries in virtually every state in the union, from upstate New York to Broward County, Florida; from Virginia to Wisconsin to Idaho to California. And, of course, to the University of Maryland, College Park, where agents visited two libraries under my responsibility, the Chemistry Library and the Engineering and Physical Sciences Library. Unlike some of the FBI's other visits to libraries, at Maryland the agents did not ask us to deny foreigners access to unclassified collections. Instead, they asked us to report to the Bureau any library users with "foreign-sounding names or accents" and to reveal the scientific interests of these foreigners. At the University of Utah, FBI agents attempted to block foreign access to the library by claiming that Soviets were attempting to use the library to gain access to the unclassified National Technical Information Service. At the University of Houston, FBI agents asked librarians to monitor their patrons because Russians were acquiring materials that could benefit them. An FBI agent visiting a Florida public library warned that agitators in the area were using the library for information.

In the Fall of 1988, Dr. Robert Park, professor of physics at the University of Maryland and Public Affairs Director of the American Physical Society, decried the FBI's "attempts to recruit snitches at scientific and technical libraries." He stated that "behind the FBI's clumsy recruitment effort is the conviction on the part of those responsible for keeping the nation's secrets that the traditional openness of American society is a weakness—and a threat to national security and economic health. Not content to restrict access through classification, the government has attempted to keep foreigners away from information termed 'sensitive but unclassified.' "[78]

In early 1989 Rep. Don Edwards (D-CA) reflected on the FBI's behavior in American libraries, warning that "government information policies now threaten the academic tradition of free access to information." Edwards claimed that "the [FBI's] library visits were tied to the troubling, though sometimes fitful, government effort to control unclassified information." Edwards, a former FBI agent, concluded: "The recent controversy over FBI visits to libraries highlights the continuing debate over government information controls. The controversy also underscores the need for a new approach to information policy. ... Our redefinition should begin with a reaffirmation of a cornerstone of our democracy: information is not a threat to a free society."[79]

Ultimately, the FBI's library surveillance programs were condemned by the library profession, ridiculed by the press, and rejected by the public at large. Yet the FBI claimed that library activists and the press exaggerated the programs' chilling effect on public access to scientific information. Predictably, the FBI characterized its critics as witting or unwitting dupes of the Soviet Union. Acting on this assumption, the Bureau began a 16-month investigation of technical librarians like myself who had openly opposed the Library Awareness Program. A secret 1989 FBI memo revealed that the Bureau had investigated these librarians in an attempt to determine whether a Soviet active measures campaign had been initiated to discredit the Library Awareness Program. The term "active measures" is intelligence jargon for foreign attempts to influence public opinion through disinformation, propaganda, or front groups.

John Berry, editor in chief of *Library Journal*, wrote: "It was predictable, alas, that agents would search for links between the suspicious librarians and the USSR. ... The FBI nearly always sees something subversive in any opposition to its efforts to protect the 'secrets' of our government or to its efforts to limit access to our libraries." Berry concluded: "We the people plant the seeds of subversion. They are there in our bill of rights, our elections, our free press, and, of course, in our libraries."[80]

Have the Library Awareness Program and the broader pattern of library surveillance been ended? No. The Bureau claims that such programs remain a legitimate part of its counterintelligence responsibilities.

The FBI continues to characterize the use of unclassified technical libraries by foreign nationals as "illegal technology transfer," even when no laws are broken. In a 1990 phone conversation with Robert Davenport, the Bureau's Inspector in Charge of Public Affairs, I asked why it was necessary to hide public domain literature. Davenport explained, "The Soviet Union is in the technological Stone Age. What is routine technical information to us may be crucial to them."

But surely the end of the Cold War destroyed any remaining pretext for the Bureau's ill-conceived program. In a 1990 letter, Davenport claimed that the Soviet threat regarding "illegal technology transfer" remained undiminished: "We are aware that, rather than decreasing its efforts, the Soviet Union has increased its campaign to acquire U.S. technology through illegal means. As such, the Soviet Union remains the most significant national threat to U.S. security. Regarding the continuation of the Library Awareness Program, the FBI does not have, nor has it ever had, a program intended to limit legal Soviet access to U.S. technology.... Soviet access to technology gained in violation of U.S. statutes, however, will remain an investigative priority."[81]

In analyzing the Bureau's rationale, the *New Scientist* wrote: "How consulting information held in a public library for anyone to see can be described as 'stealing' it is an FBI secret. So, too, must be its definition of 'sensitive.' "[82]

SCIENCE AS A COMMODITY

As national security controls on science become less credible, they are being replaced by the notion of science as a commercial commodity to be marketed or withheld from the American public and the international scientific community for purposes of profit or economic advantage. Federal policy changes in the 1980s have loosened, and in many cases eliminated, contractors' obligation to publicly report new technologies developed from federal R&D work, and also have given contractors the first rights to patents resulting from such research. In the past, contractors were required to issue detailed reports about the products and processes they had developed while working for the government. Now they have no obligation to report any nonpatentable research results, and they can take up to three years to report their patentable results.

The effects are most visible in places like NASA's Technology Utilization Program, which was created to provide for the widest practicable and appropriate dissemination of technology created under NASA contracts. NASA had previously required all contractors to promptly report any patentable inventions and significant advances resulting from federally financed research. This resulted in publication of 30 to 40 percent of NASA's most valuable research. Thousands of American companies have used this information to improve their manufacturing processes, introduce products, and incorporate new computer programs, producing commercial spin-offs in such diverse areas as solar collectors and contamination control. The new government policies have significantly reduced the number of NASA reports submitted, and contractors are now maintaining the technology they develop as trade secrets, thereby hurting American industry in general.

As industrial secrecy has moved into federal labs and American universities, it has hidden much of the nation's scientific research. In 1988, scientists and scholars expressed concern when the White House sent its Superconductivity Competitiveness Act to Congress. The Act attempted to restrict the flow of American superconductor research to foreign competitors by requiring federal agencies to withhold scientific information developed in federal laboratories whenever disclosure could reasonably be expected to harm the economic competitiveness of the United States. Robert L. Park, Director of Public Affairs for the American Physical Society, testified at Congressional hearings: "This proposal is seriously misguided. This reeks of chauvinism and ignores the international character of the research." Deborah Runkle of the AAAS warned: "There's a great urge to punish countries that are competing with us. That could spill over into the science realm."[83]

But proponents of the Superconductivity Competitiveness Act claimed that secrecy within federal laboratories, which perform research on everything from atom bombs to hybrid wheat, would protect rapid innovation within American industry. "It's a fascinating issue," said Gordon T. Longerbeam, an official at the Lawrence Livermore National Laboratory. "Should scientific inquiry be conducted in a totally open environment? Or should we contain it a little bit, in some selected areas, long enough for American industry to take advantage of it first?" In exchange for dollars, federal researchers at Livermore are now working with private companies on research in areas such as steel, biotechnology, and electronics. According to Longerbeam, the agreements call for publishing delays of up to a year and could eventually require total secrecy. "I can very easily visualize an environment where, for certain key aspects of research, we would agree never to publish." He admitted only that "it's not in our interest to go too far in that direction."[84]

At an October 1991 conference in Washington, D.C., Michelle Van Cleave of the White House Office of Science and Technology Policy revealed a new government-industry partnership with disturbing implications for American science. Van Cleave described the "inherent tension" between the need for secrecy and the values of an open society. While admitting that science is severely hindered by limiting the free exchange of ideas and technology, she warned: "[S]uch information can be used by adversaries, both military and economic, to their advantage. ... In short, we do recognize important constraints on the free flow of information." Van Cleave advocated an integrated, coherent national policy of scientific secrecy. She warned, "It's one thing for the government to identify technologies and information critical to foreign relations, military operations, or intelligence activities, but what about those things in the private sector that are also vital to the United States, such as financial and trade secrets, commercial properties, and industrial R&D?"[85]

Van Cleave proposed a shared Operations Security responsibility in a "government-industry partnership" to protect "critical technologies and strategic proprietary information." Comparing this new government role with the FBI's long-standing DECA program, from which the notorious Library Awareness Program was derived, Van Cleave concluded: "[A]cross the board I think what we may be seeing here is an emerging new intelligence mission, as the protection of the American private sector strategic information and technology is increasingly viewed as an element of the nation's security."[86]

This growing government-industry partnership offers the illusion of technological competitiveness at the price of scientific openness. A dangerous spin-off of this partnership has been the abdication of federal responsibility for information dissemination, leaving the public's right to know to the whim of the marketplace. The federal government, through the Office of Management and Budget (OMB), has for some time attempted to codify a broad, national information policy, which some regard as potentially more pernicious than the narrower national security controls. Its fundamental premise is that *all* information is a product, a commodity to be manipulated or withheld in the national interest. The Council of Library Resources declared: "Uncritical adherence to the concept of information as a commodity will distort the agendas of institutions and disciplines alike.... It is certain that the information needs of society cannot be defined by the marketplace alone."[87]

As early as 1957, OMB's predecessor, the Bureau of the Budget, issued Circular A–76, requiring government agencies to make maximum possible use of private firms for information services. This early attempt to

reduce the government's obligation to provide public information flow-
ered in the first year of the Reagan Administration with the announcement of a Presidential moritorium on new publications. In January 1983
OMB proposed that Circular A–76 be revised to define libraries as commercial activities, and contracts were quickly signed with private firms
to operate the libraries within DOE and HUD. In September 1983, OMB
drafted a circular that emphasized that "information is not a free good
but a resource of substantial economic value." In July 1984, the *Federal
Statistical Directory* was published by a private vendor for the first time
since 1939, at a cost three times that of the previous government-
published edition. In November, the EPA turned over its 20-database
Chemical Information Service to private firms.

The most comprehensive expression of federal information policy
occurred in December 1985 with the publication of OMB Circular A–
130, "Management of Federal Information Resources." Widely criticized
from the moment it was proposed, Circular A–130 required government
agencies to practice "maximum feasible reliance on the private sector"
for dissemination of information products and services, and to recover
costs for information collection and dissemination through user charges.
Questions of equitable public access to federal information were not
addressed by the circular.

The Reagan Administration's most dramatic application of the A–130
guidelines was its attempt to privatize the National Technical Information Service (NTIS). NTIS is the federal government's archive of
scientific and technical reports prepared by over 600 federal, state, and
foreign government agencies, their contractors, or grantees. The statutory mission of NTIS is to operate as a clearinghouse for the collection
and dissemination of nonclassified technical and engineering information, making such information available to industry and businesses, to
state and local governments, to other agencies of the federal government,
and to the general public.

On April 28, 1986, the Department of Commerce announced a "Study
of Alternatives for Privatizing the National Technical Information Service." The American Library Association quickly responded with a resolution emphasizing the negative implications that the privatization of
NTIS would have on the ready access to such information. Soon thereafter the Special Libraries Association adopted a similar resolution, char-
acterizing as ill-conceived the federal initiatives to privatize government
functions and services like NTIS. The resolution urged recognition that
federal government activities such as data gathering and information
sharing must be maintained for the public good.

Each time the Reagan Administration attempted to contract out NTIS operations, it was found that continued in-house operation was less expensive. In April 1986 a notice was placed in the *Federal Register* soliciting comment on the various strategies for privatizing NTIS. Ninety percent of the substantial public response was critical of the privatization proposals, yet NTIS and OMB officials forged ahead with a meeting with potential contractors. The Commerce Department's Task Force on NTIS Privatization heard overwhelmingly negative testimony from the library community, scientific organizations, and research universities. In the face of such evidence, the Commerce Department recommended against further privatization of NTIS operations, citing numerous costs and risks for the government, NTIS customers, and the information industry in general. Undaunted, OMB showed its continued commitment to privatization in early 1987 by omitting the budget line for NTIS in the President's FY1988 budget.

In January 1988 OMB proposed that NTIS be privatized through an employee stock ownership program. Congress quickly realized that a legal ban on NTIS privatization was necessary, and in March 1988 the House Science, Research and Technology Subcommittee held hearings on legislative options. A privatization ban was eventually attached to the Omnibus Trade Bill and signed into law in September 1988. A month later, a more airtight ban was included in the legislation authorizing the National Institute on Standards and Technology (NIST), effectively ending the NTIS privatization campaign.

Still, the watchdog organization OMB Watch declared: "Circular A-130 is evidence both of OMB's basic ignorance of information resources management and of the solitary imperative for OMB policies over the last eight years, namely the elimination of Federal agency information activities."[88] OMB Watch has long advocated major revision of Circular A-130 and legislative reform of the Paperwork Reduction Act to enunciate the federal responsibility to maintain the free flow of public information. But the federal government has proceeded toward privatization of its information function and abdication of its traditional, and constitutional, obligation to disseminate public information.

In January 1989, OMB proposed a revision of A-130 that would have further entrenched government privatization by applying the Circular's strictures to electronic dissemination as well as print. Agencies were also discouraged from providing "value added" products such as user guides, finding aids, or search software. The proposal viewed the proper role of government as that of wholesaler to private firms, which would then retail government information to end users, if a profit could be made.

Following extensive negative comment from the public, a change in administrations (Reagan to Bush), and a change in OMB leadership (James Miller to Richard Darman), OMB withdrew its January proposal and replaced it with a second revision containing far less emphasis on privatization.

OMB Circular A–130 is still the federal government's official statement of policy on public/private roles in the information arena. The latest OMB attempt to revise Circular A–130 was described in the March 4, 1991, *Federal Register:* "In response to interest and actions on the part of Congress, the agencies, and the public, OMB has determined that Circular No. A–130 requires a thorough revision." OMB said all proposed revisions would be published for public comment during 1991 and 1992, with first priority given to revising Circular A–130's treatment of information dissemination policy. Agencies would be required to give public notice before creating, terminating, or making significant changes in major information products, and user charges for government information products and services would be set no higher than the cost of dissemination.

Perhaps because of my work in technical libraries, I found the demise of *Scientific and Technical Aerospace Reports (STAR)* the most disturbing result of the government's information policy. This major product of NASA's Scientific and Technical Information program had always been made available to NASA offices and contractors, U.S. government agencies and their contractors, organizations in the United States and abroad, and libraries in the United States that maintain public collections of NASA documents. Many librarians and scholars protested the loss of this indispensable scientific reference tool. A letter from my library to NASA warned: "If *STAR* ceases publication, the effect would be devastating to research efforts in many areas of critical technology. This could have a major impact upon the ability of the United States to compete economically, and could even be detrimental to national security."[89] The Director of NASA's Scientific and Technical Information Division replied: "We concur on the seriousness of this hiatus and the need to resume publication as soon as possible. We were forced into this suspension by a major cut in our budget. . . . Unfortunately, at this time we cannot provide an estimated resumption schedule."[90]

Unlike other casualties of the federal government's commodity-based information policy, this story had a happy ending. Under heavy pressure from librarians, NASA announced on July 31, 1990, that it would resume publication of *STAR*, including back issues and cumulative indices. The good news was tempered the following year, when NASA reduced the number of copies of *STAR* provided to agencies and institutions while increasing the prices of *STAR* and other Scientific and Technical Information products.

The growing federal inclination to privatize goods and services traditionally produced or provided by the government raises difficult legal questions for the nation. When government attempts to privatize its responsibilities, it is subject to constitutional restraints only with respect to those activities which have been traditionally or exclusively public functions. Harold Sullivan, professor of government at John Jay College, warns: "If private flexibility and discretion are among the advantages promised by privatization, they may come at the expense of citizens' rights. If protections of the United States Constitution are to be guaranteed as services are privatized, government must severely restrict the discretion permitted to private agencies. In the end, privatization and protections of civil liberties may prove to be mutually exclusive goals."[91]

NOTES

1. *The Exploitation of Western Data Bases* (Washington, DC: Office of the Assistant Vice Chief of Staff, U.S. Air Force, 1986), IV–7.

2. Herbert S. White, "White Papers," *Library Journal,* 15 October 1988, 55.

3. " 'Sensitive,' Not 'Secret': A Case Study," *CPSR, Inc.,* January 1988, 3.

4. *National Policy on Protection of Sensitive but Unclassified Information in Federal Government Telecommunications and Automated Information Systems,* NTISSP no. 2 (29 October 1986), sec. II.

5. Office of Technology Assessment, *Science, Technology and the First Amendment: Special Report* (Washington, DC: U.S. GPO, January 1988), 8.

6. Statement of Jack Brooks, Chairman, before the House Subcommittee on Science and Technology, 27 June, 1985.

7. Testimony of Robert L. Park before the House Committee on Government Operations, 25 February 1987, 4.

8. "Reagan Seeks Controls on Data Base Access," *Boston Globe,* 20 April 1987, 35, 37.

9. National Commission on Libraries and Information Science, Hearing on Sensitive but Not Classified Information, Washington, DC, 28 May 1987, iii. Unpublished transcript released by the NCLIS.

10. Ibid., 103, 108–109, 112.

11. Ibid., 6, 11, 37–51.

12. Ibid., 72, 74.

13. *Computer Security Act of 1987: Report,* House of Representatives, 100th Cong., 1st Sess., 11 June (Washington, DC: U.S. GPO, 1987) 5.

14. Ibid., 27–28.

15. Ibid., 18–19.

16. Statement of Miriam A. Drake on behalf of the American Library Association and the Association of Research Libraries, before the House Subcom-

mittee on Legislation and National Security, on implementation of the Computer Security Act of 1987, 4 May 1989, 3.

17. Sissela Bok, *Secrets: On the Ethics of Concealment and Revelation* (New York: Vintage Books, 1984), 187–189.

18. "Senators Want Inquiry on Report of Official SDI 'Disinformation,' " *Washington Post*, 20 March 1986, A26.

19. David Wise, *The Politics of Lying: Government Deception, Secrecy, and Power* (New York: Random House, 1973), 344.

20. "U.S. Using Disinformation Policy to Impede Technological Data Flow," *Aviation Week and Space Technology*, 17 March 1986, 16–17.

21. "Yellow Rain Was Created and Sold by White House," reprinted from *Guardian*, 16 September 1987, in *The Right to Know*, vol. 2 (Oakland, CA: Data Center, 1988), 128.

22. *The KGB and the Library Target: 1962–Present* (Washington, DC: FBI Headquarters, Intelligence Division, 1988), 2.

23. *Transfer of United States High Technology to the Soviet Union and Soviet Bloc Nations*, Report of the Committee on Governmental Affairs, U.S. Senate, 15 November, 1982, Washington, DC: U.S. GPO, 1983), 54, 60.

24. "Technology Transfer at Issue: The Industry Viewpoint," *IEEE Spectrum*, May 1982, 69.

25. Eve Pell, *The Big Chill* (Boston: Beacon Press, 1984), 77.

26. "Reagan Issues Order on Science Secrecy: Will It Be Obeyed?" *Physics Today*, November 1985, 57.

27. "Soviet R&D: The True Threat to U.S. National Security," *Signal*, December 1985, 119.

28. *Export Controls, Competitiveness, and International Cooperation: A Critical Review*, Staff Report to the Committee on Science, Space, and Technology, House of Representatives, 101st Cong. 1st Sess., February 1989 (Washington, DC: U.S. GPO, 1989), 24.

29. Pell, *The Big Chill*, 76.

30. *United States v. Endler Industries*, 579 F2nd 516 (9th Cir. 1978).

31. Stephen H. Unger, "The Growing Threat of Government Secrecy," *Technology Review*, February/March 1982, 38.

32. *The Government's Classification of Private Ideas*, Hearings before a subcommittee of the Committee on Government Operations, House of Representatives, 96th Cong., 28 February, 20 March, August 21, 1980 (Washington, DC: U.S. GPO, 1981), 270.

33. Ibid., 264.

34. Ibid., 278.

35. Ibid., 273–274.

36. Ibid., 266, 285.

37. Ibid., 425, 431.

38. Ruth Greenstein, "National Security Controls on Scientific Information," *Jurimetrics Journal*, Fall 1982, 80.

39. Ibid., 81–82.

40. John Shattuck, *Federal Restrictions on the Free Flow of Academic Information and Ideas* (Cambridge, MA: Harvard University, 1985), 16–17.

41. "Administration Grapples with Export Controls," *Science*, 220 (June 1983), 1023.

42. *Export Controls, Competitiveness, and International Cooperation,* 29.

43. *A Summary and Analysis of Hearings on the National Academy of Sciences Report on National Security Export Controls,* Staff Report to the Committee on Science, Space, and Technology, House of Representatives, 101st Cong. 1st sess., February 1989 (Washington, DC: U.S. GPO, 1989), 31.

44. *Computer Security Act of 1987: Report,* 33.

45. *Export Controls, Competitiveness, and International Cooperation,* 23.

46. Ibid., 28, 30.

47. Statement of Sam Gejdenson, Chairman, Subcommittee on International Economic Policy and Trade, U.S. House of Representatives, 24 September 1991, 1.

48. Prepared statement of Richard Lehman, Director, Public Affairs, IBM Corp., before the Subcommittee on International Economic Policy and Trade, U.S. House of Representatives, 24 September 1991, 2.

49. Statement of Carleton S. Fiorina, Vice President, Strategy and Market Development, AT&T Network Systems, before the Subcommittee on International Economic Policy and Trade, U.S. House of Representatives, 24 September 1991, 1.

50. "U.S. Shifts, Agrees to Ease Fiber-Optics Export Curb," *Washington Post,* 6 March 1992, D10.

51. "U.S. Relaxes Restrictions on Technology," *Washington Post,* 22 April 1992, C2.

52. The Invention Secrecy Act of 1951, 35 USC 181–188, reads in pertinent part:

> Whenever publication or disclosure by the grant of a patent on an invention in which the Government has a property interest might, in the opinion of the head of the interested Government agency, be detrimental to the national security, the Commissioner [of Patents] upon being so notified shall order that the invention be kept secret and shall withhold the grant of a patent therefor under the conditions set forth hereinafter.
>
> Whenever publication or disclosure of an invention by the granting of a patent, in which the Government does not have a property interest, might, in the opinion of the Commissioner, be detrimental to the national security, he shall make the application for patent in which such invention is disclosed available for inspection to the Atomic Energy Commission [now DOE], the Secretary of Defense, and the chief officer of any other department or agency of the government designated by the President as a defense agency of the United States.
>
> ... If, in the opinion of the Atomic Energy Commission, the Secretary of a Defense Department, or the chief officer of another department or agency so designated, the publication or disclosure of the invention by the granting of a patent thereof would be detrimental to the national security, the Atomic Energy Commission, the Secretary of a Defense Department, or such other chief officer shall notify the Commissioner and the Commissioner shall order the invention be kept secret and shall withhold the grant of a patent for such period as the national interest requires....

53. The Atomic Energy Act of 1954, 42 U.S.C. 2181(c)–(e), provides:

> (c)...Any person who has made or hereafter makes any invention or discovery useful in the production of special nuclear material or atomic energy, shall file with the Commission [DOE] a report containing a complete description thereof unless

such invention or discovery is described in an application for patent filed with the Commissioner of Patents by such person within the time required for filing of such report. The report covering any such invention or discovery shall be filed on or before the one hundred and eightieth day after such person first discovers or first has reason to believe that such invention or discovery is useful in such production or utilization.

(d) The Commissioner of Patents shall notify the Commission [DOE] of all applications for patents heretofore or hereafter filed which, in his opinion, disclose inventions or discoveries required to be reported under subsection (c) of this section, and shall provide the Commission [DOE] access to all such applications.

54. *Science, Technology and the First Amendment: Special Report* (Washington, DC: Office of Technology Assessment, 1988), 49.

55. Letter from Thomas E. McDonnell, Associate Counsel, Naval Research Laboratory, to Herbert N. Foerstel, Engineering and Physical Sciences Library, University of Maryland, 6 March 1992.

56. "Identification and Protection of Unclassified Controlled Nuclear Information," 48 *Federal Register* 13990 (1 April 1983).

57. Statement of Herman E. Roser, Assistant Secretary for Defense Programs, U.S. Department of Energy, regarding proposed Rules on Identification and Protection of Unclassified Controlled Nuclear Information, 26 September 1983, 10.

58. Anthony Lewis, "A New Kind of Secret," *New York Times*, 30 June 1983, A19.

59. Floyd Abrams, "The New Effort to Control Information," *New York Times Magazine*, September 25, 1983, p. 22.

60. 46 *Federal Register* 31236 (August 3, 1984).

61. "Washington Feeling Insecure About Non-Secret Information," *New York Times*, 30 August 1987, E5.

62. *Soviet Acquisition of Militarily Significant Western Technology: An Update* (Washington, DC: Technology Transfer Intelligence Committee, September 1985), 17.

63. Testimony of Robert L. Park before the Committee on Government Operations, 25 February 1987, 4–5.

64. *The Exploitation of Western Databases* (Washington, DC: Office of the Assistant Vice Chief of Staff, U.S. Air Force, 30 June 1986), V–I–26.

65. National Commission on Libraries and Information Science, Hearing on Sensitive but Not Classified Information, 28 May 1987, 71.

66. Walter Gellhorn, *Security, Loyalty, and Science* (Ithaca, NY: Cornell University Press, 1950), 228.

67. Federal Bureau of Investigation, *KGB and the Library Target, 1962-Present*, Top Secret version (Washington, DC: FBI, February 1988), 2.

68. "Libraries Are Asked by FBI to Report on Foreign Agents," *New York Times*, 18 October 1987, 22.

69. U.S. Congress, House Committee on the Judiciary, *FBI Counterintelligence Visits to Libraries: Hearings Before the House Subcommittee on Civil and Constitutional Rights of the Committee on the Judiciary*, 100th Cong., 2d Sess., 20 June and 13 July 1988 (Washington, DC: U.S. GPO, 1989), 105.

70. Ibid., 292.

71. Herbert N. Foerstel, *Surveillance in the Stacks* (Westport, CT: Greenwood Press, 1991), 55, 57, 59.

72. Ibid., 59.

73. Robert L. Park, "Restricting Information: A Dangerous Game," *Issues in Science and Technology,* Fall 1988, 64.

74. Statement of Miriam A. Drake on behalf of the ALA and ARL, before the House Subcommittee on Legislation and National Security, on implementation of the Computer Security Act of 1987, 4 May 1987, 7.

75. Foerstel, *Surveillance in the Stacks,* 84.

76. U.S. Congress, House Committee on the Judiciary, *FBI Counterintelligence Visits to Libraries,* 56.

77. Foerstel, *Surveillance in the Stacks,* 51–52.

78. Park, "Restricting Information," 62.

79. Don Edwards, "Government Information Controls Threaten Academic Freedom," *Thought and Action,* Spring 1989, 87.

80. John N. Berry III, "Editorial: Little Shops of Subversion," *Library Journal,* December 1989, 6.

81. Letter from Robert B. Davenport, Inspector in Charge, Office of Public Affairs, Federal Bureau of Investigation, to Herbert Foerstel, University of Maryland, College Park, 29 March 1990.

82. "Ariadne," *New Scientist,* 7 July 1988, 104.

83. William J. Broad, "As Science Moves into Commerce, Openness Is Lost," *New York Times,* 24 May 1988, C1.

84. Ibid., C6.

85. Michelle Van Cleave, Assistant Director for National Security Affairs, White House Office of Science and Technology Policy, "National Security and Strategic Economic Information," remarks prepared for delivery, International Security Systems Symposium, Washington, DC, 28 October 1991, 9.

86. Ibid.

87. Anita R. Schiller and Robert I. Schiller, "Commercializing Information," *Nation,* 4 October 1986, 95.

88. *OMB Circular A–130: The Management of Federal Information Activities* (Washington, DC: OMB Watch, December 1988), 2.

89. Letter from Gloria Chawla, Engineering and Physical Sciences Library, University of Maryland, to Gladys Cotter, Director, Scientific and Technical Information Division, NASA, 8 March 1990.

90. Letter from Gladys A. Cotter, Director, Scientific and Technical Information Division, NASA, to Gloria Chawla, University of Maryland, College Park, 28 March 1990.

91. "Privatization of Public Services: A Growing Threat to Constitutional Rights," *Public Administration Review,* November–December 1987, 6.

CHAPTER 6

The End of the Scientific Cold War

GOODBYE TO AMERICA'S OLDEST ENEMY

At the Geneva summit in November 1985, Mikhail Gorbachev told Ronald Reagan that "a nuclear war cannot be won and must never be fought." Shortly thereafter, Gorbechev proclaimed the twin pillars of Soviet reform, *Glasnost* (openness in government) and *Perestroika* (restructuring of government), and the Cold War was programmed for meltdown. Soviet troops were soon withdrawn from Afghanistan, and when both troops and missiles were withdrawn from Eastern Europe, the fear of nuclear attack from the East began to dissipate. By the Malta summit of 1989, when Gorbachev told George Bush that "we don't consider you an enemy any more,"[1] most Americans had ceased to regard the Soviet Union as threatening or even hostile. At a June 1989 press conference, Admiral William J. Crowe, Jr., then Chairman of the Joint Chiefs of Staff, was asked if the Soviets were still our enemy. Crowe responded, "Maybe they're your enemy. They're not my enemy. I'm a military man, ... but I don't particularly look at them as an enemy. Incidentally, the last major war we were in, they were our allies."[2] The last minor war as well.

By November 1989, the most visible symbol of East/West conflict, the Berlin Wall, had fallen. By 1991, one of the most enduring remnants of the Cold War, the U.S. Distant Early Warning Line of radar posts stretching 2,000 miles across Canada, began dismantling. In that year the Soviet-led trade bloc, Comecon, was disbanded, and the Warsaw Pact was formally dissolved. A "Grand Bargain" for Western aid to Moscow was prepared jointly by Soviet and American economists. State property in the Soviet Union was denationalized, and the Soviet legislature authorized foreign investment, including 100 percent foreign ownership of Soviet businesses.

After the comitragic failed coup in 1991, the KGB was reorganized along the lines of the American CIA, and the first civilian ever to head the Soviet foreign intelligence service declared an end to the secret intelligence war with the United States. In September 1991 President Bush announced the unilateral withdrawal of all ground-based, short-range nuclear weapons and the removal of all nuclear-tipped cruise missiles from ships and submarines. In addition, *all* American strategic bombers were taken off "alert" status and a number of nuclear weapons programs were terminated. The Soviets responded with an equally dramatic set of weapons reductions.

One by one, the Soviet republics declared their independence, and finally, on December 21, 1991, the leaders of 11 former Soviet republics announced the replacement of the Soviet Union by a new Commonwealth of Independent States (CIS), paving the way for the resignation of Soviet President Mikhail Gorbechev. The agreements signed and issued at Alma Ata, Kazakhstan, stated unequivocally: "With the formation of the Commonwealth of Independent States, the Union of Soviet Socialist Republics ceases to exist." Gorbechev made a last-minute appeal to create a single commonwealth citizenship, but Russian President Boris Yeltsin made it clear that "The Commonwealth is not a state. Therefore it can have no citizenship."[3] The American government remained confused. By April 1992 the State Department was using the term "CIS," but the Agriculture Department used the term NIS (newly independent states), while the Treasury Department used FSU (former Soviet Union).

On April 27, 1992, Russia and 12 other former Soviet republics won membership in the International Monetary Fund and the World Bank, opening the door to substantial Western aid. But the transition to a market economy proved difficult within the new republics. The World Bank's chief economist, Lawrence Summers, observed: "The potential scale of the problem is staggering, the possible nightmare scernarios numerous. Imagine military disunion and civil war. Imagine the construction of Berlin Walls throughout Europe as millions of refugees attempt to flee from the [former] Soviet Union."[4] Sen. Daniel Patrick Moynihan (D-NY) saw no American advantage in exploiting such chaos. "Our problem," he stated, "is that our Cold War institutions here in Washington are still in place."[5]

SOVIET SCIENTISTS FOR SALE

The best scientists from the former Soviet Union are fleeing their country. In 1992 the Russian Academy of Sciences estimated that 12 percent of all researchers had gone abroad in the previous three years, including 40 percent of all the theoretical physicists. And the pace of the brain drain was increasing rapidly. "It's destroying some scientific schools," said Yuri Dnestrovsky, a nuclear physicist at Moscow State University. "What took decades to build up is now taking months to destroy." Dnestrovsky stated that the quality of students in chemistry and physics has declined dramatically, with the most talented now interested in business and economics: "It is my desire to pass on what I have learned. But it is very difficult, because no one is interested in continuing the great traditions of Soviet physics."[6]

Isn't this deterioration of Soviet science just what the United States has intended throughout the long history of Cold War controls on scientific communication? Apparently not. In January 1992, CIA Director Robert Gates warned Congress of a "brain drain" of scientific experts from the former Soviet Union that might enable Third World countries to expand their military capabilities: "As living conditions in the [former Soviet] republics get worse and some of these people have no alternative employment or see their families in desperate circumstances, they may be induced to emigrate ... or they may remain in place and, in exchange for cash, provide information."[7]

The following month, Secretary of State James Baker visited Chelyabinsk–70, one of two major nuclear weapons laboratories in the former Soviet Union. At a remarkable meeting, the lab's nuclear scientists presented Baker with a memo offering their scientific skills to the West. The scientists asked that a six-member U.S. committee be created to consider how to redirect the lab toward civilian high technology. Vladislaw Nitikin, Deputy Director of the Institute of Technical Physics, said that the scientists at Chelyabinsk did not want to leave the country, but "all the noise and battle about the brain drain ... is having an influence on the state of mind of our scientists and to a certain extent initiating this process." Baker assured him that it was the "highest priority" of the United States to overcome the problem of brain drain, but he recommended the "brain gain solution" that would put them back to work. Yevgeny Avrorim, chief scientist at Chelyabinsk–70, told Baker, "For a specialist it is not only important to have money for living, but important work." Baker said he understood the scientists' desire to do "interesting and intellectually rewarding work" while using their expertise to build the "new Russia."[8]

Vitaly Goldansky, Director of Moscow's Institute of Chemical Physics, said lack of money is only part of the problem faced by scientists. "For a long time, they were highly recognized, highly decorated, enjoying many privileges. Now they feel themselves abandoned." Viktor Mikhailov, deputy minister of nuclear engineering and industry, complained that workers in the nuclear industry earn below minimum wage, have no housing, and endure countless hardships. One physicist asked, "Have you ever seen a nuclear research center being forced to undertake farming so as to feed its employees? Representatives of our institute are running around the region looking for food, but everything is for barter. Does it mean we will have to trade bombs for meat?"[9]

In 1992, scientists at Russia's two preeminent atomic weapons labs were being paid six dollars a month. At Chelyabinsk, chief scientist Yevgeny Avrorim discussed with U.S. Energy Department officials the possibility of U.S. dollar stipends to keep Russian atomic scientists from emigrating. Avrorim advocated joint scientific projects and commercial endeavors that would combine Western capital with Russian brains and technology. At the Kurchatov Institute of Atomic Energy in Moscow, once the headquarters of the Soviet nuclear weapons program, there is little research being done. In desperation, some Russian scientists have formed commercial firms in an attempt to sell their scientific services for dollars.

Western governments are now considering paying scientists to continue working in the very research centers once considered the source of dangerous enemy activity. In February 1992, the United States, Russia, and Germany announced plans to establish a science and technology institute to employ nuclear scientists from the former Soviet Union in an attempt to keep them from selling their services to other nations. Among the matters discussed by Russian President Boris Yeltsin and Secretary of State James A. Baker was the sharing of technology on ballistic missile defenses. The proposed international science centers in Russia and Ukraine were described by the program's director as "clearinghouses—some call them dating services," where scientists seeking work will be matched with institutions and projects seeking help. "This is not a Russian center," he said. "It is an international center in Russia."[10] The center will seek commercial contracts, international support, and funding from foundations, academic and scientific institutions, and other nations.

Mark Prelas, a professor of nuclear engineering at the University of

Missouri, recently visited Chelyabinsk, where he spoke with Yuly Khariton, one of the founders of the Soviet atomic program. "No high-ranking scientist has ever talked so candidly and in such detail about the Soviet atomic program to outsiders," said Prelas. "We were overwhelmed by the level of sophistication and capabilities the Russians had reached in certain fields." Prelas questions the efficacy of spending millions of Western dollars to establish an institute in Moscow for Russian nuclear scientists. "The facilities and institutions already in existence are more than adequate to keep the scientists busy and productive. It would be cheaper and more directly helpful to give aid to the researchers in their own laboratories."[11] Prelas suspects American foot-dragging may reflect a reluctance to shore up the Russian defense establishment.

On February 22, 1992, Yuri P. Seminov, general director of the Russians' civilian space program, went to Capitol Hill, offering the United States the chance to buy or lease the most sophisticated Russian spacecraft and rockets at bargain-basement prices. U.S. officials were invited to lease space aboard the *Mir* space station to conduct scientific experiments. Seminov offered the *Soyuz*-TM spacecraft for use in the planned U.S. space station *Freedom,* and proposed the sale of the Russians' most powerful rocket, the Energia, which exceeds the lifting capacity of any U.S. launch vehicle. Richard Truly, outgoing administrator of NASA, then testified that there are several areas in which Russian technology could represent attractive opportunities for NASA. These would include the powerful Soviet RD–170 rocket engine, advanced automated rendezvous and docking systems, and nuclear reactor power systems.

For years, the U.S. defense industry and government labs had sporadic access to Soviet high technology, but now the independent republics are selling their recently declassified technology. John Kiser, president of an American company that has specialized in technology transfer from the former Soviet bloc, has proposed that the American government identify world-class technologies from the new Commonwealth of Independent States and import them for mutual commercial benefit. Kiser says the effort should focus on "dual use" (military or civilian) research and development that could be used directly by federal agencies or U.S. industry. Citing areas such as thermionics, electric propulsion, and combustion synthesis, Kiser says we now have the opportunity to buy, lease, or set up joint ventures to use these technologies.

In 1992, a joint venture called Turbocom Inc. was established, with the Russians owning 45 percent and John Kiser's firm, Kiser Research Inc., owning 10 percent. The Russians' contribution was know-how, not money, and they immediately began briefing the Americans on technical details that they had until then kept secret. Alexander Berlin, a Russian professor at the Moscow Physics-Technical Institute, explained, "We came out on the world market because we want to save at least a tiny portion of our science.... Today, with no money from the state, no sponsors, our great science is dying."[12]

Some in the United States believe Soviet science is already dead and cannot be revived. Joseph L. Birman, Distinguished Professor of Physics at the City University of New York, says that, rather than supporting scientific research in Russia and the neighboring republics, we should focus on employing the Soviet scientists in the West. "What kind of research is even possible in the former Soviet Union?" asks Birman. "Current journals simply are not available, so even the top laboratories may be many months or even a year behind the current state of knowledge.... [I]ntermittent electric power failures in laboratories are knocking out equipment and setting back research.... Is it any surprise that record numbers of scientists have left and are leaving the former U.S.S.R. and its wounded laboratories?"[13]

Birman opposes any Western attempt to stabilize the scientific establishment in the former Soviet Union:

> [T]here is not the slightest evidence that after the present instability scientific life can resume a pattern of high-level work.... I think the evidence is clear and the conclusion even clearer: Do not send funds to support the decaying remnants of a once-proud scientific establishment. We cannot "give" useful and meaningful work to anyone to keep them in place!... It seems fair to assert that America alone could welcome and accommodate in our laboratories, industries, and universities a good fraction of the trained scientists of the former U.S.S.R. who will want to emigrate.[14]

Indeed, many Russian scientists have already been brought to the United States, with predictable political repercussions. Rep. Bill Richardson (D-NM) complained, "What do the hundreds of American scientists at Los Alamos, Sandia, Oak Ridge, and our other national laboratories facing possible layoffs think of this practice? They have been toiling against the Soviet bear for years. Because of these scientists we won the Cold War. What is their reward? They may be fired and replaced by Russian scientists."[15]

As billions of dollars of international aid flow to Russia to support pro-Western leaders, little American technology goes with it. The high-tech conveyer belt runs only East to West, and even Russia's new "reformist" leaders are concerned. Boris Yeltsin's vice president, Alexander

Rutskoi, recently likened Western aid to "free cheese in the mousetrap."
He noted, "I don't think Americans would let me into their nuclear
weapons development center, as [James] Baker was let into Arzamas."
One legislator at the Kremlin said, "We are listening to foreigners and
foreign experts all the time. But do you think they really want our
industry and economy to develop? Surely they don't want to see us as
rivals on the world market."[16]

Ironically, the secret world of atomic energy seems to be a promising
area for post-Cold War scientific cooperation. Already, the DOE has
begun negotiations with Moscow to purchase and distribute Russian
enriched uranium. The Russians would have a market for their excess
production and DOE could supply its nuclear power plants and submarines more cheaply. Russian uranium is so cheap that some U.S.
utilities are already buying it.

But a recent incident demonstrated the continuing Cold War legacy
of atomic secrecy and the bureaucratic excesses of our export control
laws. All began innocently in early 1991, when an American scientific
consortium, partially funded by the military, began negotiations with
Moscow to buy the advanced nuclear reactor, Topaz II, for use in outer
space. The consortium, which received funding from the Air Force,
DOE, and the Strategic Defense Initiative Organization (SDIO), was
primarily interested in the reactor's application to nuclear and space
weapons, including weapons originally designed to destroy Soviet missiles. Richard Verga, Director of Key Technologies for SDIO, said, "This
would be the first of its kind of these high-tech transfers." Verga said
the aim of the proposed purchase, estimated to cost less than $10 million,
was to "jump-start" a similar reactor development program in the United
States. He anticipated using the reactor in both military and civilian
applications, including surveillance radars, lunar bases, planetary
probes, satellite tugs, and manufacturing plants.[17]

So far, so good. Stephen Aftergood, an expert on space reactors for
the Federation of American Scientists, said the proposed purchase was
a remarkable breakthrough in international cooperation and commerce.
In March 1991 an American firm, Space Power Inc., arranged for the
Russians to bring a nonworking model of the Topaz II reactor, the device
that Moscow was offering to the U.S. consortium, to Albuquerque, New
Mexico, for display at the Symposium on Space Nuclear Power Systems.
All went well until the conclusion of the conference, when the Russian
scientists prepared to take their reactor home. At that point the U.S.
Nuclear Regulatory Commission (NRC) declared that the reactor could
not be returned until the Russians obtained an "export license." Further,

the NRC claimed that an export license was prohibited by the Atomic Energy Act, under which the return of the reactor was considered illicit technology transfer. In addition, Frank Ingram, a spokesperson for the NRC, said that an export license could not be issued because Moscow and Washington have no legal agreement covering such trade. Ingram said the fact that the reactor contained no nuclear fuel and was inoperable did not exclude it from the restrictions of the Atomic Energy Act.

The Russian reactor was locked away in a guarded warehouse operated by the Smithsonian Institution, pending resolution of the dispute. "It shows how impervious the American bureaucracy is to the logic of the situation," said Stephen Aftergood. "Instead of demonstrating and enhancing... cooperation, it's providing an irritant."[18] The Russians argued that the import license was granted with assurances that the reactor would be returned. "Such actions smack of piracy," declared a commentator for TASS. "Our country has never done anything of this sort." TASS suggested that the United States was conducting a technology grab because the Russian reactor "is far ahead of similar American models."[19]

Joseph Wetch, president of Space Power Inc., said he did not research the legal code before arranging for the reactor's shipment to the United States, and the snafu caught him by surprise. Wetch said the Russian scientists who brought the reactor to the United States were "very upset, rightfully." Those scientists left the United States not only without a deal to sell the reactor but also without the reactor. Ultimately, the confrontation became such an embarrassment for the Departments of State and Commerce, which had worked to bring the reactor into the United States, that the Bush Administration felt compelled to seek a compromise. The NRC reversed its previous position by announcing that the Russian reactor did not fall under the export laws because of "the absence of fuel, moderator and coolant, the intended short stay in the United States and the intent to return it expeditiously to its country of origin."[20]

By 1992 the Russian Topaz II reactor had become a fundamental part of the technology behind America's space defense planning. In Congressional hearings, Col. Pete Worden of the SDIO testified:

> Our interest in the Russian program is to take advantage of their experience, data base and hardware to aid our own program. Fielding nuclear systems to meet U.S. needs more quickly and inexpensively is the motivation.... Pending approval, SDIO will complete the purchase of an unfueled Topaz II space nuclear reactor for use in a test program that would take place here in the United States.... Subject to positive test results from

the initial assessment, SDIO is considering a possible flight test of a mod-
ified six-kilowatt Topaz II system. This space test is intended to establish
an entry-level space reactor capability in a time frame compatible with
several SDIO missions.[21]

On March 27, 1992, the White House announced approval of a $14.3
million purchase of Russia's Topaz II reactor, satellite thrusters, and
plutonium–238 to power deep space exploration.

FINDING NEW THREATS

In January 1992, CIA Director Robert Gates told Congress that the
threat of deliberate attack from the strategic or conventional forces of
the new Commonwealth of Independent States had all but disappeared.
Just two months later a leaked DoD document revealed an imperial
blueprint for the next century. The document was classified "NOFORN,"
meaning it was to be kept from foreign nationals, including U.S. allies.
The central strategy in the new Pentagon plan was to "establish and
protect a new order" while "deterring potential competitors from even
aspiring to a larger regional or global role." The plan called for concerted
efforts to thwart the emergence of a rival superpower in Europe, Asia,
or the former Soviet Union.[22] Cold War language had always used the
vocabulary of fear, but today's threats are economic, not military. And
in economic terms, the Commonwealth of Independent States is no
threat. With the dissolution of the USSR, the American intelligence
establishment had created an imaginative new scenario to justify withholding our science, not just from the CIS but also from our traditional
allies around the world.

As early as September 1989, Oliver "Buck" Revell, the FBI's Executive
Assistant Director of Investigations, warned the American Society for
Industrial Security of America's diminishing sense of urgency in op-
posing foreign intelligence operations. He derided the popular percep-
tion that such efforts were an outmoded product of the Cold War
mentality. In his address, "Countering the Hostile Intelligence Threat
in the United States," Revell claimed that from a counterintelligence
perspective, the effects of *Glasnost* and *Perestroika* represented a frightening new challenge to the United States. "Since gaining access to Western, and above all U.S. technology, is a principal goal and indeed a
national necessity of the Soviet Union, the Soviet intelligence services
will intensify their operations to obtain embargoed technology."[23] Revell
insisted that the illegal transfer of technology continued to pose a threat

to U.S. national security. He said that the apparent reduction in the intensity of the U.S./Soviet military rivalry meant that the struggle was simply transferred to other areas. "Therefore as the military dimension of this superpower struggle becomes less important, all other dimensions of that struggle, such as the political, economic, ideological, and intelligence considerations become more crucial."[24]

In an article for *Foreign Affairs*, George Carver, Jr., a former CIA officer and Senior Fellow at the Center for Strategic and International Studies, called for continued vigilance against illegal technology transfer. "The Cold War may be ending," Carver wrote, "but there is no detente in the intelligence war." Carver claimed that there were "increasing and progressively more sophisticated attempts to acquire American technology. These attempts were mounted not just against U.S. government facilities but also directly against American corporations, by a number of nations—*including some of America's closest allies.*"[25]

Even as the Soviet Union crumbled, this new vision of an international struggle for technology came to dominate America's national security strategy. At the 1991 International Security Systems Symposium, the FBI continued to claim that the end of the Cold War signaled an *increased* threat of foreign espionage, requiring new strategies and new legislation to control technical information. The word "Communist" was no longer used, but Harry Brandon, the FBI's Deputy Assistant Director for Intelligence, said spies from the former Soviet Union were still working overtime, with their "collection level" actually increasing. He noted, however, that their targets had changed from military and strategic secrets to political, economic, scientific, and technological information. Brandon said that the United States would face severe counterintelligence problems with traditionally friendly as well as unfriendly countries. He described a new National Security Threat List being developed by the Bureau. The old list was aimed at Communist countries. The new list would contain generalized "issue threats," such as economic sabotage. Under this new approach, the FBI would be able to move more effectively against spies, regardless of their national origin.

At the same Security Systems Symposium, former CIA Director Richard Helms shared Brandon's concern about industrial espionage, but he advocated no new laws or sanctions beyond current export controls. Michelle Van Cleave, from the White House Office of Science and Technology Policy, actually saw a menace in the *breakup* of the KGB. "[I]t is possible that KGB intelligence officers may even now be circulating their résumés, looking for new work outside the former USSR. There may no longer be much demand for their ideological services, but many of these officers do have finely honed skills in the collection of technological and economic information.... Theoretically, many unemployed intelligence officers, lacking work, could reason that their future is in high technology, and attempt to sell their talents in that market."[26]

The Security Systems Symposium emphasized that we are in an age where our national security allies have become economic competitors, often using illegal methods to acquire our technology. This warning was formalized in April 1992 when CIA Director Robert Gates told a Congressional subcommittee that nearly 20 foreign governments were carrying out economic intelligence gathering that harms U.S. interests. Though he did not name the 20 countries, Gates said they included some of America's allies who sought government data on foreign trade as well as confidential contract information from U.S. companies.

Sen. David Boren (D-OK), chairman of the Senate Select Committee on Intelligence, has expressed similar concern: "An increasing share of the espionage directed against the United States comes from spying by foreign governments against private American companies aimed at stealing commercial secrets to gain a national economic advantage."[27] Boren suggested that, in the interest of national security, the U.S. government might be required to intercede to protect America's scientific and trade secrets.

But many in Congress consider the intelligence community's orchestrated clamor for more, not less, control of American technology to contradict the post-Cold War realities. The new economic rationalization for U.S. intelligence operations seems specious to some, ominous to others. Sen. Bill Bradley (D-NJ) expressed concern that President Bush would interpret the Intelligence Authorization Act of 1991 as a mandate to use U.S. intelligence agencies to give American business interests an edge in international competition. He said the Senate Select Committee on Intelligence (SSCI) had raised undue, or at least premature, claims about an emerging economic espionage threat, including the collection of U.S. proprietary and unclassified information by foreign powers. Bradley submitted his own report, drawing a sharp distinction between illegal economic espionage and "perfectly legal information-gathering by foreign powers, which we conduct ourselves and which must be tolerated."[28] He noted that because the SSCI's study on economic espionage failed to make this distinction, he remained unconvinced that illegal economic espionage was a new or growing threat. Perhaps with the FBI's notorious Library Awareness Program in mind, Bradley urged that the SSCI not allow its study to become a pretext for a new program of FBI surveillance of either foreigners or Americans.

Bradley said he was troubled by the President's suggestion that U.S. counterintelligence programs should focus on foreign threats to our industrial secrets and technologies.

> Does this mean the U.S. Government is spying on foreign-owned firms that employ millions of American workers? . . . There is no good reason why firms should expect the CIA or the FBI to protect their proprietary information against snooping by foreign competitors any more than they need such protection against similar threats from domestic American rivals. Nor should the U.S. Government use sensitive intelligence sources and methods, or scarce tax dollars, to collect economic information for the exclusive benefit of private interests. . . . Yet that is the direction the President, the Director of Central Intelligence, and the Select Committee on Intelligence seem to be headed.[29]

CIA spokesperson George Carver defends such activities, claiming that economic and technological prowess have become more significant indicators of national strength than the traditional measures of military power. "In most of the world . . . economic competition is replacing military competition—a shift that does not necessarily make the world any less Darwinian or more benign, since economic competition is often waged just as fiercely as military competition ever was." The web of economic, military, and other factors directly affecting America's national interests and security is now described as "seamless," meaning its components are inseparable. Carver concludes that traditional jurisdiction-defining distinctions between national interests are being eroded, not only foreign versus domestic but also economic versus political, military versus civilian, intelligence versus police, federal versus state, private versus public, and, in the foreign affairs field, even friend versus foe.[30]

On April 29, 1992, a series of prominent witnesses from government and business testified before a Congressional subcommittee investigating "The Threat of Foreign Economic Espionage to U.S. Corporations." Chairman Jack Brooks declared that the Cold War had given way to a new era of global competition, requiring the United States to protect its economic resources. Brooks warned: "Intelligence agencies from the former Soviet bloc nations and our allies are actively targeting U.S. companies. The information they seek is not simply technological data but also financial and commercial information."[31]

Milton Socolar, representing the U.S. General Accounting Office, testified, "[A]s the world political climate changes with the end of the Cold War, the surreptitious gathering of economic and technological information has taken on added significance. The unauthorized acquisition of U.S. proprietary or other information by foreign governments to advance their countries' economic position is growing.... The loss of proprietary information and technology through espionage activity will have broadening detrimental consequences to both U.S. economic viability and our national security interests." Citing examples of economic espionage by France, Japan, and Israel, Socolar concluded that the criminal justice and intelligence agencies have not adequately addressed this problem. "Currently, most of the discussions are being conducted within the intelligence community, without the benefit of public debate. In the final analysis, Congress may have to develop legislation to protect industry from economic espionage."[32]

James E. Riesbeck, Executive Vice President for Corning Inc., told Congress, "For the first time since the 1930s, the United States is not threatened by a foreign military power. As a result, our stature in the world will increasingly be determined by what is done in corporate boardrooms and on factory floors, rather than by the Joint Chiefs of Staff. The priorities of our national intelligence apparatus must reflect this changing circumstance by placing greater emphasis on economic security." Riesbeck said that Corning has been the target of state-sponsored industrial espionage, particularly from Europe, aimed at Corning's fiber optic technology. He concluded, "We must make sure that our technology is not knowingly or unknowingly stolen by our international competitors."[33]

Robert Gates, Director of the CIA, told the subcommittee that the November 1991 National Security Review, signed by President Bush, identified nearly 40 percent of our intelligence requirements as economic in nature. Gates noted that "some governments in Asia, Europe, the Middle East, and to a lesser degree Latin America, as well as some former communist countries . . . are involved in intelligence collection activities that are detrimental to our economic interests at some level." He concluded that while the end of the Cold War did not bring an end to the foreign intelligence threat, it did change the nature of that threat. Gates told Congress that most intelligence services—including those in former communist countries—now place a higher premium on open source collection, because advances in data processing have made it easier to aggregate, manipulate, and exploit large volumes of data.[34]

FBI Director William Sessions described how foreign nations, including tradtional allies, are "economically motivated to collect classified and unclassified scientific information" because of the growing "technological protectionism" in the leading economic countries. In response, said Sessions, the FBI created its National Security Threat List, focusing on foreign intelligence activities directed at critical American technologies or proprietary information.[35]

Stanislav Levchenko, a former KGB agent who defected to the United States, testified on the continued intelligence activities by the former Soviet Union. "[I]t would be naive to hope that President Yeltsin will decide to cut Russian intelligence substantially. In addition, practically all the new countries—the former republics of the USSR—can be expected to conduct external intelligence on their own, with U.S. technology as a prime target.... The intelligence services of the former republics will almost assuredly coordinate their work. An important point of it will be industrial espionage."[36]

FINDING NEW ENEMIES

The April 1992 Congressional hearings on economic espionage not only defined new threats to our national security, but revealed new enemies. FBI Director Sessions warned Congress: "We must recognize that the foreign intelligence threat is not confined to those foreign powers which are historically antagonistic to our national objectives.... Now and in the future, the collection strategies of adversaries and allies alike will not only focus on defense related information, but also include scientific, technological, political and economic information."[37]

CIA Director Gates testified, "Some countries with whom we have had good relations may adopt a two-track approach of cooperating with us at the level of diplomacy while engaging in adversarial intelligence collection." Gates explained that economic intelligence collection by such countries is particularly damaging to our economy because they, unlike the former communist states, are strong economic competitors.[38]

During the same month that Congress investigated economic espionage, Pulitzer Prize award-winner Jim Hoagland wrote that, with the end of the Cold War, America had become not the world's policeman, but the world's customs officer. In this context, he wrote: "Today, Japan is cited by Americans as their new Enemy Number One. France is spoken of by a White House official in interagency meetings as 'a strategic adversary.' Germany's muscular diplomacy...draws criticism in Washington for undue 'assertiveness.' "[39] By changing the context of national security from military to economic and technological, the United States has made its former allies the target of new trade restrictions and export controls on science and technology. The "techno-nationalists" in the United States have made it clear that Japan is their villain of choice, and the extremities of this obsession extend to unrestrained Japan-bashing in the popular media. A 1992 comic strip portrayed the end of the Cold War, with the American President telling the military to retarget their missiles from the air base at Minsk to the Mitsubishi plant at Nagoya.

The cartoon attack on Mitsubishi followed a more serious confrontation with Japan during the debate on the FSX aircraft deal. In 1988, Japan indicated its desire to build its own jet fighter, the FSX. The United States asked Japan instead to buy American F16s "off the shelf," but the Japanese were looking for overall performance better than the F16's. In subsequent negotiations, the United States insisted on a joint project, in which the two countries would produce a modernized version of the F16. Most important, the compromise would prevent Japan from building its own aircraft, an act the United States thought would open the door to Japanese competition in the global aeronautics trade, which is dominated by the United States.

During the negotiations on a bilateral memorandum of understanding aimed at codevelopment of the FSX, the United States insisted that Japan share any technology developed in the process of modernizing the F16. Among the specific technologies identified were compact active phased-array radar modules and a co-cured composite wing. The United States was particularly interested in any indigenous stealth technology that Japan might produce for the aircraft.

Subtle economic, rather than military, considerations quickly turned the FSX deal into a major controversy. The Pentagon and National Security Council had no problem with the FSX, but the Commerce and Energy Departments believed that building the FSX was part of a devious Japanese strategy to enter the commercial aerospace industry, over which the United States held almost monopolistic control. Many in Congress saw the deal as a giveaway of American technology to our fiercest economic rival. Sen. Jeff Bingaman (D-NM) expressed the growing Congressional sentiment that the federal government should protect America's international industrial base: "Our government approached the FSX issue from the point of view of a military and foreign policy issue. The Japanese approached it very much more from the point of view of its economic implications, particularly the impact it would have on their ambition to have a world class aerospace industry."[40] Sen. Alphonse D'Amato (R-NY) said, "The basic deal remains a bad one for the United States that will have a long-term debilitating effect on our military-industrial base."[41]

Proponents argued that the deal would divert Japan from building a commercial passenger plane. Under the FSX codevelopment project, the

United States was to supply the engine and a portion of the fuselage to the Japanese contractor, Mitsubishi Heavy Industries. Some portions of the plane, including its electronics, would be built by Japan. Other parts, such as the wings and portions of the frame, would be codeveloped, using technology supplied largely by the United States. Previous military agreements with the United States required Japan to serve merely as a manufacturer, producing all or part of an aircraft based on American specifications. Such deals were negotiated exclusively by the Defense Department, which viewed them in purely military and geopolitical terms. But America's deteriorating international economic position in the post-Cold War world has enhanced the role of the government's economic agencies in matters of technology transfer. During the FSX controversy, Commerce Secretary Robert Mosbacher proclaimed that international trade would henceforth be a key aspect of America's global politics.

On Capitol Hill, bills were introduced that would require the Pentagon to consult with the Commerce Department on all arms deals, allowing the Secretary of Commerce to stop such agreements if he believed they would have "a significant adverse impact on the international competitive position of U.S. industry."[42] Under pressure from Congress and the Commerce Department, President Bush met with his senior foreign policy and economic advisers on March 16, 1989. At that meeting, Commerce Secretary Mosbacher won a greater role for his department in monitoring the execution of the FSX deal and in negotiating future agreements in which allies are given "sensitive" technology. The Bush Administration decided to withhold America's most advanced avionics from Japan, as well as the "source codes" for the fire control computer in the aircraft. The latter would have allowed Japan to speed the development of its computer technology in an area where the United States leads.

On March 20, senior advisers to President Bush notified Japan's ambassador to the United States of the changes desired in the FSX agreement. One of Bush's demands was that "sensitive" technological data shared with Japan would have restrictions preventing Japan from applying that technology to other aircraft. Again, the ironic twist was that military applications of American technology were no longer of concern, but any diversion of that technology to Japan's civil aviation industry was a threat to America's national security.

Under the new guidelines, Japan would budget $1.2 billion to develop six FSX prototypes between 1989 and 1995, and U.S. firms would be guaranteed 40 percent of the work. But critics of the deal still complained that it guaranteed the United States no particular share of the *production* phase, leaving that share to be negotiated after the prototypes were developed. The rhetoric employed by Congressional critics remained particularly shrill. Rep. Duncan Hunter (R-CA) wrote: "How can we approve a program that would give our most sensitive military technology to a company that helped Moammar Gadhafi build chemical weapons that might one day be used against American citizens? . . . For now, we must keep our sensitive military technology away from Mitsubishi Heavy Industries. The FSX should be scrapped."[43]

A Japanese spokesperson denied any Mitsubishi involvement with Gadhafi: "This kind of action—hurling unsubstantiated, inflammatory charges without real evidence—is a McCarthyite tactic."[44] In testimony before the House Foreign Affairs Committee, Deputy Secretary of State Lawrence Eagleburger also denied the Mitsubishi/Gadhafi connection, but Congress paid no heed. The debate went pretty far afield, with Sen. Jesse Helms (R-NC) harkening back to World War II in his criticism of the Japanese: "They skinned us many a time. They skinned us real bad in 1941, and they are skinning us with the FSX."[45]

Eventually, Congress passed legislation imposing a broad new set of conditions on the FSX agreement, including constraints on the American negotiating position in future talks on FSX production. President Bush vetoed that legislation, rejecting "binding provisions" that would tie the hands of the executive branch. Sen. Richard Gephardt (D-MO) said, "With his veto of the bipartisan bill to safeguard America's interests in the FSX deal with Japan, President Bush is giving away our best technology and our best jobs."[46]

On September 14, 1990, the Senate voted 66 to 34 to override the President's veto, one vote short of the necessary two-thirds majority. President Bush had already extracted substantial compromises from Japan, which, among other things, introduced a delay of two years in the program. The scheduled first flight of an FSX prototype had slipped to 1995, the start of production to 1997, and delivery of the first plane to 1999. Japan's estimated costs for the FSX had increased 50 percent, to about $1.9 billion, due to the American insistence on a production role for General Dynamics as well as Mitsubishi. Still, there remained hard feelings on both sides. Shintaro Ishihara, Japanese Congressman and candidate for Prime Minister, charged that Japan gave away the store when it allowed the United States to quash its independent development of the FSX. He felt that Japan should have proceeded, even without the powerful engine the United States was to provide. "If America gets really nasty, Japan could buy engines from France," he concluded.[47]

Now that the FSX deal has collapsed, Harold Brown, former Secretary of Defense, says the affair was characterized by confused decision making and bad feeling on both sides, and that the potential consequences of such antagonism will become more severe in the post-Cold War world. He claims that Japan and the United States are, overall, at technological parity, a situation that offers new opportunities for the two nations to share knowledge and collaborate in developing technologies: "Rather than relying on a U.S. technological supremacy, which no longer exists ... or trying to block foreign access to our know-how (which would be self-defeating), we should recognize how much we stand to gain from rapidly expanding technological links with Japan."[48]

Instead, economic xenophobia continues to drive America's technological fear. In June 1991 a report titled *Japan: 2000* was prepared for the CIA by the Rochester Institute of Technology (RIT). RIT's President, M. Richard Rose, had a cozy relationship with the CIA, which had given the university over $5 million to conduct research exclusively for the CIA. In a foreword to the report, Rose said Americans must "counteract Japan's national vision and their pursuit of world economic domination." The report, written by Rose's executive assistant, was even more explicit, describing the Japanese as "creatures of an ageless, amoral, manipulative and controlling culture."[49] In case the reader is not clear about what kind of "creature" the Japanese resemble, the RIT report says that the Japanese function "as does the lamprey eel, living on the strength of others." The report says that Japan is preparing "an economic sneak attack from which the U.S. may not recover," and it warns of the need to defend America. "In 1776, a brave American patriot took it upon himself to warn the sleeping colonists that an invasion of our shores had begun.... Two hundred years later, another type of attack has begun, launched by a different adversary.... *Japan 2000* should provide notice that 'the rising sun' is coming—the attack has begun."[50]

A Cadillac commercial on American TV took a similar view, featuring World War II footage of Japanese kamikaze attacks on American targets. Close-ups showed leering, giggling Japanese pilots, guns blazing, swooping in on seemingly defenseless targets ... *Cadillac automobiles*. As the Cadillac logo appears in the Japanese gun sight, the announcer proclaims: "For forty-one years Cadillac has defended our shores as America's luxury sales leader. Now, from out of the land of the rising sun come the luxury cars of rising prices. But Cadillac fights back with...." At this point the screen shows a besieged Cadillac suddenly spouting gunfire from its grille and headlights. The attacking Japanese warplanes explode in flame and plummet to earth.

On the "MacNeil Lehrer News Hour," Paul Salmon said the ad may
have been meant in fun, but it reinforces a disturbing trend in America
these days: "The revival of a once popular image of Japan the malevolent,
a nation of kamikaze pilots whom we had better take care of before they
take care of us.... By now Japan has come to be seen as economically
invincible, and therefore threatening once again.... Some Americans
even think we're back at war, only this time we're losing."[51] The American
techno-nationalists may not see the hostility within their political and
economic positions, but the Japanese do. A recent poll in Japan asked
people who they thought was the most likely opponent Japan might face
in a future war. The answer overwhelmingly was "the United States."[52]

The end of the Cold War has brought changes to Western Europe
that America may not find entirely congenial, including the emergence
of the European Common Market as a major economic competitor even
more formidable than Japan. In 1992, the United States threatened
Western Europe with the largest trade retaliation in history, amid skir-
mishes over aid to the former Soviet Union and international economic
cooperation. Hobart Rowen, financial columnist for the *Washington Post*,
warned Americans to look to France and Germany for Economic Enemy
Number One. Jim Hoagland noted, "NATO was invented, it was said
half in jest, to keep the Americans in, the Russians out and the Germans
down. The American era in Europe is ending. Today the Russians are
gone, the Germans are up, and America is starting home."[53] Robert
Hunter, of the Center for Strategic and International Studies, explained,
"With the collapse of the Cold War, a fundamental part of the glue that
bound the United States to Europe is gone."[54]

America's European allies are now being submitted to a cool American reassessment concerning their access to U.S. technologies. One visible result of such thinking is the American government's increasing
application of the restrictive designation NOFORN (no foreigners) on
unclassified scientific meetings previously available to European allies.
Aviation Week and Space Technology reports Europeans are now considering a NOAMER restriction on technical meetings in Western Europe.

President Bush has accused the European Community of hiding behind an "iron curtain" of protectionism, and France was his major target.
A senior American official stated, "It's certainly no exaggeration to say
that we have more problems with France than with any other ally."
French President François Mitterand responded angrily, "France is not
ready to bow to American demands, nor submit to the interests of any
other country, and will not give way."[55]

The suspicion and acrimony generated in America by Japan's ineffective attempt to enter the world aerospace market by way of the FSX project has been more than duplicated by the appearance of the European Airbus. Airbus is a consortium of French, German, British, and Spanish companies that receive subsidies from their governments. Columnist George Will claims that the United States has a national security interest in maintaining Boeing's leadership of the commercial aircraft industry, a crucial component of America's economic vitality. After decrying Europe's "arrogant aggression," Will concludes: "The Airbus dispute is a suitable occasion for America to say what Americans said about some overbearing Europeans 216 years ago: If they mean to have war, let it begin here."[56] Just two months after Will's call to arms, Airbus approached three Japanese aerospace companies—Mitsubishi, Kawasaki, and Fuji—concerning a deal to jointly develop a twenty-first-century supersonic passenger plane that would carry more than 600 passengers.

With visions of a new evil economic axis, American technological paranoia generated new strategies for information control. Many Americans believe the fierce trade war with Europe has evolved, or degenerated, into industrial espionage as devious and threatening as the Cold War spy stuff. An oft-cited example concerns a U.S. sales team that traveled to Paris to offer Air France a high-tech device to upgrade its aircraft. At its meeting with the U.S. sales team, it became obvious that the Air France representatives had already read the report on the device. It was subsequently determined, according to the U.S. company's security director, that while one American executive was out of his Paris hotel, the maid, working for French intelligence, had removed, copied, and replaced the document. French intelligence then gave the copy to government-owned Air France.

The scenario described above has never been confirmed, but American suspicions of French industrial espionage have grown to a fever pitch. In September 1991, NBC TV presented a prime time "Exposé" on the subject. The Wall Street Journal claimed that French employees working for U.S. companies in France were either planted or recruited there by French intelligence. FBI reports claimed that staff from the French consulate in Houston, Texas, had been searching trash to find documents discarded by U.S. corporate executives living nearby. The French Consul General said he and an assistant were simply picking up bags of grass cuttings to fill a hole near the consulate.

In May 1992, the Pentagon intervened to prevent a French company, Thomson-CSF, from purchasing an American corporation's missile division. The Pentagon insisted that Thomson establish a special all-American board of directors to "insulate the management from active participation of foreign owners." Angry Thomson officials initially rejected such an arrangement, saying it would make it impossible to integrate the new company into Thomson's global business. But, alarmed by a Senate bill that would halt the sale, Thomson virtually accepted the idea of an all-American board. The French company asked only that it be allowed to name a single person to its own board. In addition, Thomson promised to allow only Americans with proper security clearance to review classified contracts. "We have always respected American laws in these matters and we would continue to do so under this special security agreement," pleaded Thomson. "We are not trying to steal secrets."[57] The Pentagon remained unconvinced. Frank Carlucci, former U.S. Secretary of Defense serving as an investment banker for the group negotiating the Thomson purchase, reminded the Senate Armed Services Committee that Thomson had worked on dozens of military contracts for the American and European governments, with no complaints heard. Carlucci accused the American government of "dressing protectionist positions in the cloak of national security."[58]

During the Congressional hearings, James Bell, president of Thomson's U.S. operations and an American citizen, was asked if French officials had ever requested him to spy on U.S. companies. Bell said that had never occurred, but he had been "approached by the U.S. government" to do industrial espionage against foreign companies. The Defense Intelligence Agency nonetheless concluded that the Thomson purchase posed a significant risk that crucial military technology would be compromised. A classified report claimed that the risk to national security was in fact greater than that posed by any of the 200 proposed foreign transactions it had previously reviewed. Although Congress has no official role to play in such transactions, it, too, lined up against the Thomson deal. Sen. John Danforth (R-MO) said, "This company is an extension of the government of France, which is busily trying to make itself the major force in the international defense market." Sen. Lloyd Bentsen (D-TX) questioned the extent of America's alliance with France, claiming, "In economic matters, we are not allied."[59]

Today, the American government regards the growing threat of industrial espionage as ample justification for maintaining the network of government controls on science. Oliver Revell, until recently FBI Deputy Director, claims that foreign intelligence services "are gearing their whole apparatus to collect our proprietary information." James

Geer, former head of the FBI's Counterintelligence Division, has been hired by DuPont to shore up the company's security. The Bureau's Deputy Assistant Director, R. Patrick Watson, says the FBI is reorganizing its Counterintelligence Division with the new goal of covering, "across the board," foreign intelligence agencies that might steal corporate technology that is "unclassified but still critical." He adds that FBI agents will begin interviewing scientists and engineers at U.S. companies to try to determine how to stop the loss of American technology.[60]

The government's position is that information is a significant international product that can no longer be regarded as free, and should, at the least, be bartered in international agreements. And since individual researchers and commercial corporations currently exercise controls over the dissemination of technical information for reasons that have no relationship to national security, why should the government hesitate to do the same? The government report *The Exploitation of Western Data Bases* states, with smug confidence: "[T]he military departments are quite prepared to weigh and balance the risk of endangering our national technological health versus the risk of offering free technical assistance to our adversaries."[61] Others are not quite so prepared to leave that judgment in the hands of military departments or federal agencies, the last constituency one could expect to moderate federal power over information.

Scientific information is increasingly considered useful to a nation only if it is exclusive to that nation. Information shared is information lost; in some mysterious way it ceases to exist if it cannot be used for scientific hegemony. A look back at the Cold War should be ample warning against the imposition of scientific secrecy. Professor George Davida has documented areas of scientific research where the United States and the Soviet Union had practiced absolute secrecy; despite the overall American lead in technology during the Cold War, the accomplishments of both nations were about the same in these fields. Given the general superiority of American science, Davida concludes: "This implies that if we were to impose secrecy in other areas . . . then what we can expect is that we will do about as well as [did] the Soviets. Secrecy, it seems, has only one thing in store for us: Mediocrity."[62]

NOTES

1. Don Oberdorfer, "Winning and Losing by CNN," *Washington Post*, 3 January 1992, A23.

2. "U.S-Soviet Pact to Curb Incidents," *Washington Post,* 7 June 1989, A12.

3. "Ex-Soviet Republics Sign Charter," *Washington Post,* 22 December 1991, A1.

4. Hobart Rowen, "U.S. Must Lead Soviet Rescue—Now," *Washington Post,* 8 December 1991, H1.

5. Interview with Daniel Patrick Moynihan on "This Week with David Brinkley," ABC-TV, 9 June 1991.

6. "Exodus of Researchers Stirs Fears over Fate of Science in the Former Soviet Union," *Chronicle of Higher Education,* 4 March 1992, A44.

7. "Gates Fears Soviet 'Brain Drain,' " *Washington Post,* 16 January 1992, A22.

8. "Atom Scientists at Ex-Soviet Lab Seek Help," *Washington Post,* 15 February 1992, A1.

9. Fred Hiatt, "Russian Nuclear Scientists Seek Business, Food," *Washington Post,* 18 January 1992, A20.

10. "Russian Scientist Aid Is Developing," *Washington Post,* 24 April 1992, A10.

11. Debra E. Blum, "Into the 'Gold Mine' of Russia's Weapons Labs," *Chronicle of Higher Education,* 22 April 1992, A5.

12. Ibid.

13. Joseph L. Birman, "The Fate of Scientists from the Soviet Union," *Chronicle of Higher Education,* 12 February 1992, B1.

14. Ibid.

15. "U.S. Urged to Act 'Aggressively' to Aid Researchers in Former Soviet Union," *Chronicle of Higher Education,* 18 March 1992, A49.

16. "Resentment of West Rising to Surface in Russian Congress," *Washington Post,* 9 April 1992, A18.

17. "Consortium to Buy Soviet Nuclear Reactor," *Washington Post,* 8 January 1991, A6.

18. "U.S. Won't Let Soviets Take Reactor Back Home," *Washington Post,* 20 April 1991, A6.

19. "U.S. Agency to Let Soviets Take Their Reactor Home," *Washington Post,* 22 May 1991, A14.

20. Ibid.

21. Statement by Col. Pete Worden, Deputy for Technology, Strategic Defense Initiative Organization, before the House Science, Space and Technology Committee, 12 March 1992, 3–4.

22. "Keeping the U.S. First," *Washington Post,* 11 March 1992, A1, A4.

23. "Countering the Hostile Intelligence Threat in the United States," remarks by Oliver B. Revell, Associate Deputy Director, Investigation, Federal Bureau of Investigation, at the 35th Annual Seminar of the American Society for Industrial Security, 11–14 September 1989, 4–5.

24. Ibid., 6–7.

25. George A. Carver, Jr., "Intelligence in the Age of *Glasnost*," *Foreign Affairs,* Summer 1990, 160. (Emphasis added).

26. Michelle Van Cleave, Assistant Director for National Security Affairs, White House Office of Science and Technology Policy, remarks prepared for delivery at International Security Systems Symposium, Washington, DC, 28 October 1991.

27. Carver, "Intelligence in the Age of *Glasnost*," 153–154.

28. *Congressional Record—Senate,* 4 August 1990, S12459–12460.

29. Ibid.

30. Carver, "Intelligence in the Age of *Glasnost,*" 153–154.

31. Opening statement of Congressman Jack Brooks before the House Subcommittee on Economic and Commercial Law, Committee of the Judiciary, 29 April 1992, 1.

32. Statement of Milton J. Socolar, Special Assistant to the Comptroller General, before the House Subcommittee on Economic and Commercial Law, Committee on the Judiciary, 29 April 1992, 1, 8.

33. Statement of J. E. Riesbeck, Executive Vice President, Corning, Inc., before the House Subcommittee on Economic and Commercial Law, House Committee on the Judiciary, 29 April 1992.

34. Statement of Robert M. Gates, Director of the Central Intelligence Agency, before the House Subcommittee on Economic and Commercial Law, Committee on the Judiciary, 29 April 1992, 8.

35. Statement of William S. Sessions, Director of the Federal Bureau of Investigation, before the House Subcommittee on Economic and Commercial Law, Committee on the Judiciary, 29 April 1992, 5.

36. Statement by Stanislaw Levchenko before the House Subcommittee on Economic and Commercial Law, Committee of the Judiciary, 29 April 1992, 7.

37. Statement of William S. Sessions, 29 April 1992, 5.

38. Statement of Robert M. Gates, 29 April 1992, 9–10.

39. Jim Hoagland, "Keeping Our Allies from Becoming Our Adversaries," *Washington Post,* 26 April 1992, C1.

40. "U.S.-Japan Collaboration on Jet Draws Fire," *Washington Post,* 15 March 1989, D7.

41. "Senators Step up Attack on FSX Deal with Japan," *Washington Post,* 11 May 1989, A5.

42. "Bush Is Pressed to Kill Japan Jet Deal," *Washington Post,* 16 March 1989, A5.

43. Letter from Rep. Duncan Hunter (R-CA) to *Washington Post,* 20 April 1989, A18.

44. "Stop Using McCarthyism to Kill the FSX Deal," *Washington Post,* 4 April 1989, A24.

45. "Senators Step up Attack on FSX Deal with Japan," A5.

46. "Bush Vetoes Measure on U.S.-Japan Fighter," *New York Times,* 1 August 1989, D1.

47. Hobart Rowen, "Japanese 'No' Man," *Washington Post,* 18 January 1990, A23.

48. Harold Brown, "Compete—and Cooperate—with Japan," *Washington Post,* 26 March 1990, A11.

49. "Cap and Gown, Cloak and Dagger at RIT," *Washington Post,* 20 June 1991, A3.

50. Bruce Cumings, "C.I.A.'s *Japan 2000* Caper," *The Nation,* 30 September, 1991, 367.

51. "MacNeil/Lehrer News Hour," National Public Television, 1 April 1991.

52. Charles Freund, "Has the Cold War Chilled Out?" *Washington Post,* 6 December 1988, A19.

53. Jim Hoagland, "Coming Home," *Washington Post,* 18 February 1992, A17.

54. "U.S. Vows Duties on EC Imports," *Washington Post,* 1 May 1992, B1, B4.

55. "Tensions Between France and U.S. Said to Turn Allies into Rivals," *Washington Post,* 22 January 1992, A25.

56. George F. Will, "Free Trade, or Trade War," *Washington Post,* 29 September 1991, C7.

57. "Thomson Offers Security Guarantees in Purchase of LTV Unit," *Washington Post,* 20 May 1992, F1.

58. "Pentagon Cites Security Issues in Sale of LTV to Thomson," *Washington Post,* 1 May 1992, B1–B2.

59. "Sale of LTV Missile Unit to French Firm Poses Risk, U.S. Agency Says," *Washington Post,* 15 May 1992, A15.

60. "Corporate Targets: As Cold War Fades, Some Nations' Spies Seek Industrial Secrets," *Wall Street Journal,* 17 June 1991, A1, A5.

61. *The Exploitation of Western Data Bases,* (Washington, DC: Office of the Assistant Vice Chief of Staff, U.S. Air Force, 1986), Appendix J–8.

62. U.S. House of Representatives, Committee on the Judiciary, Subcommittee on Courts, Civil Liberties and the Administration of Justice, *1984: Civil Liberties and the National Security State,* Hearings, 98th Cong., 1st Sess., November 3, 1983 (Washington, DC: U.S. GPO, 1984), 58, 98.

Selected Bibliography

Alderman, Ellen, and Kennedy, Caroline. *In Our Defense*. New York: Morrow, 1991.

Bamford, James. *The Puzzle Palace: A Report on America's Most Secret Agency*. Boston: Houghton Mifflin, 1982.

Bickel, Alexander. *The Morality of Consent*. New Haven: Yale University Press, 1975.

Bok, Sissela. *Secrets: On the Ethics of Concealment and Revelation*. New York: Vintage Books, 1984.

Cole, Leonard A. *Politics and the Restraint of Science*. Totowa, NJ: Rowman and Allanheld, 1983.

Dandeker, Christopher. *Surveillance, Power and Modernity*. New York: St. Martin's Press, 1990.

The Exploitation of Western Data Bases. Washington, DC: Office of the Assistant Vice Chief of Staff, U.S. Air Force, 1986.

Foerstel, Herbert N. *Surveillance in the Stacks: The FBI's Library Awareness Program*. Westport, CT: Greenwood Press, 1991.

Gellhorn, Walter. *Security, Loyalty, and Science*. Ithaca, NY: Cornell University Press, 1950.

Gervasi, Tom. *Soviet Military Power: The Pentagon's Propaganda Document, Annotated and Corrected*. New York: Vintage Books, 1988.

Grove, J. W. *In Defense of Science: Science, Technology, and Politics in Modern Society*. Cheektowaga, NY: University of Toronto Press, 1989.

The Government's Classification of Private Ideas. Hearings, 96th Cong., 28 February, 20 March, 21 August 1980. Washington, D.C.: U.S. Government Printing Office, 1981.

Johnson, Loch K. *America's Secret Power: The CIA in a Democratic Society*. New York: Oxford University Press, 1989.

Katz, Steven D. *Government Secrecy: Decisions Without Democracy*. Washington, DC: People for the American Way, 1987.

Mukerji, Chandra. *A Fragile Power: Scientists and the State*. Princeton, NJ: Princeton University Press, 1989.

National Commission on Libraries and Information Science. *Hearing on Sensitive but Not Classified Information*, Washington, DC, 28 May 1987. Unpublished manuscript.

1984: Civil Liberties and the National Security State. Hearings before the House Subcommittee on Courts, Civil Liberties and the Administration of Justice, 3 November 1983. Washington, DC: U.S. GPO, 1984.

O'Brien, David M. *The Public's Right to Know: The Supreme Court and the First Amendment*. New York: Praeger, 1981.

Pell, Eve. *The Big Chill*. Boston: Beacon Press, 1984.

Reingold, Nathan. *Science, American Style*. New Brunswick, NJ: Rutgers University Press, 1991.

Stern, Philip M. *The Oppenheimer Case: Security on Trial*. New York: Harper & Row, 1969.

U.S. Congress, Office of Technology Assessment. *Science, Technology and the First Amendment: Special Report*. Washington, DC: U.S. GPO, 1988.

Wiener, Tim. *Blank Check: The Pentagon's Black Budget*. New York: Warner Books, 1990.

Wise, David. *The Politics of Lying: Government Deception, Secrecy, and Power*. New York: Random House, 1973.

Wulff, Keith M., ed. *Regulation of Scientific Inquiry: Societal Concerns with Research*. Boulder, CO: Westview Press, 1979.

Index

About the Author

HERBERT N. FOERSTEL is Head of Branch Libraries and Head of the Engineering & Physical Sciences Library at the University of Maryland. He holds degrees from Hamilton College, Rutgers University, and Johns Hopkins University, and is the author of *Surveillance in the Stacks: The FBI's Library Awareness Program* (Greenwood, 1991).